James Kennedy

Modern Poets and Poetry of Spain

James Kennedy

Modern Poets and Poetry of Spain

ISBN/EAN: 9783337243524

Printed in Europe, USA, Canada, Australia, Japan

Cover: Foto ©Thomas Meinert / pixelio.de

More available books at **www.hansebooks.com**

MODERN POETS

AND

POETRY OF SPAIN.

By JAMES KENNEDY, Esq.,

HER BRITANNIC MAJESTY'S JUDGE IN THE MIXED COURT
OF JUSTICE AT THE HAVANA.

WILLIAMS AND NORGATE,
14, HENRIETTA STREET, COVENT GARDEN, LONDON;
AND
20, SOUTH FREDERICK STREET, EDINBURGH.
1860.

TO

THE RIGHT HONOURABLE

GEORGE, EARL OF CARLISLE,

&c. &c.

My Lord,

I HAVE sought permission to inscribe your Lordship's name on this page, as a favour appropriate to my work, under the considerations in which it originated.

I began these translations, partly as a means of acquiring an accurate knowledge of the Spanish language, and partly as a relaxation from other studies and pursuits, about the time when your Lordship, in the course of your statesmanlike visit to America, made, in 1842, a lengthened stay in Cuba, studying the circumstances of those countries, which are soon, perhaps, to take a yet more prominent place, than they do at present, in the history of the world.

The discussions I heard respecting that visit—for it was then considered an extraordinary one—raised in my mind many suggestions, as to the benefits that must accrue to the public from the observations of individual travellers. Accordingly as each one might have his special object in view, his sphere of action or opportunities of learning, so the knowledge he acquired might be proportionately imparted. The community at large had always evinced the greatest interest in the accounts given by travellers of their visits to foreign countries, as was shown by the favourable reception uniformly given to their works. Of these many that were published were well deserving of the popularity they obtained, especially as with regard to Spain there were several that left little for any future writer to supply of ordinary information. In one respect, however, all such works appeared to me to be deficient, though their failure was almost unavoidable, in the case of transient visitors, in their being unable to convey any adequate idea of the state of mental culture among the people they visited.

Yet this, to a philosophic reader, would be undoubtedly the truest test of the state of civilization to which any nation had attained. Such a reader would not be contented with merely a recital of the everyday occurrences of travelling, nor yet with general or statistical information respecting any people, obtained from ordinary sources. He would rather seek to follow them into the occupations of private life and into their favourite courses of thought and feeling, judging of these by the studies of their better classes of society, in their hours of relaxation or for domestic enjoyment. As the sagest of the Roman emperors, M. Antoninus, observed, To know any people's minds and inclinations, we should examine their studies and pursuits,—τὰ ἡγεμονικὰ αὐτῶν διάβλεπε, καὶ τοὺς φρονίμους, διὰ μὲν φεύγουσιν, διὰ δὲ διώκουσιν.

Few persons going abroad for a short period, or for a specific purpose, could be expected to acquire such an intimate knowledge of the literature of any country as to be able to render a satisfactory account of it. Where, however, any one had the means and the leisure to do so, that seemed to me the task most worthy for him to undertake.

As a servant of the public, I considered this more peculiarly a duty; and I therefore ventured, by extending my studies, to attempt giving a comprehensive view of Modern Spanish Poetry, and so complete the representations of Spanish society and manners given by other writers. This I thought best to be done, first, by compiling some critical and biographical notices of the principal modern poets; and, next, by endeavouring to transfuse into English verse the most favourable specimens of their productions, by which the English reader might in some degree be enabled to judge of their merits.

Such was the task I then set before me, the results of which I now offer to the public as my contribution to the store of general knowledge. For such a work there can be little merit claimed, except that for patient industry. But as a naturalist or collector of works of art patriotically endeavours to bring home the most valuable productions or treasures of other countries, so I trust that this work may also be favourably accepted, as a praiseworthy attempt to enrich our English literature with what was most interesting in the Spanish.

I have relied on your Lordship's approval of the design, from your well-known anxiety and constant efforts to improve the moral and social condition of the people, by literary as well as by legislative means. Sharing in the public respect for those efforts on their behalf, and with much thankfulness for the sanction afforded me, I have the honour to subscribe myself,

Your Lordship's

Most obedient,

Humble Servant,

J. KENNEDY.

London,
May 6, 1852.

INTRODUCTION.

THOSE writers are very much mistaken who suppose, that, consequent upon the long domination of the Moors in Spain, there are to be found in Spanish literature any of the exuberances of style which are considered the principal characteristics of Eastern poetry. In all the Moorish ballads that have been handed down to us, those characteristics, both in thought and expression, abound as much as in the poems of more Eastern nations. But in even the earliest Spanish ballads, contemporary with the Moorish, a very decided difference is to be observed, as they show, on the contrary, a simplicity of expression and propriety of thought, which present an extraordinary contrast, not only to the Moorish, but also to the early poetry of other European countries. This favourable distinction has continued to the present day. The poetry of the Northern nations of Europe has been marked by extravagances throughout, as contrary to common sense as to good taste and nature. That of the French school has been distinguished by an affectation, a sentimentality and straining after effect, to say nothing of its peculiar ribaldry and licentiousness, all equally removed from the true feeling of poetry. Even the Italians, in their poetical works, have indulged in strange absurdities, the more remarkable from the good taste that has pervaded their other works of genius. It is only in English literature that we can find writers imbued with the same vigour of thought and depth of poetic feeling as the Spanish, and it is therefore only with them that the latter can be classed in considering the relative merits of the poetry of different modern nations.

If the character of the poetry may be taken as the criterion by which to judge of the degree of civilization to which any people had attained in the earlier period of their history, Spain has a good right to claim the first place among the nations of Europe, when emerging from that period denominated the Dark Ages. While the popular poetry of other nations at that period was almost entirely occupied with childish stories of giants and supernatural beings, or in magnifying the outrages of their heroes, and even of their outlaws, as if they were honourable exploits, instead of merely murder and rapine, the Spanish bards were engaged in celebrating the patriotism and prowess of their Christian warriors in strains not unworthy of the deeds they commemorated. Those strains have been made sufficiently well-known to the English reader by the labours of Southey and Lockhart, for which the student of Spanish literature must feel the utmost respect and gratitude, as well as by those of Rodd, Bowring and others. From their translations the character of those warriors will be found to have been distinguished, differently from those of other nations in that age, for the milder virtues combined with pure chivalrous enterprise. If, as apparently was the case, the great champion, known as the Cid, especially was deserving of the eminently honourable character depicted for him by the poets, the popular feeling must have attained something of the same tone when he was adopted as the first object of national regard. Coming of a chivalrous race, engaged in a sacred warfare, the Cid combined in his character all that was most noble in human conduct, and gave to his countrymen a fame which they knew full well how to appreciate. Thus the spirit which the ballads breathed in recounting his exploits was one in unison with that of the people. Each Spaniard of after-times, in listening to those recitals, felt he had no need to connect himself with fabulous narratives. He could say, like Diomede,—" Of this race and blood do I boast myself to be "—

Ταύτης τοι γενεῆς τε καὶ αἵματος εὔχομαι εἶναι,

and so feeling could identify himself truly with his heroes.

Formed originally of very different races, Celts and Goths, mixed with the descendants of Romans and Phœnicians or Carthaginians, the Spaniards had against the Moors become amalgamated into one people, whose great bond of union was their religion more even than their country. This holy cause ennobled their conduct, and gave them higher aims and motives than any ordinary warfare could do; so that acting constantly under the sense of such feelings, their national character assumed the staid bearing, which has always since so favourably distinguished it. Hence also the national literature, even in its lightest productions, assumed the tone of high moral and practical tendency which it has generally borne, far removed from the comparatively trifling topics which formed the staple subjects of the literature of neighbouring countries.

There is another mistake into which some writers have fallen, in supposing that Spain owed her civilization entirely to the Moors. The Arab conquest undoubtedly entailed on her for many ages a succession of enlightened as well as warlike rulers, who are justly to be classed among the greatest patrons of literature and art; but they fostered rather than founded the sciences that afterwards flourished under their rule, and which they found preparing to burst forth in the country they conquered. Though their forefathers might have come from the seats of learning in the East, such as they then were, the immediate conquerors of Spain were natives of the neighbouring parts of Africa, where the sciences had not flourished in any remarkable degree before the conquest, and where they did not rise subsequently to any eminence. The learned Lampillas, who has given us a very able Vindication of Spanish Literature, in answer to the attacks of some Italian critics, might justly have gone further than he has done as to its merits under the Moorish domination. Rather than as owing her advances in learning and civilization to the Moors, it is more probable that these were the remains of former civilization, existing among the Roman colonies on the dissolution of the empire. At that time Spain was essentially inhabited by descendants of Romans, as it still continues to be, mainly, to the present day. Latin had become the language of the country, and the best of the later Latin authors, Seneca, Lucan, Martial, Quinctilian and others, were natives of the Peninsula. The Romans had planted sixty-seven colonies there, and in the time of Vespasian could enumerate 360 cities inhabited by them. These would undoubtedly retain their municipal institutions, and were perhaps more retentive of Roman manners than were even the towns of Italy. The original inhabitants had been driven into the mountains of Catalonia, Cantabria and Lusitania. They were of Celtic origin, and their descendants in those provinces still show that origin by a different pronunciation of the language imposed on the country by the Romans; while the Castillians, being of purer descent from them, speak even now a language little different from that in common colloquial use under the Emperors. The lower orders, in fact, speak an idiom nearer to it than do the educated classes, showing that the main race of the people, in Madrid for instance, remains essentially Roman. In Betica or Andalusia and the South of Spain, the descendants of Romans had become incorporated with those of Phœnician or Carthaginian and a few Greek colonists, forming together a race perhaps still more civilized than the new-comers. Thus the Moors found the people they had conquered in a high state of civilization, scarcely affected by former conquests, and they had only the merit of accepting and continuing the mental culture which they found there, and which they had not possessed in their native deserts.

The Goths and Vandals had swept like a hurricane over Spain; but they passed over it without leaving any considerable traces of their conquest. This is clear from the circumstance of so few Northern words remaining in the language of the country. At the entrance of the Moors into Spain, the dominant party there was certainly of Gothic descent; but they had already lost their Northern idioms, and were immerged in the mass of the people they had conquered, in the usual course of such events, as the Scandinavians soon did in Normandy and the Normans in England. When the races had begun to amalgamate in Spain, the distinctive lines might have been longer discernible in the South, if it had not been for the Moorish invasion. This soon repeated the events of former conquests, in the extermination of the fighting men and the enslaving of the other classes, who became feudatories or worse. Those who escaped to the mountains of the North constituted a nucleus of resistance, which was no doubt much strengthened in their subsequent contests by the aid of the

Christian population left of necessity among the Moors, who thus became dangerous as internal enemies, though they had been tolerated at first as valuable dependents. The war that then arose in Spain, and continued for upwards of 600 years, was imbued, on the part of the Christians, with all those ingredients of religious as well as patriotic feeling that render wars remarkable for desperate conflict. On the part of the Moors, it is but justice toward them to say, that for chivalrous honour and bravery they proved themselves in no respect inferior to their opponents, who, thus engaged in generous rivalry, became distinguishable for the same virtues.

The circumstances of the wars between the Christians and the Moors were too near to the every-day experience of the people to allow of any imaginary addition to the legends of the times, and they were too engrossing in importance and interest to require any heightening. The ballads founded upon them, therefore, assumed almost the matter-of-fact air of history, and this seemed hence to become the characteristic of all the subsequent literature of Spain. It is true that romances abounded in which giants and other absurdities of knight-errantry might be found, but they were principally of foreign origin, and did not become incorporated in the national poetry. This national poetry was always true to its mission, for it may be observed that the poets of Spain have seldom or never gone beyond their own history for their heroes; they have rather instinctively followed the maxim of the great lyrist of old, not to select objects of admiration from strangers, but to seek them at home,—

> Οὐδ' ἀλλοτρίων ἔρωτες
> Ἀνδρὶ φέρειν κρέσσονες,
> Οἴκοθεν μάτευε.

Thus also they were secure of the sympathy of their audience, and found patriotism the best inspirer of poetry.

None of the Spanish poets, of either former or present times, can be said to have attained the highest rank; yet as they have always shown a predilection for subjects of real incident and passion or feeling, they have gained, in perhaps a greater degree than those of any other modern nation, that hold upon the popular affections which arises from all earnest participation in kindred sentiments. This might arise partly from the national character developed, as before intimated, in the Moorish wars, and partly from the personal tendencies of the respective individuals. Whilst in other countries the poets were generally to be found among the classes dependent upon the rich and powerful, in Spain they were persons generally of the highest classes. Some were of royal rank, others were eminent as statesmen, and others, if not of the same high station, were yet equally engaged in military service or the active business of life. Three of the most favourite poets, Garcilasso de la Vega, Manrique, and Cadahalso, died the death of soldiers from wounds received in warfare. Ercilla, author of the chief poem in the Spanish language, which may be considered an Epic, was a participant in the wars he so graphically describes. Cervantes received three wounds at the battle of Lepanto, by one of which he lost an arm. Calderon de la Barca passed many years of his life in the campaigns in the Low Countries, where he gained great military reputation; and Lope de Vega was one of the few adventurers in the "Invincible Armada" who were fortunate enough to return to their native country. Such men were not likely to indulge in dreamy idealities, or idle reveries, and fantastic imaginations, the offspring of morbid temperaments and sedentary habits. On the contrary, they were only calculated to adopt that peculiar manliness of style and sentiment, which their successors, from example, from national character, and from being placed in similar circumstances of life, have continued.

How far those circumstances have affected the modern literature of Spain may be best seen from the memoirs hereafter detailed of the principal poets individually. Our present purpose in this Introduction is only to make general observations to lead to the conclusions that may be deduced from them.

Spain, as it has been already observed, cannot boast of having ever produced a poet of the highest class, meaning by that term, one of such high creative genius as to stamp his character, not only on the literature of his own age and country, but also on that of all successive ages within his possible influence. Of such poets the world has only seen four or five at the utmost, with the exception of the inspired writers, referring to Homer, Dante, Shakespeare, Milton, and perhaps we may add, Byron. With these, Virgil and other imitators must not be classed, however great the talents they may have displayed, nor yet other writers of greater originality and even genius, who have, however, confined themselves to minor works or those on less important subjects. Of such writers of great original genius, who did not aim at works of the highest order, Spanish literature may claim as many as that of any other couutry. With them the English reader has been made acquainted more fully than with the writers of most other modern countries, by the works of Bouterwek and Sismondi, translated respectively by Mrs. Ross and William Roscoe, and now by the more comprehensive work of Mr. Ticknor (New York, 1849; London, 1850), who has supplied the deficiencies the others had left in the course of their inquiries. Of these works Sismondi's is little more than a repetition of Bouterwek's, without the ackuowledgement made which was in justice due to his original. That however was in reality so jejune in treating of the materials at the command of the writer, as almost to warrant the use of his materials for a livelier production. Another work has been lately published on Spanish literature by Mr. A. F. Foster (Edinburgh, 1851), compiled in like manner from former writers, which, for succinct and able treatment of the subject, may perhaps be recommended as the one best suited to the general reader. But Mr. Ticknor's book must remain the great work of reference to the older Spanish authors, as he has left little for future writers to supply respecting them. Yet neither has he gone scarcely any further than Bouterwek, who wrote at the beginning of this century, and since whose time so many writers have arisen in Spain superior to any perhaps that have preceded them. In such works we have more cause to congratulate ourselves on having any one to undertake the labour of going over so wide a field, than to complain of his stopping short at a point where less was known of Spanish literature, and where it became so much more interesting as connected with our own times. But as all the compilers now mentioned have so confined their labours to works written previously to the present century, it may be considered acceptable, in continuation of them, that the present essay should be offered to the public. This is, however, also undertaken on a more extended and somewhat different plan; not merely giving short notices of the several authors and their works, as in the nature of a catalogue or dictionary, but taking only the principal poets for a particular account of their history, and giving translations from their works most characteristic of their genius or best suited for translation, for the purpose of enabling the critical notices respecting them to be better understood.

In treating of the literature of any country historically, it may perhaps be considered necessary to give a catalogue of every person who has published a book of any pretensions to notice, whatever the different gradations of talent between the authors; but for the general reader, the better course seems rather to be to pass by those works which the nation had not accepted as to be incorporated in the national literature, and to dwell extendedly on those which, by repeated editions, were entitled to be considered of that character. Bouterwek's work on Spanish literature, which appears to have been his own performance, and which certainly does great credit to his industry, is an exemplification of the former course. The volume on Portuguese literature, under his name, which he acknowledges to have been the contribution of a friend, is not so liable to the same objection, and may be considered written according to the other. It is so difficult a task, and so enviable a lot for any one to attain to excellence above his fellows, that beyond its being due to his own merits, it is an advantage to others to show them by his example the way to attain to the same eminence. Johnson, in his Lives of the English Poets, has given us a work admirable for its criticisms as well as for the other lessons it conveys for general conduct in life; but those criticisms would have lost much of their effect, if they had not had appended to them the works to which they referred. Biography, to be worthy of study, should be something more than a mere enumeration of those particulars of a man's life which are of the common class of every-day events, so as to be the reflex of every one's in his station. If any man's life be at all more memorable than that of ordinary mortals, the means by which he obtained his reputation alone merit a lengthened consideration for an example for others. With authors those claims must rest on their writings, which will speak for themselves; but this cannot be the case with foreign authors, as few readers of other nations can ever be expected to have acquired their language so perfectly as to understand the essential beauty of their poetry. To enable such readers therefore to understand their works, or even the criticisms upon them, a translation is necessary, on which again much depends, not only in respect of faithfulness but also of felicity of transcript, to render the beauties of the original sufficiently perceptible.

Many rules have been given by critics for the benefit of translators from the earliest times till now, to which it is not necessary here to refer further than to state the plan upon which these translations have been made. In a didactic or historical work, the more precisely the translation is made according to the letter of the original, the greater merit may it be considered to possess. But in works of imagination, especially of poetry, it may be more important to attend to the spirit of the original than to the literal construction. The main thoughts contained in each passage should be as faithfully given in the one case as in the other, though it may not be necessary, and sometimes not even becoming, to have the same regard to details. With poetry, the translator should make it his great aim to consider how his author would have expressed the same thoughts if he had been writing in English verse, and thus mould the original ideas into synonymous poetical expressions, as far as the idioms of the two languages and the requirements of metre will allow. It would be a poor vanity in a translator to think of improving on his original, so far as to make any alteration or addition merely for that purpose. But where any words admit of synonyms with different shades of meaning, it is certainly his right, if not his duty, to adopt the one he thinks most suitable. Sometimes it may seem to him accordant with good taste to make a more decided alteration, and in every language there are many expressions sufficiently poetical and appropriate, which if construed literally into another would appear otherwise. These the author, it may be supposed, would have altered himself, under the same circumstances, and the other, therefore, in so

b

doing, would be only acting on his presumed wishes. In all cases much must be left of necessity to the translator's judgement, and he, with every care he can take, must still be content to share, with Pope and Dryden and the greatest masters of rhyme, the consciousness of scarcely ever being able fully to convey the conceptions of a foreign author. The shackles of rhyme also require something to be sacrificed to them, so as of themselves alone to prevent any exact copy being given in verse. Yet still acting on the above considerations, and by rejecting expletives in some cases and adding a few in others, in following up the train of ideas suggested by the original, we may hope to succeed perhaps not only in giving the meaning, but something also of the spirit even of foreign authors.

It is fortunate for any writer to have his works sent forth to the world in any language of more than usual ascendency, such as the Latin or English, whereby to obtain for himself, if he can claim it, the most extended reputation. But it is more fortunate for a translator under similar circumstances, because languages of such a character are almost of necessity mixed languages, acquiring from that cause an extraordinary nerve and richness, which render translations into them to be made more easily and satisfactorily than from them into a poorer. The English is essentially suited for such a purpose, as, being compounded of the French and German languages, it becomes a double one, combining the nerve of the one with the facility of expression of the other, and the copiousness arising from the union of both. The Latin is still more a mixed language, the roots of which are yet to be developed, notwithstanding all the labours of philologists, who have erred in wandering after imaginary extinct languages for its derivations, instead of looking into those yet existing. Considering the Spanish to be the direct descendant of the Latin, it may be a matter of surprise that, though a very sonorous language, it cannot be termed a rich one. Abounding in long words (sesquipedalia verba), it loses in precision and strength what is gained in sound, and thus the ideas are encumbered when simplification was required. The comparatively monosyllabic character of the English language has in this respect an immense advantage for the translator, as it enables him to give the sentiments of the original more concisely than one from it into another. Having also more synonyms with different shades of meaning, a greater precision may be lost or gained, according to the circumstances and the judgement applied to them. Thus a translation may sometimes be even superior to the original, from its giving the ideas more distinctly, and as it is the test of good writing to find how it reads in another language, so with really superior authors it may be a matter of little importance in what version their thoughts are expressed. "Words are the daughters of earth, but thoughts are the sons of heaven." It is not presumed hereby that the following translations all come under this consideration, but with the advantages above expressed, it may be hoped that, as exotics in a greenhouse, these flowers of Spanish poetry may be found pleasing representations of what they were in their native soil, even if they cannot be made entirely denizens of our own.

Differing entirely from those writers who suppose that the best days of Spanish literature have gone by, and believing, on the contrary, that it never has been more truly original and flourishing than during the present and preceding ages, it might be justly considered presumptuous in any new author to present such opinions to the world without showing the grounds on which they were founded. Bouterwek and his copyist, Sismondi, together with their criticisms on the several Spanish poets, contented themselves with giving merely a few lines from the more favoured ones in their original language, without any translation whereby to enable those ignorant of it to judge even of the thoughts they contained. They thus resemble the wiseacre in Hierocles (the Σχολαστικὸς, which word Johnson has strangely translated 'pedant,' taking the primary for the intended meaning), who brought a stone as a description of a building. In so doing, they have seldom given even favourable specimens; but if they had, there are few authors who can be rightly estimated by isolated passages, or even by any one short poem. Almost all authors are unequal in their productions, and many seem, by an accidental felicity, to have produced some one effusion to which none of their other efforts could ever approach. As instances of this, we may note Heber's 'Palestine;' Pringle's lines, 'Afar in the Desert,' and Leyden's 'Ode to an Indian Gold Coin,' which Colton has pronounced, in his opinion, "to come as near to perfection as the sublunary Muse can arrive at."

It is only by several well-sustained efforts that any author has a right to be placed among poets, and it would not be just, therefore, to judge of any without such a consideration of their productions. In all the translations here given, the most characteristic specimens of the style of each writer have been sought, particularly those containing what seemed to be his favourite course of thought, while selecting entire, though generally short, poems for that purpose. With the exception of the Duke de Rivas, the poets enumerated in this work have not published poems of any great length, and therefore the plan adopted may be considered altogether appropriate to the object in view.

With regard to the metres chosen, no rule has been attempted of taking the original strictly for a guide, where the style of verse, in a different language, would not admit of it easily. Perhaps the truest definition of Poetry may be given in the words of our great poet—

> "Thoughts that voluntary move
> Harmonious numbers—"

for it may be observed, that the finest passages are generally the easiest for translation and for rhyme. Thus keeping the original constantly in view as the guide, the verse has been adopted as the thoughts seemed to indicate the metre most appropriate.

With the disadvantage of rhyme, in a foreign language, no apology is requisite for the ruggedness of any lines which the critic may point out. I differ totally from those writers, Coleridge and others, who affect a contempt for finished versification, and rely entirely on the brilliancy of their ideas. Whatever is worth doing at all is worth doing well, according to the writer's best capability, and the reader's ear ought surely to be as much consulted as his mind is sought to be engaged. Those who have had to write "nonsense verses" at school or college, have no right to excuse themselves from labouring to make their lines run smoothly. If, therefore, any of the following translations are not so rendered, it will occasion the writer much regret that his best efforts for that purpose have been unsuccessful.

Another complaint may be anticipated, that this work does not comprehend authors either in prose or the drama. The fault, if it be one, must be admitted, with the observation, that the task undertaken was felt sufficient of itself to require the best exertions of the writer. According to the plan laid down of giving only entire pieces, in the case of including either prose or dramatic writers, the work would have been increased to an inordinate extent, or the plan must have been adopted of giving extracts, which would be contrary to the opinion expressed of the best course to be pursued. If this attempt should meet with public approbation, some one else may be induced to continue the further service. If it should not, the labour expended on a larger work would be so much more given in vain. In the one case, the failure might be ascribed to having attempted too much; in the other, the approbation might not have been gained but for the efforts having been directed undividedly to what was thus only within the reach of accomplishment.

In sequence of the remark before made, of the manly style of thought, feeling and expression which had characterized the older Spanish writers, from their having been persons generally who had engaged in the active affairs of life, the reader may perhaps feel interested in tracing how the same causes have produced the same effects with their successors. From the memoirs hereafter detailed, it may be seen that no fewer than six out of the twelve had to suffer the evils of exile for public or private opinions, of whom three so died unhappily in foreign countries. Three others, though not actually exiled, were subjected to long and cruel imprisonment for the same causes, while two out of the remaining three had to take their share of burdens in the public service during the troubled state of the country. Such men could have no mawkish sentiments to develope, and no fantastic feelings to indulge. What they felt, they felt deeply; what they observed, they observed distinctly, and thus were enabled to give their thoughts and feelings clearly and strongly.

But in addition to the causes assigned for the superior character of modern Spanish poetry in particular, there is one other to be suggested, the association of which may perhaps occasion some surprise, though it may not be for that the less indubitable. This is the fact of the later Spanish writers having, perhaps unconsciously, but unmistakenly, taken better models than their predecessors by preferring the study of English literature to that of the French. This fact, though without the full inference that might have been drawn from it, has been observed by a German author, F. J. Wolf, of the Imperial Library at Vienna, who has published a collection of modern Spanish poetry, with biographical notices, Paris, 1837, in two volumes—' Floresta de Rimas Modernas Castellanas.' It is an interesting collection, but being all given in the Spanish language, is only available to those who are acquainted with it. In the introduction to this work, Wolf treats of the "efforts of Melendez and the Salamanca school to give a new splendour to Spanish poetry, partly by the study and imitation of the ancient and good Spanish writers, taking advantage of the national forms, and partly by making it more profound and substantial, imitating not only and exclusively the French, but also and especially the English." (Page 15.)

During the early part of the last century, consequent upon the accession of the Bourbons to the throne, the writers of verse in Spain, who obtained most favour among their contemporaries, formed their style avowedly upon the model of what was called the French school, and thus taking examples unworthy of imitation, became still more wretched as copyists. Towards the end of the century, however, a feeling arose, on the other side, in favour of the study of English literature, which has led to the happiest results. Of the twelve poets whose lives and poems it is the purpose of this work to delineate, no fewer than ten may be observed acquainted in no inconsiderable degree with the best English authors and proficient in the English language. Two only, Breton de los Herreros and Zorrilla, seem not to have extended their studies so far. With the peculiar humorous vein of the former, perhaps the deficiency may not be considered as leaving any merit to be supplied. But it does seem a matter of regret that a person of Zorrilla's exalted genius should have confined his studies so much to French writers, and so have deprived himself of the expansion necessary for the highest flights of poetry. France has never produced a great painter or a great poet. The very language, so monotonous and unmusical, in having the accent almost invariably on the last syllable of the words, seems opposed to rhythmical cadence, and not to admit of the highest excellence either in oratory or poetry. Whatever may be the cause, it is evident that such excellence has not been attained in the language, and therefore the best works in it cannot be models for imitation when they are only themselves of an inferior value.

Beyond the writers enumerated hereafter, whose memoirs and writings are to be considered worthy of fuller notice, there are several others who, as especially coming under the consideration above suggested, may here be noticed in further corroboration of the statements we have made.

1. Juan de Escoiquiz, tutor to Ferdinand VII., one of the most upright, if not most successful, public men of his time, published, in 1798, an epic poem 'On the Conquest of Mexico,' which showed considerable poetical ability, though it did not obtain much popular favour. In 1797 he published a translation of Young's 'Night Thoughts,' from the English into Spanish verse, and in 1814 a translation of Milton's 'Paradise Lost.' Of the former, a translation in prose had been previously published by Cristoval Caldera. Escoiquiz died in 1814.

2. Josè de Cadalso or Cadahalso, born 1741, was a person of rank and fortune, who had travelled much in his youth, and become proficient in various foreign languages and literatures, especially the English. He wrote several works, both in prose and verse, which were received with great

favour at the time, and have been republished frequently since his death. The last edition was in 1818, in three volumes, under the editorship of the late learned Navarrete, who appended to them an interesting biography of the author. Among the miscellanies are several translations from the English, which language, we are informed, Cadalso not only studied himself assiduously, but induced Melendez Valdes to adopt for peculiar study also. This eminent poet was in early life so assisted by Cadalso as to have been pronounced his "best work," and he, as may be seen hereafter, seems sedulously to have followed the good counsels and example given him by his friend. Cadalso, like so many other of the principal poets of Spain, had embraced a military career, in which, having been ordered with his regiment to the siege of Gibraltar, he there received a wound of which he died a few days after, the 27th February, 1782. His death was a great loss to Spanish literature, and it was equally lamented by the English in the besieged fortress, by whom he was much esteemed from previous friendly communications.

3. The Conde de Noronia, born 1760, died 1816, another poetical writer of considerable reputation, was also engaged in military service, in which he attained high rank, and with the division of the Spanish army under his command, gained the victory at the battle of San Payo over the French. He was appointed ambassador successively at Berne and St. Petersburgh, and was celebrated as a diplomatist for his knowledge of English and other languages. Notwithstanding an active life in the public service, he found leisure for literary pursuits, and in 1800 published a collection of poems in two volumes. Among these are to be observed several translations from the English, of which one of Dryden's celebrated 'Ode for St. Cecilia's Day,' rendered into Spanish verse with

much spirit, deserves particular mention. The best of his poems seems an 'Ode on the Death of Cadalso,' by whose side he was present when he received his wound. The Conde further attempted an epic, in twelve cantos, entitled 'Ommiada,' detailing the events in the reign of Abderaman, the last of the Ommiades, which poem was published in two volumes in 1816. For the purpose of assisting him in this work, he had translated several pieces from the Arabic and other eastern languages into Spanish verse, published since at Paris in 1833.

4. Juan Maria Maury, who died in 1846, was another writer of considerable talent. He was sent early in life to France, and completed his education in England, becoming thereby well acquainted with the language and literature of both countries. His principal work is a poem entitled, 'Esvero y Almedora,' in twelve cantos, published at Paris in 1840. It is founded on the adventures of a passage-at-arms, held against all comers, in 1434, at the bridge of Orbiza, near Leon, and contains several interesting scenes spiritedly described. His earliest work was a poem he called 'British Aggression,' published in 1806, the sentiments of which he seems afterwards to have considerably modified. Maury appears to have been a person of very amiable character, and much esteemed by all who knew him, judging by the manner in which Del Rio and others write respecting him. In his latter years he resided almost entirely at Paris, and gained for himself the extraordinary merit of being esteemed also a correct writer of French verse, by his translations of the principal Spanish poets into that language. This work, published in two volumes at Paris in 1826, entitled, 'Espagne Poétique, Choix de Poésies Castellanes depuis Charles Quint jusqu'à nos jours,' is, as the name imports, a selection of Spanish poetry with critical and biographical notices, made with much

taste and judgement, and forming altogether a very interesting work for the French student of Spanish literature. It is dedicated to his friends Arriaza and Quintana, in a poetical epistle, from which the following extract may be considered acceptable in corroboration of the previous remarks:—

> " Sans doute, Emmanuel, aux champs de Tamise
> Triomphe une vertu qu'ailleurs tu crus permise,
> Et qui là fier génie a ravi le trident.
> Jeune j'y respirai l'orgueil indépendant ;
> Là, j'admirai l'accord, merveille alors unique,
> Qui règle et garantit, sur le sol britannique
> Au trône ses splendeurs, aux grands l'autorité,
> Aux citoyens leurs droits, qu'on nomma liberté,
> Et le temps destructeur y consacre, y conserve
> Le plus beau monument élevé par Minerve."

5. Josè Joaquin Mora, born at Cadiz, 1783, and yet happily surviving, is another modern poet of great merit. When the French invaded Spain, he entered a regiment of dragoons in the national cause, and was made prisoner in 1809, in consequence of which he was detained in France six years. He took advantage of this residence in that country to pursue his studies, and on the return of peace he undertook the editorship of the 'Scientific and Literary Chronicle of Madrid,' which, in 1820, he converted into 'The Constitutional.' In 1823 he had to emigrate to London, where he wrote and published several periodical and other works, under the auspices of Messrs. Ackerman, besides various translations. He afterwards went to Buenos Ayres, Chili and Bolivia, from which last republic he returned to London as Consul-General, and published, in 1840, his principal work, entitled 'Spanish Legends.' This work, which is highly praised by Ochoa, gives, as the title imports, descriptive accounts of various events in the history of Spain, according to what seems to be the favourite formula of modern Spanish poetry. Another work he published, in 1826, entitled 'Poetical Meditations,' is

founded principally on Blair's celebrated poem, 'The Grave.' Wolf pronounces him excelling in his satirical essays, which, he says, are full of grace and ease.

In addition to the writers mentioned above, and those whose works form the main purpose of this work hereafter in detail, many others have appeared, both during the latter part of the last century and during the present, who have shown much talent, and have been deservedly received with much favour by their countrymen. It will be sufficient for us here to give the names of Cienfuegos, Tapia, Lista, Gallego, S. Bermudez de Castro, Garcia Gutierrez and Pastor Diaz among them; and to meet any observation that may be suggested on account of no fuller notice being taken of them, it may be allowed me to state, that I have notwithstanding read and examined carefully all their works, and those of many others whose names it is needless to recapitulate. I would further add, that in so doing, although there was certainly much in them to admire, yet there was nothing in them, in my judgement, suited for translation to interest English readers, whose tastes it was my duty principally to consult. Some of those just mentioned and others omitted, I have personally known and appreciated in private life, but in all the selections and criticisms made or repeated, I have allowed no consideration to weigh with me, except the respect due to superior merit alone. So much of this superior merit seemed to me to exist in modern Spanish literature, that I ventured to think the English public would receive favourably this attempt to make them acquainted with it. If it should fail, the blame must attach to the translator; if it be received favourably, there is yet a rich mine of intellectual wealth in store to reward the labours of those who choose to undertake it.

The student who wishes to follow in the same course, will

find the way much prepared for him in the various collections of ancient and modern poetry lately published. Those by Maury and Wolf have been already mentioned. Quintana has, in the late edition of his great work, brought down the series of national poets to the beginning of this century; and Ochoa has, lastly, given a very valuable addition to his other labours of criticisms and compilation, in his Notices for a Library of contemporary Spanish writers;—'Apuntes para una Biblioteca de Escritores Españoles contemporaneos,' in two volumes, Paris, 1847. Ferrer del Rio has also conferred a great service on the national literature, by giving a series of biographical sketches, ably written, of the principal Spanish writers of the present day, 'Galeria de la Literatura Española,' published by Mellado, at Madrid, 1846. From these works, when no other authority is mentioned as of distinct character, the notices in this work have been compiled, except in a few instances, which will be found also generally stated when they have been obtained from private information. The facts, of necessity, could not but be learned from such sources, and the translator is only answerable for the selection of those he thought worthy of being repeated, and the arrangement, in addition to the criticisms that coincided with his own judgement, for his adoption.

In conclusion of these introductory remarks, it now only remains necessary further to observe, that the rules of Spanish versification are very similar to the English, being dependent upon accents, according to the rhythm adopted on certain syllables of each line, whether alternately or further removed. The rule as to rhyme is also the same, admitting of single or double rhymes, used in one case or the other, according as the accent is on the last syllable of the final word or the penultimate. The latter, however, is more common in Spanish than in English, where it seems only suited for the livelier strains of verse.

But in addition to the usual method of using rhymes, dependent in English and most other languages upon the consonants rather than the vowels, the Spaniards have a form of verse of which the rhyme is dependent on the vowel only, and the consonants may be entirely dissimilar. This form of verse they call Asonantes, in contradistinction to the other, which they call Consonantes, or full and perfect rhyme. Thus in the first stanza of the 'Alcazar of Seville,' the words *prolijas* and *cornisas* are Consonantes or full rhymes, but in the following verses *miran* and *distintas* are Asonantes, as also *risa* and *evitan*. The Spaniards conceive the Asonantes to be a form peculiar to themselves, but it is one common to many other nations, in the earlier stages of poetical composition. In the earliest Spanish poems, asonants and consonants were used together promiscuously, as may be observed particularly in the early poems in the Galician dialect; and it is curious to trace in this respect, as well as in many of their words, vestiges of their Celtic descent, this same form being also one of the prominent features of Celtic versification. In their modern asonante verse, the Spanish poets usually exclude consonantes, and that form continues in much favour, probably on account of the words in their language, as in the Latin, having generally so much the same sound as to make a variation pleasing to the ear, to break the monotonous effect of a too frequent recurrence of similar terminations. For this reason, no doubt, it was that the Latin poets did not adopt the system of rhymes, and for the same also it is common now in Spanish poems to have lines occasionally to which no other line presents a rhyme, giving thereby a pleasing effect to the whole. In our language, on the contrary, where, from the ruggedness of its character, the terminations vary so exceedingly as to make them often even difficult to be found for the purposes of rhyme, the recurrence of rhyme gives a more pleasing sound to the ear from the degree of surprise that is thus occasioned. In Spanish they might easily be made of one vowel termination for a long poem, so that the difficulty in it is to avoid the too frequent recurrence of the same sound.

Martinez de la Rosa has boasted of the variety of rhymes in Spanish; but he refers to double as well as single rhymes, and in this and in other respects is carried away by his ardour, in admiration of his country's language, much further than the facts will be found to support him. Thus he also praises the number and variety of metres used in it as extraordinary, when in fact they are no more. so than any other neighbouring language could present. It may be justly conceded, that poetry has been cultivated lately in Spain with much assiduity and success; but there is no peculiarity in the language to give it an advantage over others in respect to metres. The strict censorship which has weighed down the energies of the country, with regard to most subjects of public discussion, has had the effect of directing talent to the cultivation of poetry, as almost the only road to literary reputation. This it is, combined with the sensitive character of the nation, that has made their poets attain the eminence we are bound in justice to award them; and it is fortunate for them that they have in their language so admirable an exponent of their genius, as it must in fairness be allowed, though the merit still remains peculiarly their own.

The following is a summary list of the principal Modern Spanish Poets whose memoirs and writings it is the object of this work more particularly to make known to the English public, given with a statement of dates respecting their lives, for the purpose of enabling the reader to compare more easily the periods in which they flourished. They are, it will be observed, twelve in number, and the list has been divided into two parts, as marking an evidently distinctive character of the poetry in the former and latter part of the epoch which they have rendered memorable.

PART I.

I. Jovellanos . . . . Born 1744. Died 1811. Age 67.

II. Iriarte . . . . . . Born 1750. Died 1791. Age 41.

III. Melendez Valdes . . Born 1754. Died 1817. Age 63.

IV. Leandro Moratin . . . Born 1760. Died 1828. Age 68.

V. Arriaza . . . . Born 1770. Died 1837. Age 67.

VI. Quintana . . . . . . Born 1772. Living 1851. Age 79.

PART II.

VII. Martinez de la Rosa . . Born 1789. Living 1851. Age 62.

VIII. The Duke de Rivas . . Born 1791. Living 1851. Age 60.

IX. Breton de los Herreros Born 1796. Living 1851. Age 55.

X. Heredia . . . . Born 1803. Died 1839. Age 35.

XI. Espronceda . . . . Born 1810. Died 1842. Age 32.

XII. Zorrilla . . . . Born 1817. Living 1851. Age 34.

PRELIMINARY NOTE.

For readers unacquainted with the Spanish language, it may be perhaps most advisable, in this place, to affix a few short instructions for the proper pronunciation of such names and words as are to be found in the following pages.

1. The vowels in Spanish have each invariably their peculiar sound; not as in English, where each has two or more sounds, making them in fact so distinct as strictly requiring to be designated by different characters, or after the manner of the Hebrew points. Thus *a* has always the broad open sound found in the English words *arm, arrack*.

e, long or short, as in the English words *ere, ever*.

i and *y*, as in *machine, syntax*.

o, long or short, as in *ore, host, hostage*.

u has uniformly the sound of *oo* in *food*. The Celtic sound of this vowel, preserved in France and Portugal, is unknown in Spain, and also in the Basque or Biscayan language.

2. Of the consonants, *b* has a softer sound than in English, and approaches to *v*, which again is made to sound like *b*. Thus the city of the Havana is, in Spanish spelling, La Habana, and the river Bidasoa is written Vidasoa.

c, before *a, o, u*, is to be pronounced hard, as in English; before *e* or *i*, it is to be sounded like *th* in *thin*, though in the provinces

c

this pronunciation is giving way to the French and English mode of sounding the letter. Thus the name of the great Roman orator is pronounced Thithero. *ch* has always the soft sound it usually has in English, as in *chat, check, chin, choke, chum.*

d, at the end of a word, is generally pronounced like *th*: thus Madrid is Madrith; *ciudad*, a city, is pronounced *thiudath*; otherwise, both *d* and *t* are spoken as in English, or slightly more dentally.

f has the same sound as in English.

g is an aspirate, like our *h*, more or less guttural, according to the word. The soft sound of this letter, as in *gem*, left by the Celts in Italy and Portugal, is unknown in Spain, as is also the soft sound of the letter *j*.

h may be said to be invariably a silent letter, and seems only used to prevent two vowels running into each other, so as to form a diphthong.

j is a very harsh guttural, like the Hebrew *Cheth*. Thus Juan (John) is to be pronounced strongly, Hwan; Josè (Joseph) also strongly, Hosè.

The letters *k, l, m, n, p,* are the same as in English.

q or *qu* has the sound of our *k*: thus *que* (that) is the same as the Italian *che*.

r, s, t have the same sounds as in English, except that the first has one somewhat rougher, especially when two come together.

x is a strong guttural, for which *j* is now generally used, as Don Quijote.

z is pronounced as *th*: thus Cadiz is sounded Cadith.

The Spaniards consider their *ll* and *ñ*, or *n* with a circumflex, distinct letters, but they are in fact only the letters *l* or *n* with the sound of *i* after them, as in the English words *million, minion,* being the same sound that the French and Italians express by *gn*, or *gl*. Several names may be found in the body of this work altered according to our mode of spelling, though in the headings retained as in the original, as Padillia instead of Padilla. For the sake of preserving the sound free from constant explanation or confusion, the like course has been sometimes adopted with regard to other words, as, for instance, the name of the river Genil or Xenil, represented in English as Henil.

Two or more vowels coming together are enunciated so as to form one syllable generally in Spanish, and especially in poetry, yet nevertheless so as to allow of each vowel to be sounded distinctly, as each syllable is also.

With regard to accents, the general rule is, that it should be placed on the penultimate syllable. There are many exceptions, but in print these are always marked by the accent (') on the vowel indicated, except in words of two syllables, which, if ending in a consonant, have generally the accent on the last syllable, if ending in a vowel, on the first, without being notified.

From these notices it may be observed, that the Spanish language is remarkable for two sounds, the guttural and the predominating *th*, which distinguish it from the two sister dialects of Italy and Portugal, while it is deficient in the soft sound of *g* and *j*, found so frequently used in the latter. These two assimilate so much to each other that natives of either country understand those of the other readily, while they cannot those of Spain, showing that the influence of the Gothic and Moorish invaders was impressed there on the pronunciation of the common language, though it was not extended to altering materially the language itself.

Besides the soft sound of the *g*, there are two other sounds unknown in Spanish, though common in Portugal and France, left by their former Celtic inhabitants, those of the *sh* or French *j*, and the disagreeable nasal pronunciation of the letter *n*. The latter is very slightly given in *Don*, and a few other words, but the other is unknown. In Portuguese it is so prevalent that they even use it for Latin words which it would be difficult to recognize at first as the originals from which the others were derived; thus the words *pluvia*, *plorare*, transformed in Spanish into *lluvia*, *llorar*, are in Portuguese further transformed into *chuva* (*shuva*), *chorar* (*shorar*). The natives of Galicia speak a dialect more allied to Portuguese than the Spanish, being of more decided Celtic descent, like the Portuguese, than the rest of the people of the Peninsula. The natives of Catalonia speak a dialect half French, half Spanish, which may be considered the representative of the ancient Provençal or Limoisin. It is very guttural as well as nasal. The Basque or Biscayan language is entirely distinct from the modern Spanish, and also from the Latin, the Celtic, or that of any neighbouring country, and is well deserving of study. It has no harsh or disagreeable sounds in it, and abounds in vowels, many words having not a single consonant in them.

ERRATA.

Page xxii line 30, *instead of* association, *read* assertion.
— 11, — 18, —— "make it a well," *read* "use it for a well."
— 60, — 7, —— suffice *read* suffices.
— 66, — 11, —— sensibly *read* sensitively.
— 157, — 23, —— sage *read* shade.
— 271, — 29, —— nineteen *read* eighteen.
— 301, — 12, —— "of Lord Byron's," *read* "in Lord Byron's."

Page 145, line 4, "has been announced," &c. This statement is erroneous, the reference having been made to Mr. J. Russell's Life of Gonzalo de Còrdova, translated from Quintana's first volume, London, 1851.

CONTENTS.

	Page
DEDICATION	iii

INTRODUCTION. On the character of Spanish Poetry, Ancient and Modern.—Causes affecting it suggested from considerations of Roman civilization, Moorish wars, and personal history of the principal Poets.—Works on Spanish literature: Remarks on translation and language.—References to other modern Poets.—Spanish metres and versification vii

PRELIMINARY NOTE. On the pronunciation of Spanish names and words xxxiii

PART I.

1. GASPAR MELCHOR DE JOVELLANOS.

Memoir of	3
Epistle to Cean Bermudez, on the Vain Desires and Studies of Men	18
To Galatea's Bird	30
To Enarda.—I.	32
To Enarda.—II.	33

II. TOMAS DE IRIARTE.

	Page
Memoir of	37
Epistle to Don Domingo de Iriarte, on his Travelling to various Foreign Courts	46
The Bear, the Monkey and the Hog	53
The Ass and the Flute	55
The Two Rabbits	56
The Lamb and his Two Advisers	58
The Flint and the Steel	59

III. JUAN MELENDEZ VALDES.

Memoir of	61
Juvenilities	77
The Timid Lover	79
My Village Life	81
Remembrances of Youth	84
Of the Sciences	87
The Disdainful Shepherdess	90

IV. LEANDRO FERNANDEZ MORATIN.

Memoir of	95
Dedication of the Mogigata to the Prince of the Peace	106
Epistle to Don Gaspar de Jovellanos, sent from Rome	108

V. JUAN BAUTISTA DE ARRIAZA.

Memoir of	113
Tempest and War, or the Battle of Trafalgar	123
The Parting	132

VI. MANUEL JOSE QUINTANA.

Memoir of	141
To the Spanish Expedition for the Promotion of Vaccination in America, under Don Francisco Balmis	152
On the Battle of Trafalgar	158

PART II.

VII. FRANCISCO MARTINEZ DE LA ROSA.

	Page
Memoir of	169
Remembrance of Spain, written in London in 1811	183
Return to Granada, October 27, 1831	185
Epistle to the Duque de Frias, on the Death of the Duquesa	190
Anacreontic	199
Bacchanalian	200

VIII. ANGEL DE SAAVEDRA, DUKE DE RIVAS.

Memoir of	203
The Alcazar of Seville	224

IX. MANUEL BRETON DE LOS HERREROS.

Memoir of	249
Satirical Letrillias.—III.	258
Satirical Letrillias.—IV.	260
Satirical Letrillias.—VII.	262

X. JOSE MARIA HEREDIA.

Memoir of	265
Sonnet. Dedication of the Second Edition of his Poems, to his Wife	275
To his Horse	276
The Season of the Northers	277
Poesy, an Ode	280
Ode to Night	285

XI. JOSÈ DE ESPRONCEDA.

	Page
Memoir of	291
To Spain, an Elegy. London, 1829	305
The Condemned to Die	308
The Song of the Pirate	314
To Harifa, in an Orgy	318

XII. JOSE ZORRILLA.

Memoir of	323
The Christian Lady and the Moor	336
Romance, The Waking	339
Oriental Romance, Boabdil	343
The Captive	345
The Tower of Munion	347
The Warning	350
Meditation	352

NOTES 357

MODERN POETS

AND

POETRY OF SPAIN.

PART I.

GASPAR MELCHOR DE JOVELLANOS.

AN able and distinguished writer in the Madrid Review has observed, that if the question were asked as to which is the first great name in modern Spanish literature, the answer must unquestionably be—Jovellanos. It seems, therefore, only a just deference to his merits, though it is but a fortuitous coincidence in the order of dates, that we have to place his name first in the series of modern Spanish poets. It is, however, to his State Papers and his writings on Political Economy that he principally owes his reputation; though it is a proud consideration for Spanish literature, that, as regards him, as well as Martinez de la Rosa and the Duke de Rivas, she has to place the names of eminent statesmen among her principal poets.

Jovellanos was born the 5th of January, 1744, at Gijon, a town in the Asturias, of which his father was Regidor or one of the chief Magistrates. His family connections were of the class called Nobles, answering to the Noblesse of

France, and were moreover very influential and sufficiently wealthy. To take advantage of the preferments these offered him, he was destined in early youth, being a younger son, for the church, in which he entered into the first orders for the purpose of holding several benefices that were given him. He studied consecutively at Oviedo, Avila and Osma, where he distinguished himself so much to the satisfaction of those interested in his fortunes, that he was removed, in 1764, to the University of Alcalà de Henares, and shortly afterwards to Madrid to study law. His friends and relatives, having become aware of his great talents, had now induced him to abandon the clerical profession and engage in secular pursuits. A person of his rank in those days was not at liberty to practise as an advocate, though the young Noble, under court favour, might administer the law; and thus he was, in 1767, when only in his twenty-fourth year, appointed judge of criminal cases at Seville. In this office he conducted himself with great ability and humanity, appearing to have been the first to abandon the employment of torture for obtaining confessions, which system has scarcely yet been discarded on the Continent. As characteristic of him, it may here be added, that he is reported to have been the first of the higher magistrates in Spain who gave up the use of the official wig; so that his unusual dress, combined with his youth, made him on the bench more observed than perhaps even his talents would at first have rendered him.

Whatever objections might have been made, if cause could be found, he seems, after having served nearly ten years as judge in the criminal courts, to have been advanced, with the approbation of all parties, to the office of judge in civil cases, also at Seville. This was an office much more agreeable to his inclinations, though the salary was no higher than what he had previously enjoyed. He had, however, other duties also entrusted to him of minor character, though of proportionate emolument, and thereupon he resigned his benefices in the church, which he had held till then, and to the duties of which he had strictly attended. Beyond this act of disinterestedness, he seems to have given his brother magistrates no inconsiderable inquietude at the same time by refusing some emoluments of office to which they considered themselves entitled. But their minds were soon relieved from the apprehensions his conduct might occasion them, as at the end of four years he was, in 1778, appointed judge of criminal cases at Madrid; an office generally considered of eminent promotion, but which he accepted with regret.

In after times, every letter and every notice of Jovellanos that could be found was eagerly sought and treasured up; and from these and his own memorandums, it appears he had good reason to consider the years he passed at Seville as the happiest of his life. Honoured in his public capacity and beloved in his social circle, he passed whatever time he could spare from his official or private duties in literary pursuits. It was then he wrote or prepared most of the lighter works which entitle him to be ranked among the poets of the age; the tragedy of "Pelayo," and comedy of "The Honourable Delinquent," both which were highly esteemed by his countrymen, as well as most of his minor poems. He did not however confine himself to such recreations, but at the same time entered on graver studies for the public service, on which his fame was eventually established.

Shortly after Jovellanos joined the courts at Seville, he had for one of his colleagues Don Luis Ignacio Aguirre, a person of high literary attainments, who had travelled much, and brought with him, as stated by Bermudez, many works in English on Political Economy. To understand these, Jovellanos immediately, under Aguirre's guidance, proceeded to learn the English language, of which he soon obtained a competent knowledge. He then studied the science, then newly dawning, from the works his friend afforded him, and made himself a master of it, so as to give him a name among the most eminent of its professors. Not contented with these pursuits, his active mind was still further engaged in whatever could tend to the benefit of society in the place of his labours. He seems indeed to have always had before him the consideration of what might be the fullest duties his station imposed on him, beyond the mere routine of official services. Not confining himself to these, much less giving himself up to passive enjoyments, however harmless or honourable in themselves, he seemed then and through life as ever acting under the sense of a great responsibility, as of the requirements of Him "who gave his servants authority, and to every man his work." Thus he instituted a school at Seville for children, reformed the course of practice at the hospitals, attended to the keeping of the public walks and grounds in good order, and was foremost in every case where charity called or good services were required. Artists and men of genius found in him a friend, who, by advice and other aid, was always ready to their call; and it was observed that his only passion was for the purchase of books and pictures, of which respectively he formed good collections.

On giving up his duties at Seville, Jovellanos travelled through Andalusia, and, as was his custom in all the places he visited, made notes of whatever useful information he could obtain respecting them, many of which were afterwards published in a topographical work he assisted in bringing forward. On arriving at Madrid, where his fame had preceded him, he was at once chosen member of the different learned societies, to several of which he rendered valuable services. At Seville he had already prepared a sketch of his great work, entitled "Agrarian Law," in which he treated of the law and tenure of land, its cultivation, and other topics connected with it. This work he then published in an extended form, in which it has been reprinted several times, separately as well as in his collected works. In the several societies he also read many papers, one of which, "On Public Diversions," deserves to be named particularly, as containing much curious information, as well as many excellent suggestions for public advantage, on points which statesmen would do well to remember more frequently than they are in the habit of doing.

On leaving Seville, Jovellanos regretted that he had to engage again in criminal cases, for which he had a natural aversion. After fulfilling these duties at Madrid a year and a half, he therefore sought another appointment, and obtained one in the Council of Military Orders, more agreeable to his inclinations. In this office it was his duty to attend to the affairs of the four military orders of Spain, and in his visits to their properties and other places on their behalf, he was entrusted with various commissions, which he fulfilled with his accustomed zeal. In those visits he had to go much to his native province, and he took advantage of his influence to make roads, which were much needed there, and the benefits of which he lived to see appreciated. He incited the members of the Patriotic Society of Oviedo, and others connected with the Asturias, to explore the mineral wealth of the country, rich in mines of coal and iron, then scarcely known. For the study of such pursuits he founded the Asturian Institute, and raised subscriptions to have two young men educated abroad in mathematics and mining, who were afterwards to teach those sciences at the Institute. Every day of his life indeed seems to have been employed on some object of public

utility, or in studies connected with such objects; following the ancient maxim to do nothing trifling or imperfectly:—
Μηδὲν ἐνέργημα εἰκῆ, μηδὲν ἄλλως ἢ κατὰ θεωρήμα συμπληρωτικὸν τῆς τέχνης ἐνεργεῖθω.
Though exact in the fulfilment of his official duties, and other various commissions entrusted to him by the government to report on the state of the provinces, it is wonderful to consider the industry with which he followed other pursuits. He studied botany and architecture, on which he wrote several treatises; and though each of those subjects would have been a sufficient task for ordinary men, to him they were only relaxations from his favourite science of political economy.

Bent on the promotion of law and other reforms in the state, he became connected with the Conde de Cabarrus, who, though a Frenchman by birth, had obtained high employments in Spain, and who, as a person of superior talent and discernment, was also convinced of the necessity of such measures. As too often is the case with able and honest statesmen, the Conde de Cabarrus fell, while attempting to effect these reforms, under the intrigues of his enemies, and Jovellanos became involved in his disgrace. He had been sent, in 1790, into the provinces in fulfilment of the duties of his office; when, having heard on the road of his friend's ill fortune, he returned at once to offer him whatever assistance he might have in his power. He had, however, no sooner arrived in Madrid, where the Conde was under arrest, than, without being allowed to communicate with him, Jovellanos received a royal order to return immediately to his province.

The terms in which this order was conveyed convinced Jovellanos that he was to share in the disgrace of his friend, and to consider himself banished from court. He therefore proceeded philosophically to settle himself in his paternal abode with his brother, their father being now deceased, with his books and effects, and engaged in the improvement of their family estates. His expectations proved correct, as in this honourable exile he had to pass seven years, though not altogether unemployed, as he had several commissions entrusted to him similar to those he had previously discharged. But still Jovellanos, unbowed by political reverses, continued the same ardent promoter of public improvement. For the Asturian Institute, which he had founded for the purpose of teaching principally mineralogy and metallurgy, and which he personally superintended, he wrote his very able work on Public Instruction, and compiled elementary grammars of the French and English languages, in which he showed himself proficient to a degree truly astonishing.

In his official duties, having to go carefully in inspection over the Asturias and other neighbouring provinces, he noted his observations in diaries, which have been fortunately preserved, and which contain much valuable information. In these he has gathered all he could learn relative to the productions of the provinces, and the state in which he found them and the people, as embodied in his reports thereon to the government, with an account of the ancient remains and public buildings, making copies of whatever he found most interesting in the archives of the several convents, cathedrals and corporations. Some of these copies now possess a peculiar value, from the damages that have since accrued to many of the originals from time and the events of the subsequent wars.

If it were not for the disparagement of being considered in banishment, Jovellanos could have felt himself contented. He had not only honourable employment, as before stated, but he also received several notices of approbation from the government, especially as regarded the Institute, to which notices he perhaps paid a higher regard than they deserved. He seems himself to have felt this; for in one of his letters he writes—"I will not deny that I desire some public mark of appreciation by the government, to gain by it that kind of sanction which merit needs in the opinion of some weak minds. But I see that this is a vain suggestion, and that posterity will not judge me by my titles, but by my works."

This was written on a rumour having reached Gijon of the probability of his being soon restored to favour at court. Those under whose intrigues he had fallen had now passed away in their turn: a favourite of a more powerful grade was in the ascendant, Godoy, the Prince of the Peace, to whose mind had been suggested the advisability of gathering round him persons of acknowledged probity and knowledge, for the support of his government. Jovellanos had returned home, in October 1797, from one of his journeys of inspection, when he found the whole town in a state of rejoicing. On inquiring the cause, he was told it was because news had been received of his nomination as ambassador to Russia. A few days afterwards the rejoicings were renewed, on the further intelligence of his being nominated a member of the government itself, as Minister of Grace and Justice.

In this office it might have been hoped that a happier career was before him; but evil fortune on the contrary now followed him, and more fatally than ever. His former banishment from court was owing to the endeavours he had made to remove those abuses into which all human institutions have a tendency to fall, rendering frequently necessary a correction of those abuses, to preserve what was most valuable in the institutions themselves. His next misfortune arose from personal differences with the reigning favourite, whose greater influence it was his error not to have perceived. Jovellanos had been restored to favour at the instance of Godoy; but as this was without his seeking, he felt himself under no obligation to maintain him as the head of the government, for which he was totally unfit. Jovellanos joined in an opposition to him, which for a short time succeeded in depriving Godoy of office. But his influence at court continued, and thus Jovellanos was in his turn dismissed, after holding the office of minister only about eight months, and ordered to return to Gijon.

Unhappily the favourite carried his resentment further; and Jovellanos was, on the 13th of March, 1801, arrested in his bed at an early hour of the morning, and sent as a prisoner through the country to Barcelona, thence to Mallorca, where first in the Carthusian convent, and afterwards in the castle of Bellver more strictly, he was closely confined, without any regard paid to his demands to know the accusation against him. Here his health was severely affected, as well as his feelings outraged, by the unjust treatment to which he was subjected. Still he was not one to sink under such evils. He was rather one of those "who, going through the valley of misery, make it a well." He turned accordingly to the resources of literature, and employed himself in writing and translating from Latin and French several valuable treatises on architecture, and other works, on the history of the island, and of the convent, besides several poems, among which the Epistle to Bermudez, his biographer, deserves particular notice.

Another work he then wrote is no less deserving of mention, showing the attention he had paid to English affairs, entitled "A Letter on English Architecture, and that called Gothic," in which he treated of English architecture from the time of the Druids, dividing it into the Saxon, Gothic and modern periods. He describes the buildings according to the epochs, especially St. Paul's and others of the seventeenth century, coming down to the picturesque style of gardening then adopted in England, with notices of the different sculptors, painters and engravers, as well as architects, and also of the authors who had written on the Fine Arts in England. This work has not been published, but Bermudez states he had the manuscript.

After being seven years a prisoner, Jovellanos was in 1808 released on the abdication of Charles IV. and the consequent fall of Godoy. This release was announced to him in terms of official brevity, and he replied by an earnest demand to be subjected to a trial, for the purpose of having the cause of his imprisonment made manifest. Before, however, an answer could be returned, Ferdinand had, under Napoleon's dictation, also ceased to reign, and Jovellanos was called upon to take a prominent place in the intrusive government of king Joseph. This he could not be supposed from his antecedent character to be willing to accept. On the contrary, being chosen by the National party a member of the Central Junta, he engaged with his accustomed energy on the other side until the Regency was formed, principally under his influence, to carry on the struggles for independence.

On this being effected, Jovellanos wished to retire to his native city apart from public affairs. At his advanced age, with cataracts formed in his eyes, and after his laborious life and painful imprisonment, rest was necessary for him; but he could not attain it. One of his first efforts in the Central Junta was to draw up a paper on the form of government to be adopted, and this he strongly recommended to be founded as nearly as possible on the model of the English constitution. But he was far too enlightened for the race of men with whom he had to act, and his prepossessions for English institutions were made a reproach against him, observes the editor of the last edition of his works, even by those who were striving to introduce the principles of the Constituent Assembly into Spain.

The miserable intrigues and jealousies of the leading members of the National party caused Jovellanos much anxiety. But he had fulfilled his duties as a Deputy, and those having ceased, he left Cadiz in February, 1810, to return to the Asturias, in a small sailing vessel. After a long and dangerous passage, during which they were in great danger of shipwreck, they arrived at Muros in Galicia, in which province he had to remain more than a year, in consequence of the Asturias being in the possession of the French, to whom he had now become doubly obnoxious.

In July, 1811, however, the French having left that part of Spain, Jovellanos was enabled to return to his native city, where he was again received as he always had been with every token of popular respect. He seems to have been always looked upon there with undeviating favour and gratitude, as their most honourable citizen and public benefactor. No one knew of his coming, says his biographer, but he was observed to enter the church, and kneel before the altar near his family burying-place, when the whole town was roused simultaneously, and a spontaneous illumination of the houses took place, with other tokens of public congratulations and rejoicing.

Here he now hoped to have a peaceful asylum for his latter years, engaged in the objects of public utility for which he had formerly laboured. But those labours were to be begun again. His favourite "Asturian Institute," which he truly said, in one of his discourses, was identified with his existence, had been totally dismantled and used for barracks by the French. Having obtained authority from the Regency to do so, he began to put the building again into repair, and collect together the teachers and scholars. Having done this, he announced by circulars that it would be reopened the 20th of November following, when the news of the French returning compelled him again to fly on the 6th of that month. He set sail in a miserable coasting vessel for Ribadeo, where a ship was ready to take him to Cadiz or England as he might desire, in virtue of instructions given by the Regency, and in accordance with the English government. But further misfortunes only awaited him. The vessel in which he had to take refuge was cast on shore in a storm near the small port of Vega, on the confines of Asturias; and there, worn out with fatigue, and under a pulmonary affection, brought on by exposure to the weather, he died the 27th of November, 1811, a few days after his landing.

The news of his death was spread rapidly through Spain, notwithstanding the interrupted state of communications, and was everywhere received with regret as a national calamity. Those who had opposed his views did justice to the uprightness of his motives and character; and the Cortes, now assembled, passed a decree, by which in favour of his patriotism and public services, he was declared Benemerito de la Patria. This beautiful and classical acknowledgement of his worth was then also remarkable as a novelty, though it has been since rendered less honourable, by being awarded to others little deserving of peculiar distinction.

The life of Jovellanos, as intimately connected with the history of his country, is well deserving of extended study. But our province is rather to consider him as a poet. Eminent as a statesman for unimpeachable integrity and for wise administration of justice, he carried prudent reforms into every department under his control, in which, though subjected to many attacks, he proved himself, by a memoir published shortly before his death, in justification of his public conduct, to have been fully warranted. This memoir, for heartfelt eloquence, deserves to be ranked with Burke's Letter to the Duke of Bedford. Jovellanos has been compared by his countrymen to Cicero. A writer in the Foreign

Quarterly Review has instituted an ingenious parallel between him and Montesquieu. With either, or with Burke, he may be observed to have possessed the philosophy and feeling, which give eloquence its chief value and effect.

As a prose writer, Jovellanos, for elegance of style and depth of thought, may be pronounced without a rival in Spanish literature. As a dramatist, he only gave the public a tragedy and comedy, both of which continue in much favour with the public. The latter, "The Honourable Delinquent" is particularly esteemed; but it is a melodrame rather than a comedy, according to our conceptions. It turns on the principal character having been forced into fighting a duel, and who, having killed his opponent, is sentenced to die; but after the usual suspenses receives a pardon from the king. There are several interesting scenes and much good writing in the piece; but no particular delineation of character, to bring it any more than the other into the higher class of dramatic art. It has, however, been observed, that it only needs to have been written in verse to make it a perfect performance, and this alone shows the hold it must have on the Spanish reader.

As a poet, Jovellanos is chiefly to be commemorated for his Satires. Two of these, in which he lashes the vices and follies of society at Madrid,—"girt with the silent crimes of capitals,"—are pronounced by the critic in the Madrid Review to be "highly finished" compositions. They were, in fact, the only poems he himself published, and those anonymously. With the strength of Juvenal, they have also his faults, and abound too much in local allusions to be suited for translation. In somewhat the same style were several epistles he addressed to different friends, of which the one written to his friend and biographer Bermudez has been chosen for this work, as most characteristic of the author. Like his other Satires, it is written in blank verse; which style, though not entirely unknown in Spain, he had the merit of first bringing into favour. He probably gained his predilection for it from his study of Milton, for whose works he had great admiration, and of whose Paradise Lost he translated the first book into Spanish verse.

The Epistle to Bermudez is remarkable as written with much earnestness, in censure not only of the common vices and follies of mankind, but in also going beyond ordinary satirists into the sphere of the moralist, to censure the faults of the learned. What our great modern preacher Dr. Chalmers has termed the "practical atheism" of the learned, was indeed the subject of rebuke from many English writers, as Young and Cowper, but may be looked for in vain in the works of others. Jovellanos had no doubt read the former, at least in the translation of his friend Escoiquiz, and meditated on the sentiment,—"An undevout astronomer is mad," even if not in the original. It can scarcely be supposed that he was so well acquainted with English literature as to have read Cowper; but there are several passages in his Epistles of similar sentiments. The praise of wisdom especially, in the one to Bermudez,—by which we may understand, was meant the wisdom urged by the kingly preacher of Jerusalem, or the rule of conduct founded on right principles, in opposition to mere learning,—is also that of our Christian poet:—

> Knowledge and wisdom, far from being one,
> Have ofttimes no connexion. Knowledge dwells
> In heads replete with thoughts of other men;
> Wisdom in minds attentive to their own.

In his hours of leisure, Jovellanos employed himself in composing occasional verses at times, for the amusement of the society in which he lived, without thinking of their being ever sought for publication. These, however, have been lately gathered together with much industry and exactness in the last edition of his collected works, published by Mellado at Madrid in five volumes, 1845. As the last and fullest, it is also the best collection of them, four other editions of them previously published having been comparatively very deficient with regard to them. Besides those, there were various reprints of several others of his works, which were all received with much favour, both in Spain and abroad.

Jovellanos was never married, and in private life seems to have considered himself under the obligations of the profession for which he was originally intended. His character altogether is one to which it would be difficult to find a parallel, and is an honour to Spain as well as to Spanish literature. His virtues are now unreservedly admitted by all parties of his countrymen, who scarcely ever name him except with the epithet of the illustrious Jovellanos, to which designation he is indeed justly entitled, no less for his writings, than for his many public and private virtues and services to his country. These may be forgotten in the claims of other generations and succeeding statesmen; but his writings must ever remain to carry his memory wherever genius and worth can be duly appreciated.

The charge of writing a memoir of Jovellanos was entrusted by the Historical Society of Madrid to Cean Bermudez, who fulfilled it with affectionate zeal, Madrid, 1814; several other notices of his life have appeared in Spain, including that by Quintana, which has been copied by Wolf. The English reader will find an excellent one in the Foreign Quarterly Review, No. 10, February, 1830; and the Spanish scholar a further very eloquent encomium on his talents and merits in Quintana's second Introduction to his collection of Spanish Poetry.

JOVELLANOS.

EPISTLE TO CEAN BERMUDEZ,
ON THE VAIN DESIRES AND STUDIES OF MEN.

Arise, Bermudo, bid thy soul beware:
Thee raging Fortune watches to ensnare;
And, lulling others' hopes in dreams supine,
A fell assault she meditates on thine.
The cruel blow which suffer'd from her rage
Thy poor estate will not her wrath assuage,
Till from thy breast her fury may depose
The blissful calm to innocence it owes.
Such is her nature, that she loathes the sight
Of happiness for man in her despite.
Thus to thine eyes insidious she presents
The phantasies of good, with which she paints
The road to favour, and would fain employ
Her arts thy holds of virtue to destroy.
Ah! heed her not. See her to rob thee stand
Ev'n of the happiness now in thy hand.
'Tis not of her; she cannot it bestow:
She makes men fortunate;—but happy? No.

Thou think'st it strange! Dost thou the names confound
Of Fortune with felicity as bound?
Like the poor idiots, who so foolish gaze
On the vain gifts and joys which she displays,
So cunning to exchange for real good.
O cheat of human wisdom! say withstood,
What does she promise, but what beings born
To our high destiny should hold in scorn?
In reason's balance her best offers weigh,
And see what worthless lightness they betray.

There are who, burning in the track of fame,
Wear themselves ruthless for a sounding name.
Buy it with blood, and fire, and ruin wide;
And if with horrid arm is death descried,
Waving his pennon as from some high tower,
Their hearts swell proud, and trampling fierce they scour
The field o'er brothers' bodies as of foes!
Then sing a triumph, while in secret flows
The tear they shed as from an anguish'd heart.

Less lofty, but more cunning on his part,
Another sighs for ill-secure command:
With flatteries solicitously plann'd,
Follows the air of favour, and his pride
In adulation vile he serves to hide,

To exalt himself; and if he gain his end
His brow on all beneath will haughty bend;
And sleep, and joy, and inward peace, the price
To splendour of command, will sacrifice:
Yet fears the while, uncertain in his joy,
Lest should some turn of Fortune's wheel destroy
His power in deep oblivion overthrown.

Another seeks, with equal ardour shown,
For lands, and gold in store. Ah! lands and gold,
With tears how water'd, gain'd with toils untold!
His thirst unquench'd, he hoards, invests, acquires;
But with his wealth increased are his desires;
And so much more he gains, for more will long:
Thus, key in hand, his coffers full among;
Yet poor he thinks himself, and learns to know
His state is poor, because he thinks it so.

Another like illusion his to roam
From wife and friends, who flying light and home,
To dedicate his vigils the long night
In secret haunts of play makes his delight,
With vile companions. Betwixt hope and fear
His anxious breast is fluctuating drear.
See, with a throbbing heart and trembling hand,
There he has placed his fortune, all to stand

Upon the turning of a die! 'Tis done:
The lot is cast; what is it? has he won?
Increased is his anxiety and care!
But if reverse, O Heaven! in deep despair,
O'erwhelm'd in ruin, he is doom'd to know
A life of infamy, or death of woe.

And is he happier, who distracted lies
A slave beneath the light of beauty's eyes?
Who fascinated watches, haunts, and prays,
And at the cost of troubles vast essays,
'Mid doubts and fears, a fleeting joy to gain?
Love leads him not: his breast could ne'er profane
Admit Love's purer flame; 'tis passion's fire
Alone that draws him, and in wild desire
He blindly headlong follows in pursuit:
And what for all his toils can he compute?
If gain'd at length, he only finds the prize
Bring death and misery ev'n in pleasure's guise.

Then look on him, abandon'd all to sloth,
Who vacant sees the hours pass long and loth
O'er his so useless life. He thinks them slow,
Alas! and wishes they would faster go.
He knows not how to employ them; in and out
He comes, and goes, and smokes, and strolls about,

To gossip; turns, returns, with constant stress
Wearying himself to fly from weariness.
But now retired, sleep half his life employs,
And fain would all the day, whose light annoys.
Fool! wouldst thou know the sweetness of repose?
Seek it in work. The soul fastidious grows
Ever in sloth, self-gnawing and oppress'd,
And finds its torment even in its rest.

But if to Bacchus and to Ceres given,
Before his table laid, from morn to even,
At ease he fills himself, as held in stall:
See him his stomach make his god, his all!
Nor earth nor sea suffice his appetite;
Ill-tongued and gluttonous the like unite:
With such he passes his vain days along,
In drunken routs obscene, with toast and song,
And jests and dissolute delights; his aim
To gorge unmeasured, riot without shame.
But soon with these begins to blunt and lose
Stomach and appetite: he finds refuse
Offended Nature, as insipid food,
The savours others delicacies view'd.
Vainly from either India he seeks
For stimulants; in vain from art bespeaks
Fresh sauces, which his palate will reject;
His longings heighten'd, but life's vigour wreck'd;

And thus worn out in mid career the cost,
Before life ends he finds his senses lost.

O bitter pleasures! O, what madness sore
Is theirs who covet them, and such implore
Humbly before a lying deity!
How the perfidious goddess to agree
But mocks them! Though perhaps at first she smile,
Exempt from pain and misery the long while
She never leaves them, and in place of joy
Gives what they ask, with weariness to cloy.
If trusted, soon is found experience taught
What ill-foreseen condition they have sought.
Niggard their wishes ever to fulfil,
Fickle in favour, vacillating still,
Inconstant, cruel, she afflicts today,
And casts down headlong to distress a prey,
Whom yesterday she flatter'd to upraise:
And now another from the mire she sways
Exalted to the clouds; but raised in vain,
With louder noise to cast him down again.
Seest thou not there a countless multitude,
Thronging her temple round, and oft renew'd,
Seeking admittance, and to offer fraught
With horrid incense, for their idol brought?
Fly from her; let not the contagion find
The base example enter in thy mind.

Fly, and in virtue thy asylum seek
To make thee happy: trust the words I speak.
There is no purer happiness to gain
Than the sweet calm the just from her attain.
If in prosperity their fortunes glide,
She makes them free from arrogance and pride;
In mid estate be tranquil and content;
In adverse be resign'd whate'er the event:
Implacable, if Envy's hurricane
O'erwhelm them in misfortunes, even then
She hastes to save them, and its rage control;
With lofty fortitude the nobler soul
Enduing faithful; and if raised to sight,
At length they find the just reward requite,
Say is there aught to hope for prize so great
As the immortal crown for which they wait?

But is this feeling then, I hear thee cry,
That elevates my soul to virtue high,
This anxious wish to investigate and know,
Is it blameworthy as those passions low?
Why not to that for happiness repair?
Wilt thou condemn it? No, who would so dare,
That right would learn his origin and end?
Knowledge and Virtue, sisters like, descend
From heaven to perfect man in nobleness;
And far removing him, Bermudo, yes!

From vice and error, they will make him free,
Approaching even to the Deity.
But seek them not, in that false path to go
Which cunning Fortune will to others show.
Where then? to Wisdom's temple only haste;
There thou wilt find them. Her invoke; and traced,
See how she smiles! press forward; learn to use
The intercession of the kindly Muse
To make her be propitious. But beware,
That in her favour thou escape the snare,
The worship, which the vain adorer pays.
She never him propitiously surveys,
Who insolently seeking wealth or fame,
Burns impure incense on her altar's flame.
Dost thou not see how many turn aside
From her of learning void, but full of pride?
Alas for him, who seeking truth, for aid
Embraces only a delusive shade!
In self conceit who venturing to confide,
Nor virtue gain'd, nor reason for his guide,
Leaves the right path, precipitate to stray
Where error's glittering phantoms lead the way!
Can then the wise hope happiness to feel
In the chimæras sought with so much zeal?
Ah, no! they all are vanities and cheats!
See him, whom anxious still the morning greets,

Measuring the heavens, and of the stars that fly
The shining orbits! With a sleepless eye,
Hasty the night he reckons, and complains
Of the day's light his labour that detains;
Again admires night's wonders, but reflects
Ne'er on the hand that fashion'd and directs.
Beyond the moons of Uranus he bends
His gaze; beyond the Ship, the Bear, ascends:
But after all this, nothing more feels he:
He measures, calculates, but does not see
The heavens obeying their great Author's will,
Whirling around all silent; robbing still
The hours from life, ungratefully so gone,
Till one to undeceive him soon draws on.

Another, careless of the stars, descries
The humble dust, to scan and analyse.
His microscope he grasps, and sets, and falls
On some poor atom; and a triumph calls,
If should the fool the magic instrument
Of life or motion slightest sign present,
Its form to notice, in the glass to pore,
What his deluded fancy saw before;
Yields to the cheat, and gives to matter base
The power, forgot the Lord of all to trace.
Thus raves the ingrate.

Another the meanwhile
To scrutinize pretends, in learning's style,
The innate essence of the soul sublime.
How he dissects it, regulates in time!
As if it were a subtile fluid, known
To him its action, functions, strength and tone;
But his own weakness shows in this alone.

'Twas given to man to view the heavens on high,
But not in them the mysteries of the sky;
Yet boldly dares his reason penetrate
The darksome chaos, o'er it to dilate.
With staggering step, thus scorning heavenly light,
In error's paths he wanders, lost in night.
Confused, but not made wise, he pores about,
Betwixt opinion wavering and doubt.
Seeking for light, and shadows doom'd to feel,
He ponders, studies, labours to unseal
The secret, and at length finds his advance;
The more he learns, how great his ignorance.
Of matter, form, or motion, or the soul,
Or moments that away incessant roll,
Or the unfathomable sea of space,
Without a sky, without a shore to trace,
Nothing he reaches, nothing comprehends,
Nor finds its origin, nor where it tends;

But only sinking, all absorb'd may see
In the abysses of eternity.

   Perhaps, thence stepping more disorder'd yet,
He rushes his presumptuous flight to set
Ev'n to the throne of God! with his dim eyes
The Great Inscrutable to scrutinize;
Sounding the gulf immense, that circles round
The Deity, he ventures o'er its bound.
What can he gain in such a pathless course
But endless doubts, his ignorance the source?
He seeks, proposes, argues, thinking vain,
The ignorance that knew to raise, must fain
Be able to resolve them. Hast thou seen
Attempts that e'er have more audacious been?
What! shall an atom such as he excel
To comprehend the Incomprehensible?
Without more light than reason him assign'd,
The limits of immensity to find?
Infinity's beginning, middle, end?
Dost Thou, Eternal Lord, then condescend
To admit man to Thy councils, or to be
With his poor reason in Thy sanctuary?
A task so great as this dost Thou confide
To his weak soul? 'Tis not so, be relied,
My friend. To know God in His works above,
To adore Him, melt in gratitude and love;

The blessings o'er thee lavish'd to confess,
To sing His glory, and His name to bless;—
Such be thy study, duty and employ;
And of thy life and reason such the joy.
Such is the course that should the wise essay,
While only fools will from it turn away.
Wouldst thou attain it? easy the emprise;
Perfect thy being, and thou wilt be wise:
Inform thy reason, that its aid impart
Thee truth eternal: purify thy heart,
To love and follow it: thy study make
Thyself, but seek thy Maker's light to take:
There is high Wisdom's fountain found alone:
There thou thy origin wilt find thee shown;
There in His glorious work to find the place
'Tis thine to occupy: there thou mayst trace
Thy lofty destiny, the crown declared
Of endless life, for virtue that's prepared.

Bermudo, there ascend: there seek to find
That truth and virtue in the heavenly mind,
Which from His love and wisdom ever flow.
If elsewhere thou dost seek to find them, know,
That darkness only thou wilt have succeed,
In ignorance and error to mislead.
Thou of this love and wisdom mayst the rays
Discern in all His works, His power and praise

That tell around us, in the wondrous scale
Of high perfection which they all detail;
The order which they follow in the laws,
That bind and keep them, and that show their cause,
The ends of love and pity in their frame:
These their Creator's goodness all proclaim.
Be this thy learning, this thy glory's view;
If virtuous, thou art wise and happy too.
Virtue and truth are one, and in them bound
Alone may ever happiness be found.
And they can only, with a conscience pure,
Give to thy soul to enjoy it, peace secure;
True liberty in moderate desires,
And joy in all to do thy work requires;
To do well in content, and calmly free:
All else is wind and misery, vanity.

TO GALATEA'S BIRD.

O silly little bird! who now
   On Galatea's lap hast got,
My unrequited love allow
   To envy thee thy lot.

Of the same lovely mistress both
　　Alike the captives bound are we;
But thou for thy misfortune loth,
　　Whilst I am willingly.

Thou restless in thy prison art,
　　Complaining ever of thy pains;
While I would kisses, on my part,
　　Ev'n lavish on my chains.

But, ah! how different treating us,
　　Has scornful Fate the lot assign'd!
With me she's always tyrannous,
　　But with thee just as kind.

A thousand nights of torment borne,
　　A thousand days of martyrdom,
By thousand toils and pains, her scorn
　　I cannot overcome.

Inestimable happiness,
　　A mere caprice for thee has got;
So bathed in tears, in my distress,
　　I envy thee thy lot.

And there the while, with daring heel,
　　Thou tread'st in arrant confidence,
Without a heart or hope to feel,
　　Or instinct's common sense,

In the embraces, which my thought,
   Not even in its boldest vein,
Could scarce to hope for have been brought,
   Presumptuous to attain.

TO ENARDA.—I.

Lovely Enarda! young and old
   All quarrel with me daily:
Because I write to thee they scold,
   Perhaps sweet verses gaily.

"A judge should be more grave," they say,
   As each my song accuses;
"From such pursuits should turn away
   As trifling with the Muses."

"How wofully you waste your time!"
   Preach others; but, all slighting,
The more they scold, the more I rhyme;
   Still I must keep on writing.

Enarda's heart and mind to praise,
   All others far excelling,
My rustic pipe its note shall raise,
   In well-toned measures telling.

I wish, extolling to the skies,
   Her beauty's high perfection
To sing, and all her witcheries
   Of feature and complexion:

With master pencil to portray
   Her snowy neck and forehead,
And eyes that round so roguish play,
   And lips like carmine florid.

And let the Catos go at will,
   To where they most prefer it,
Who withering frowns and sneerings still
   Give me for my demerit.

In spite of all, with wrinkled pate,
   The censures each rehearses,
Enarda I will celebrate
   For ever in my verses.

TO ENARDA.—II.

CRUEL Enarda! all in vain,
   In vain, thou view'st with joyful eyes
The tears that show my grief and pain,
   Thyself exulting in my sighs.

The burning tears that bathe my cheek,
   With watching shrunk, with sorrow pale,
Thy lightness and caprice bespeak,
   Thy guilt and perfidy bewail.

Those signs of sorrow, on my face,
   Are not the obsequies portray'd
Of a lost good, nor yet the trace
   Of tribute to thy beauties paid.

They are the evidence alone
   There fix'd thy falsehood to proclaim;
Of thy deceits the horror shown,
   Of my delirium the shame.

I weep not now thy rigours o'er,
   Nor feel regret, that lost to me
Are the returns, which false before
   Thou gavest, or favours faithlessly.

I weep o'er my delusions blind;
   I mourn the sacrifices made,
And incense to a god unkind
   On an unworthy altar laid.

I weep the memory o'er debased
   Of my captivity to mourn,
And all the weight and shame disgraced
   Of such vile fetters to have borne.

Ever to my lorn mind return'd
  Are thoughts of homage offer'd ill,
Disdains ill borne, affection spurn'd,
  And sighs contemn'd, recurring still.

Then, ah, Enarda! all in vain
  Thou think'st to please thee with my grief:
Love, who now looks on me again
  With eyes of pity and relief,

A thousand times has me accost,
  As thus my tears to censure now,
"To lose them thou hast nothing lost;
  Poor creature! why then weepest thou?"

II.

TOMAS DE IRIARTE.

Of all the modern Spanish poets, Iriarte seems to have obtained for his writings the widest European reputation. He was born the 18th September 1750, at Teneriffe in the Canary Islands, where his family had been some time settled, though the name shows it to have been of Basque origin. His uncle, Juan de Iriarte, also a native of the same place, was one of the most learned men of his age, and to him the subject of this memoir was indebted for much of the knowledge he acquired, and means of attaining the eminence in literature he succeeded him in possessing. Juan de Iriarte had been partly educated in France, and had afterwards resided some time in England, so as to acquire a full knowledge of the language and literature of those countries. He was also a proficient in classical learning, and wrote Latin with great precision, as his writings, published by his nephew after his death, evince; Madrid, two volumes, 4to. 1774. Having been appointed keeper of the Royal Library at Madrid, he enriched it with many valuable works, in upwards of 2000 MSS. and 10,000 volumes. He was an active member of the Royal Spanish Academy, and one of the principal assistants in compiling the valuable dictionary and grammar published by that learned Society, as well as other works.

At the instance of this uncle, Tomas Iriarte went to Madrid in the beginning of 1764, when not yet fourteen years of age, and under that relative's able guidance completed his studies, learning at the same time the English and other modern languages. He was already far advanced in a knowledge of classical literature, and it is stated that some Latin verses he wrote, on leaving his native place, showed such proficiency as to surprise his friends, and make them entertain great expectations of his future success. Some of his Latin compositions, published afterwards among his works, prove him to have been a scholar of very considerable acquirements. Classical literature does not seem in modern times to be much studied in Spain, and Iriarte is the only distinguished writer among the modern Spanish poets who can be pointed out as conspicuous for such attainments. Thus they have failed in apprehending one of the chief beauties of modern poetry, so remarkable in Milton and Byron, and our other great poets, who enrich their works with references that remind us of what had most delighted us in those of antiquity.

In 1771 his uncle died, and Tomas Iriarte, who had already been acting for him in one of his offices as Interpreter to the Government, was appointed to succeed him in it. He was afterwards, in 1776, appointed Keeper of the Archives of the Council of War; and these offices, with the charge of a paper under the influence of the government, seem to have been the only public employments he held. From one of his epistles, however, he appears to have succeeded to his uncle's property, and thus to have had the means as also the leisure to give much of his time to the indulgence of literary tastes. He was very fond of paintings and of music, to which he showed his predilection, not only by his ability to play on several instruments, but also by writing a long didactic poem on the art, entitled 'Musica.' This he seems to have considered as giving him his principal claim to be ranked as a poet, though the world preferred his other writings.

When yet under twenty years of age, Iriarte had already appeared as a writer of plays, some of which met with considerable approbation. Of these it will be sufficient for us here to observe, that Moratin, the first great dramatic poet of Spain in modern times, pronounced one of them, 'The Young Gentleman Pacified,' to have been "the first original comedy the Spanish theatre had seen written according to the most essential rules dictated by philosophy and good criticism."

Besides several original plays, Iriarte translated others from the French, from which language he also translated the 'New Robinson' of Campe, which passed through several editions. From Virgil he translated into Spanish verse the first four books of the Æneid, and from Horace the Epistle to the Pisos. These, though censured by some of his contemporaries so as to excite his anger, were altogether too superior to those attacks to have required the vindication of them he thought proper to publish. Horace seems to have been his favourite author; but he had not learned from him his philosophical equanimity, wherewith to pass over in silent endurance the minor miseries of life. Thus he allowed himself, throughout his short career, to be too much affected by those ungenerous attacks, which mediocrity is so apt to make on superior merit. The names of those censurers are now principally remembered by his notices of their writings; an honour, which men of genius, in their hours of irritation, too often confer on unworthy opponents. Thus a large portion of his collected works consists of these controversial notices, which, as usual in such cases, only impair the favourable effect produced by the remainder on the mind of the reader. Those works were first published in a collected form in six volumes, in 1786; afterwards in eight volumes, in 1805.

From Iriarte's poetical epistles, which are eleven in number, he appears to have been a person of a very kindly disposition, as Quintana describes him, living in friendly intercourse with the principal literary characters of Spain, especially with the amiable and ill-fated Cadahalso, to whom, in one of those epistles, he dedicated his translations from Horace. The others also are mainly on personal topics, and display his character advantageously, though, as poetical compositions, they have not been received so favourably as some of his other works.

The fame of Iriarte may be said to rest on his literary fables, which have attained a popularity, both at home and abroad, equalled by few other works. They are eighty-two in number, and all original, having, as their title indicates, a special reference to literary questions, though they are also all sufficiently pointed to bear on those of ordinary life. Like Sir Joshua Reynolds's Discourses on Painting, they convey general instructions to all, while professing an application to one particular pursuit. They are written with much vivacity and ease, yet with an appropriate terseness that adds to their effect. Martinez de la Rosa, equally eminent as a statesman, a poet and a critic, observes of them, that if he had not left compositions of any other class, they would have extended his reputation as a poet; and adds, " that they abound in beauties, though frequently wanting in poetical warmth, so as to recommend this valuable collection, unique in its class, as one of which Spanish literature has to be proud."

Of these fables, first published in 1782, so many editions have appeared, that it would be a very difficult task to enumerate them. There is scarcely a provincial town in Spain, of any consequence, in which they have not been reprinted. Several editions have appeared in France, two in New York, and three in Boston, where they have been used in teaching Spanish. Several of the fables have been imitated by Florian, and translations have been made into other languages. Of these translations, one in French verse was published by M. Lanos, Paris, 1801, and another, in prose, by M. L'Homandie, ibid. 1804: into German they were translated by Bertuch, Leipzic, so early as 1788, and into Portuguese, by Velladoli, in 1801.

I am not aware of more than one edition of them in England, that published by Dulau, 1809; but there have been no fewer than three translations of them into English verse; first by Mr. Belfour, London, 1804, another by Mr. Andrews, ibid. 1835, and a third by Mr. Rockliff, ibid. 1851.

The same popularity attended another work which Iriarte prepared for the instruction of youth, named 'Historical Lessons,' published posthumously, about twenty editions of which have since appeared, principally from its having been adopted as a text-book for schools. Of this also an edition has been published in London by Boosey, and a translation into English. Iriarte's industry appears to have been of the most practical character, and his endeavours were as wisely as they were unremittingly directed to make his countrymen wiser and better in their future generations. If a man's worth may be estimated by such labours, few persons have ever lived who were so entitled to the gratitude of posterity, as few have ever effected so much as he did in the short career that was afforded him.

In private life, in the leisure allowed from his studies and duties, he indulged much, as has been already stated, in the recreation of music; and in praise and explanation of that favourite art he wrote his largest work, 'Music,' a didactic poem, in five cantos. Of this work, which was first published in 1780, the fifth separate edition appeared in 1805, since which I have not heard of any other. It has, however, had the good fortune to be translated into several foreign languages; into German by Bertuch, in 1789; into Italian by the Abbé Garzia, Venice, 1789; into French by Grainville, Paris, 1800; and into English by Mr. Belfour, London, 1807. The last-mentioned translation is made with much exactness and elegance into heroic verse; though, as the original had the fault usual to all didactic poems of not rising to any high poetical power, the translation must share the fault to at least an equal extent.

In the Italian version, a letter is quoted from the celebrated Metastasio, in which he speaks of the style of Iriarte's poem as "so harmonious, perspicuous and easy, as to unite the precision of a treatise with the beauties common to poetry." It is said also that Metastasio further pronounced the poem to be "not only excellent, but to be considered uncommon, in having successfully treated a subject so difficult, and apparently so little adapted to poetry." It is to be observed that Iriarte had warmly eulogized Metastasio in the book, so as to merit the commendation. The first canto is confined to treating the subject artistically, and will therefore prove less to the taste of the general reader than the other cantos, which are of a more interesting character, and may be read with pleasure by persons who do not understand music as a science. The third canto especially is written with much spirit in its praise, as connected with devotion. The second canto treats of the passions as they may be expressed by music, including martial music. The fourth minutely discusses theatrical music, with its excellences and defects. The fifth explains it, as calculated for the amusement of societies, or individuals in solitude. The poem concludes with pointing out what ought to be the study of a good composer, and by a proposal for the establishment of an academy of music, or scientific body of musicians, anticipating the benefit to science that would result from such an institution.

This poem, the 'Musica,' and the Epistles, are written in a very favourite style of versification in Spain, denominated the Silva, which consists of lines of eleven syllables, varied occasionally with others of seven, rhyming at the pleasure of the writer. The 'Literary Fables' are written in various metres; Martinez de la Rosa observes in upwards of forty different kinds, appropriate to the characteristics of the subjects, which may be more perceptible to a native ear than to a foreigner's. It is certainly true that this gives a variety to the work which is well suited to the purposes the author had in view. He was wise enough to know that truths hidden in the garb of fiction will often be felt effectually, where grave precepts would not avail,

> Καὶ ποῦ τι καὶ βρότων φρενὰς
> Ὑπὲρ τὸν ἀληθῆ λόγον,
> Δεδαιδαλμένοι ψεύδεσι ποικίλοις
> Ἐξαπάτωντι μῦθοι,

and thus conveyed his lessons in examples, with a moral, which could be quickly understood and easily remembered.

With regard to the objection made to these fables, that they are often deficient in poetical warmth or colouring, it may be observed that the subjects would scarcely admit of any. Iriarte was certainly a writer of more poetic taste than talent, and it must be acknowledged that his genius, judging by the works he left, was not one to soar to the higher flights of poetry. He felt this himself, as he intimates in his Epistle to his brother; and, choosing a subject like Music for a didactic poem, or writing familiar epistles on occasional subjects, did not give himself much scope for fancy, much less for passion. But as applied to the fables, the objection was unnecessary. If they deserved praise for their vivacity of style, that very circumstance, independent of the subjects, rendered them passionless, ἀπαθέστατα, as Longinus remarks, where stronger feelings could scarcely be brought into connexion with such discussions. The great difficulty in such cases is, when metres are chosen to suit the subject, abounding in pyrrhics, trochees, and such measures, as the same great critic adds, to guard, lest the sense be lost in too much regard to the sound, raising only attention to the rhythm, instead of exciting any feeling in the minds of the hearers.

Of the five fables chosen for translation, the two first were taken from Bouterwek, and the third on account of its having been particularly noticed by Martinez de la Rosa. The Epistle to his Brother was selected partly on account of its notices of other countries, as a foreigner's judgement of them; and partly as being most characteristic of the writer, showing his tastes and dispositions more perhaps than the rest. The reader generally feels most interested in such parts of the works of favourite writers, especially when their private history gives the imagination a right to ask sympathy for their sufferings.

Nothing is to be found in Iriarte's works to show any peculiar opinions on religion, though the tendency of his mind is everywhere clearly seen, as leading to freedom of thought, instead of subjection to dogmas. In his poem on Music, as already intimated, some devotional rather than freethinking principles are developed; yet it is said that it was from a suspicion of his being affected by the French philosophy of the day he fell under the censure of the Inquisition, and was seized in 1786, and imprisoned three years in the dungeons of that institution. What was the particular offence imputed to him has not been stated. It could be no question of a political character, for he was in the employment of the government, and was amenable to it for any misdeeds. It probably was from some private cause, under the cloak of a question of faith, that he had to undergo this imprisonment, during which it is said he had to submit to severe penances before he could obtain his liberty. After he had obtained it, he returned to his studies and wrote further, a monologue, entitled 'Guzman,' and some Latin maccaronic verses on the bad taste of some writers then in vogue. But his spirits were no doubt broken down, as his health and strength were undermined; and thus it was that he died two years after, though his death was imputed to his sedentary habits and gout, the 17th of September, 1791, when he had just completed his forty-first year.

This untimely death was a serious loss to Spanish literature. With his great and varied acquirements and unremitting industry, the world might have expected still more valuable works from him, when, at the age of thirty-six, in the best period of a man's existence for useful labours, he was cast into that dungeon, from which he seems to have been permitted to come out only to die. The last Auto da fe in Spain was celebrated in 1781; but the Inquisition had other victims whose sufferings were no less to be deplored, though not made known. If Iriarte was one, he had unquestionably the consciousness of being enabled to feel, though not dying "an aged man," yet that in his comparatively short life, he had not lived in vain for his own good name, and the benefit of posterity.

TOMAS DE IRIARTE.

EPISTLE TO DON DOMINGO DE IRIARTE,

ON HIS TRAVELLING TO VARIOUS FOREIGN COURTS.

He who begins an instrument to play,
   With some preludings, will examine well
   How run the fingers, how the notes will swell,
And bow prepares, or breath for his essay;
   Or if to write the careful penman's aim,
He cuts and proves his pen, if broad or fine;
And the bold youths, to combat who incline,
   Strike at the air, as trial of the game:

The dancer points his steps with practised pace;
The orator harangues with studied grace;
   The gamester packs his cards the livelong day;
I thus a Sonnet, though worth nothing, trace,
   Solely to exercise myself this way,
   If prove the Muse propitious to my lay.

It seems to me, dear brother, that Apollo
A course divine now does not always follow,
Nor please to dictate verses of a tone,
Worthy a sponsor such as he to own;
But rather would be human, and prefer
To prose in rhymes of warmthless character;
Without the enthusiasm sublime of old,
And down the wings of Pegasus would fold,
Not to be borne in flight, but gently stroll'd.

You who forgetful of this court now seek
Those of the east and north to contemplate,
  Forgive me, if in envy I may speak,
That to indulge it has allow'd you fate
  The tasteful curiosity! to view
With joy the land, so famed and fortunate,
  Which erst a Tully and a Maro knew,
To which Æmilius, Marius service paid,
Which Regulus and the Scipios obey'd.
  Long would it be and idle to recall
The triumphs, with their blazonries unfurl'd,
  Matchless of her, that once of Europe all
Was greater part, metropolis of the world.

I only ask of you, as you may read,
How in Avernus, destined to succeed,
Anchises show'd Æneas, in long line,
The illustrious shades of those, who were to shine
One day the glory of the Italian shore,
Now you, more favour'd than the Trojan chief,
Not in vain prophecy, but tried belief,
From what you see, by aid of history's lore,
To admire the lofty state which Rome possess'd,
The which her ruins and remains attest.

From our Hispanian clime I cannot scan
With you the column of the Antonine,
The fane or obelisk of the Vatican,
Or the Capitol, and Mount Palatine;
I cannot see the churches, or the walls,
The bridges, arches, mausoleums, gates,
The aqueducts, palaces, and waterfalls,
The baths, the plazas, porticos, and halls,
The Coliseum's, or the Circus' fates;
But still the immortal writings 'tis for me,
Of Livy, Tacitus, Cicero, to see;
I see Lucretius, Pliny, Juvenal,
Augustus, Maro and Mæcenas all;
With their names is the soul exalted high,
Heroic worth and honour to descry;

And so much more that model imitates
   A nation now, so much more to be gain'd,
Is seen it but to approach the lofty heights
   Of splendour, wealth, fame, power, that Rome attain'd.

From the benignant lands that richly gleam
Beneath the Tiber's fertilizing stream,
You next will pass, where borne as he arose,
Through colder realms the mighty Danube flows.
Girded in pleasant borders 't is for you
The Austrian Vienna there to view;
To admire the monarch, warlike, good and wise,
With the magnanimous Prussian king who vies
An army brave and numerous to sway;
Chosen and hardy, forward to obey,
Whom as companions honour'd he rewards,
And not as slaves abased a lord regards.
There agriculture flourish you will see;
Public instruction is promoted free;
The arts extended rapidly and wide;
   And these among, in culture and esteem,
That with which Orpheus tamed the furious pride
   Of forest beasts, and cross'd the Lethe's stream:
There all the tales of wonderful effect,
Of music's art divine, with which are deck'd
The ancient Greek and Latin histories,
No longer will seem fables in your eyes,

When near you may applaud the loftiness,
The harmony, and the consonance sublime,
　All that in varied symphonies to express
Has power the greatest master of our time;
　Haydn the great, and merited his fame,
　Whom to embrace I beg you in my name.

But now the confines of the German land
I see you leaving, for the distant strand
Of Britain's isle your rapid course to take,
And tour political around to make.
　There in the populous court, whose walls' long side
Bathes the deep Thames in current vast and wide,
A nation's image will before your eyes
In all things most extraordinary rise.
Not rich of old, but happy now we see
By totally unshackled industry.
　A nation liberal, but ambitious too;
Phlegmatic, and yet active in its course;
　Ingenuous, but its interests to pursue
Intent; humane, but haughty; and perforce
　Whate'er it be, the cause it undertakes,
Just or unjust, defends without remorse,
　And of all fear and danger scorn it makes.
There with inevitably great surprise,
　What in no other country we may see,
You will behold to exert their energies
　Men act and speak with perfect liberty.

The rapid fortune too you will admire
Which eloquence and valour there acquire;
Nor power to rob has wealth or noble birth
The premiums due to learning and to worth.
   You will observe the hive-like multitude
Of diligent and able islanders,
   Masters of commerce they have well pursued,
Which ne'er to want or slothfulness defers;
   All in inventions useful occupied,
In manufactures, roads, schools, arsenals,
Experiments in books and hospitals,
   And studies of the liberal arts to guide.
There you will know in fine what may attain
   An education wise; the skilful mode
Of patriotic teaching, so to train
   Private ambition, that it seek the road
Of public benefit alone to gain:
   The recompense and acceptation just,
   On which founds learning all its hope and trust;
And a wise government, whose constant aim
Is general good, and an eternal fame.

   Midst others my reflections I would fain,
In some description worthy of the theme,
   (If it were not beyond my powers) explain,
The varied scenes, enchantment all that seem,

Which the Parisian court on your return
. Prepares, and offers you surprised to learn.
Polish'd emporium of Europe's courts,
The which with noble spectacles invites,
With public recreations and resorts,
That give to life its solace and delights;
Brilliant assemblages! and these among,
The chief and most acceptable to gain,
Of all to this new Athens that belong,
To enjoy the fellowship of learned men;
With useful science, or with taste alone;
Who enlighten foreign nations, and their own.

But I, who from this narrow corner write,
In solitude, while shaking off the dust
From military archives, ill recite
What I, O travelling Secretary! trust
Yourself will better practically see,
Whilst I can only know in theory.
Continue then your journey on in health;
From tongue to tongue, from land to land proceed:
To be a statesman eminent your meed.
Acquire each day with joy your stores of wealth,
Of merit and instruction; I the while,
As fits my mediocrity obscure,
Will sing the praise of quiet from turmoil;
Saying, as Seneca has said of yore;—

"Let him, who power or honours would attain,
On the high court's steep precipice remain.
I wish for peace, that solitude bestows,
Secluse to enjoy the blessings of repose.
To pass my life in silence be my fate,
Unnoticed by the noble, or the great:
That when my age, without vain noise or show,
Has reach'd the bounds allotted us below,
Though a plebeian only to pass by,
Perhaps I yet an aged man may die.
And this I do believe, no death of all
Than his more cruel can a man befall,
Who dying, by the world too truly known,
Is of himself most ignorant alone."

FABLES.

THE BEAR, THE MONKEY AND THE HOG.

A BEAR, with whom a Piedmontese
    A wandering living made,
A dance he had not learn'd with ease,
    On his two feet essay'd:

And, as he highly of it thought,
    He to the Monkey cried,
"How's that?" who, being better taught,
    "'Tis very bad," replied.

"I do believe," rejoin'd the Bear,
    "You little favour show:
For have I not a graceful air,
    And step with ease to go?"

A Hog, that was beside them set,
    Cried, "Bravo! good!" said he;
"A better dancer never yet
    I saw, and ne'er shall see."

On this the Bear, as if he turn'd
    His thoughts within his mind,
With modest gesture seeming learn'd
    A lesson thence to find.

"When blamed the Monkey, it was cause
    Enough for doubting sad;
But when I have the hog's applause,
    It must be very bad!"

As treasured gift, let authors raise
    This moral from my verse:
'Tis bad, when wise ones do not praise;
    But when fools *do*, 'tis worse.

THE ASS AND THE FLUTE.

This little fable heard,
   It good or ill may be;
But it has just occurr'd,
   Thus accidentally.

Passing my abode,
   Some fields adjoining me,
A big Ass on his road
   Came accidentally;

And laid upon the spot,
   A Flute he chanced to see,
Some shepherd had forgot,
   There accidentally.

The animal in front,
   To scan it nigh came he,
And snuffing loud as wont,
   Blew accidentally.

The air it chanced around
   The pipe went passing free,
And thus the Flute a sound
   Gave accidentally.

"O! then," exclaim'd the Ass,
　"I know to play it fine;
And who for bad shall class
　The music asinine?"

Without the rules of art,
　Ev'n asses, we agree,
May once succeed in part,
　Thus accidentally.

THE TWO RABBITS.

Some shrubs amidst to shun
　The dogs he saw pursue,
I will not call it run,
　But say a rabbit flew.

From out his hiding-place
　A neighbour came to see,
And said, "Friend, wait a space:
　What may the matter be?"

"What should it be?" he cried;
　"I breathless came in fear,
Because that I espied
　Two scoundrel greyhounds near."

"Yes," said the other, "far
    I see them also there;
But those no greyhounds are!"
    "What?"—"Setters, I'll declare."

"How, setters do you say?
    My grandad just as much!
They are greyhounds, greyhounds, they;
    I saw them plainly such."

"They are setters; get along:
    What know you of these matters?"—
"They are greyhounds; you are wrong:"—
    "I tell you they are setters."

The dogs while they engage
    In these contentious habits,
Come up, and vent their rage
    On my two thoughtless rabbits.

Who minor points affect,
    So much about to quarrel,
And weightier things neglect,
    Let them take the moral.

THE LAMB AND HIS TWO ADVISERS.

A FARM there was, with a poultry-yard,
    Where roved an old bantam about;
And laid at his ease, a pig was barr'd
    In a sty close by without.

A lamb moreover was raised up there;
    We know it does so befall:
Together in farms these animals fare,
    And in good company all.

" Well, with your leave," said the pig one day
    To the lamb, " what a happy life!
And healthful too, to be sleeping away,
    One's time without cares or strife!

" I say there is nothing, as I am a pig,
    Like sleeping, stretch'd out at ease;
Let the world go round with its whirligig,
    And cares just as it may please."

The other the contrary chanced to tell
    The same little lamb, to take heed;
" Look, innocent! here, to live right well,
    Sleep very little indeed.

"Summer or winter, early to rise
　　With the stars the practice seek;
For sleeping the senses stupefies,
　　And leaves you languid and weak."

Confused, the poor lamb the counsels compares,
　　And cannot perceive in his mind,
That contrary each advising declares,
　　But how he himself is inclined.

And thus we find authors the practice make,
　　To hold, as infallibly true,
The rules they fancy themselves to take,
　　And in their own writings pursue.

THE FLINT AND THE STEEL.

CRUELLY bent, it chanced the Flint
　　Ill-treated the Steel one day;
And wounding, gave it many a dint,
　　To draw its sparks away.

When laid aside, this angry cried
　　To that, "What would your value be
Without my help?" the Flint replied,
　　"As much as yours, sir, but for me."

This lesson I write, my friends to incite;
   Their talents, however great,
That they must study with them unite,
   To duly cultivate.

The Flint gives light with the help of the Steel,
And study alone will talent reveal;
For neither suffice if found apart,
Whatever the talent or the art.

III.

JUAN MELENDEZ VALDES.

For a hundred years after the time of Calderon de la Barca, who died in 1687, there appeared in Spain no writer of sufficient merit to be classed among those eminent characters, who had done so much honour to Spanish literature in the seventeenth century. Verses were published in sufficient abundance, which found readers and even admirers, merely from the necessity the public felt of having something to read and to admire, as of the fashion of the day. But they were written with a perversion of taste and a deficiency of talent, which was truly astonishing, in the successors of such authors, as had immediately preceded them.

This depression of literature, however, could not be expected to continue long, among a people of such imaginative and deep passioned character as the Spanish, whose native genius was by far too buoyant, to be affected for any length of time by inferior models, even under dynastic influences. Accordingly, towards the end of the eighteenth century, it might have become apparent to an attentive observer, that another order of writers was about to be called forth, and that the nation was prepared to welcome the advent of true genius whenever it was to be recognized. Learned societies had been established throughout Spain; education on a sound basis had been sedulously promoted; and the country was wealthy, and sufficiently flourishing to give incitement to the arts, which are the attendants of public prosperity.

At this epoch appeared Melendez Valdes, the restorer of Spanish poetry, as his admirers with much justice termed him; who then showed by his writings, that the old inspiration of the national genius was yet capable of being revived in all its former grace and strength; and who by the influence of his example further roused the energies of other men of genius to follow in his steps.

This highly gifted poet was born the 11th of March, 1754, at Ribera del Fresno in the province of Estremadura, where his parents were of what was called noble families, and, what was more important, in respectable circumstances. The good disposition noticed in the son determined them to destine him for study, and to award him a becoming education. Thus, having learned the rudiments of Latin at home, he was sent to study philosophy, or what was called philosophy, at Madrid, under the charge of the Dominican Fathers of St. Thomas, where his application and advancement gained him the esteem of his tutors and fellow-pupils. Thence he was sent by his parents in 1770 to Segovia, to study with his only brother, who was private secretary to the bishop of that city, and with whom he was confirmed in that fondness for reading, and taste for acquiring books, which might be called the passion of his whole life. The bishop, who was a distant relation, pleased with his talents and inclination for study, sent him in 1772 to Salamanca, the alma mater of Spain, and assisted him to proceed in the study of law, in which he distinguished himself wherever he had an opportunity; so that, says his biographer, " appearing absorbed in the pursuit of that career, no one would have judged him the same young man, whose inclination for poetry and learning was soon after to place him at the head of the elegant literature of his country."

Fortunately for Melendez, continues his biographer, there happened then to be at Salamanca Don Jose de Cadalso, "a man celebrated for extensive erudition, combined with more than ordinary talent for poetry and letters, and a zeal for the glory and advancement of his country, learned in the school, and under the inspiration of virtue. Generous and affable, always lively, and at times satirical without branching off into maliciousness, his conversation was kind and instructive, and his principles indulgent and steadfast." This eminent individual, already well known in the literary world by several works published in 1772 and 1773, immediately recognized the value of Melendez: he took him to his house to live with him, showed him the beauties and defects of the older writers, taught him how to imitate them, and opened to him the road to become acquainted with the literature of the learned nations of Europe. "He afforded him an instruction yet more precious, in the beautiful example he gave him to love all writers of merit, to rise superior to envy, and to cultivate letters without degrading them by unworthy disputations. The eulogies Cadalso bestowed on his contemporaries are a public testimony of this noble character; and the works of Melendez, where there is not a single line detracting from the merit of any one, and his whole literary career, exempt from all attack, show how he profited by the lessons of his master."

The Anacreontic style, in which Cadalso excelled, was also that first cultivated by Melendez; and the former, seeing the progress of his pupil, and the first efforts of his Muse, unreservedly acknowledged him his superior, and in prose and verse announced him as the restorer of good taste and the better studies of the University. This kindly union was maintained until the death of Cadalso, at the siege of Gibraltar; and the "Elegiac song of Melendez on this misfortune, will be, as long as the Spanish language endures, a monument of affection and gratitude, as well as an example of high and beautiful poetry."

Beyond the instructions which he received from Cadalso, Melendez was aided by the example and counsels of other distinguished persons then residing at Salamanca, among whom were two, favourably known as writers of verse, Iglesias and Gonzalez. These, though they were soon eclipsed by the young poet, admitted him to their friendship. By the latter he was brought into communication with the illustrious Jovellanos, then Judge of the High Court at Seville; and between them soon was instituted a correspondence, which has been in great part preserved, though as yet unpublished; a valuable monument, says Quintana, in which are seen, "livingly portrayed, the candour, the modesty and virtuous feelings of the poet, the alternate progress of his studies, the different attempts in which he essayed his talents, and above all, the profound respect and almost idolatry with which he revered his Mæcenas. There may be seen how he employed his time and varied his tasks. At first he applied himself to Greek, and began to translate Homer and Theocritus into verse; but learning the immense difficulty of the undertaking, and not stimulated to it by the bent of his genius, he shortly abandoned it."

He then dedicated himself to the English language and literature, for which he was said to have ever had an exceeding great predilection, observing, "that to the Essay on the Human Understanding, he should owe all his life the little he might know how to acquire." As books came to his hands, he went on reading and forming his judgements upon them, the which he transmitted to his friend. Thus "by all the means in his power he endeavoured to acquire and increase that treasury of ideas, which so much contributes to perfection in the art of writing, and without which verses are nothing more than frivolous sounds."

His application to study, however, soon proved more than his health and strength would permit. He was obliged to leave Salamanca, and repair to the banks of the Tormes, which he has made famous in song, and there, by long attention to the regimen imposed on him, he fortunately recovered. About this time his brother died in 1777, their parents having died previously; and Melendez suffered much grief, as might naturally be expected, on being thus left alone of his family, the more painful in his state of health. Jovellanos urged him to join him at Seville, but he declined the invitation, observing, that "the law of friendship itself, which commands us to avail ourselves of a friend in necessity, also commands that without it, we should not take advantage of his confidence."

Study, to which he now returned to engage himself with more intensity than ever, was the best alleviant of his sorrow, and time as usual at length allayed it. " He then gave himself up to the reading and study of the English poets: Pope and Young enchanted him. Of the former, he said that four lines of his 'Essay on Man' were worth more, taught more, and deserved more praise than all his own compositions." The latter he attempted to imitate, and in effect did so, in the poem on 'Night and Solitude,' but in remitting it to his friend, expressed with much feeling his sense of its deficiencies compared with the original. Thomson also he studied, and Gesner, in his lonely exercises by the Tormes, and acknowledged how much he was indebted to the former for many thoughts with which he subsequently enriched his pastoral poems.

Thus having prepared himself to appear before the literary world as a candidate for fame, an opportunity soon occurred for him to obtain distinction. The Spanish Academy had been proposing subjects for prizes, and then having given one for an Eclogue, 'On the happiness of a country life,' Melendez felt himself in his element, and sent in his Essay for the prize. This succeeded in receiving the first. The second was awarded to Iriarte, who showed his mortification on account of the preference, more sensibly than was becoming, under the circumstances.

In the following year, 1781, Melendez went to Madrid, where his friend Jovellanos had already been appointed Councillor of the Military Orders, when for the first time they met. Melendez was already in the road to fame, which his friend had foretold for him; and Jovellanos, delighted with the realization of his hopes and endeavours, received him into his house, introduced him to his society, and took every opportunity of advancing his interests. It was the custom of the Academy of San Fernando to give triennial celebrations, with much solemnity, for the distribution of prizes, when eloquence, poetry and music were tasked to do honour to the fine arts. One of these celebrations was about to take place; Jovellanos was engaged to pronounce a discourse, and Melendez was invited to exercise his genius on the same subject, as the first literary characters of preceding times had already given the example. Melendez acceded, and delivered accordingly his Ode on the Glory of the Arts, which was received with rapturous admiration, and ever since seems to have been considered his masterpiece.

In the midst of these successes, Melendez received the Professorship of Humanities in his University, and in the following year, 1782, proceeded to the degree of Licentiate, and in 1783 to that of Doctor of Law, having shortly before the last married a lady of one of the principal families of Salamanca. But as his professorship gave him little occupation, and his marriage no family, he remained free to continue his favourite studies.

In 1784, on the occasion of peace being made with England, and the birth of twin Infantes, to give hopes of secure succession to the throne, the city of Madrid prepared magnificent celebrations of rejoicings, and among the rest, a prize was proposed for the two best dramatic pieces that might be offered within sixty days, under the condition that they should be original, appropriate, and capable of theatrical pomp and ornament. Out of fifty-seven dramas that were offered, the prize was awarded to the one sent in by Melendez, 'The Bridals of Comacho the Rich,' a pastoral comedy, which, however, though abounding in poetical passages, was found on representation wanting in effect, so as to be coldly received on the stage, where it has not since been attempted.

This ill-success gave occasion to several detractors of Melendez to pour forth the effusions of envy or disappointment against him, to which he gave no other answer than by the publication of his poems in a collected form. This was in 1785; and the manner in which they were received, it could be said, had had no parallel in Spain. Four editions, of which three were furtive, were at once taken up, and all classes of persons seemed to have the book in hand, commenting on its excellences. The lovers of ancient poetry, who saw so happily renewed the graces of Garcilasso, of Leon and Herrera, and "even improved in taste and perfection," saluted Melendez as the restorer of the Castillian Muses, and hailed the banishment of the prosaic style which had previously prevailed. The applauses extended beyond the kingdom, and found especially in Italy the admiration repeated, as well as in France and England, where several of the poems are said to have been imitated.

Great as was his success in literature, it was not enough provision for his daily needs, notwithstanding the help of his professorship; and Melendez accordingly applied for and obtained an office as a local judge at Zaragoza, of which he took possession in September 1789. The duties of this office were too onerous to admit of much study; but he was soon removed, in 1791, to the chancery of Valladolid, where he had more leisure, and where he remained till 1797, when he was appointed Fiscal of the Supreme Court at Madrid. During this time he wrote apparently little; but he prepared, and in 1797 published, another edition of his works with two additional volumes, enriched with many new poems, in which he "had elevated his genius to the height of his age;" —"descriptive passages of a superior order, elegies powerful and pathetic, odes grand and elevated, philosophic and moral discourses and epistles, in which he took alternately the tone of Pindar, of Homer, of Thomson, and of Pope, and drew from the Spanish lyre accents she had not previously learned."

But notwithstanding the great merit of many of these poems, the biographer of Melendez had it to confess that this publication was not so favourably received as the first had been; and attempts to account for it partly by the circumstances of the times, and partly by what was new not being on the whole so finished and well-sustained in interest as his former poems. Some of them also met with decided disfavour; especially one, 'The Fall of Lucifer,' which showed that his genius was not of the severer cast calculated for graver and higher subjects allied to the epic, any more than to the dramatic. But the merits of Melendez in his own sphere are too great, and his fame is too well-founded to lose by acknowledgements which must be made in truth and justice. It is not improbable that he had been urged by his admirers to these attempts, to which his own inclinations would not have led him, and it might thus have been the easiness of his disposition that made him yield to suggestions which ended in failure.

In the prologue which he affixed to this edition, Melendez attempted to prove that poetic studies derogated nothing from the judicial dignity, and that they had no incompatibility with the duties and talents of a public man or man of business. But without following him or his biographer into such a discussion, we may concede the point so far, that any one undertaking responsible duties from the State, is bound to give them his best and undivided energies. If, however, he has any hours of leisure free from those responsibilities, it is surely only an extension of his duty for him to employ them in attempting to make his fellow-men wiser and better, or happier, in the manner most congenial to his disposition or talents. Melendez certainly had no need to exculpate himself in this respect, having been "long remembered at Zaragoza and Valladolid as a model of integrity and application, for his zeal in arranging amicably all disputations in his power, for his affability and frankness in listening to complaints, and for the humane and compassionate interest with which he visited the prisoners, accelerating their causes, and affording them assistance, with an inseparable adhesion to justice." It was for his detractors,—and Melendez had them, notwithstanding the amiability of his character and the superiority of his talents,—to make these objections, if they could have done so. His resorting to such apologies only gave the appearance of a consciousness of weakness, which was not becoming either in the one character or the other.

Shortly after the publication of this edition, Melendez went to Madrid to take possession of his new office. The advanced age of his predecessor in it had for some time prevented his due attention to its duties, so that Melendez had many arrears to dispose of in addition to the ordinary services, through all which he laboured with much assiduity and credit. But they were the last satisfactory events of his life, which was henceforth to be passed in reverses and misery. Yet at that time he seemed to be in the height of prosperity. Holding an elevated post under the government, of which his friend Jovellanos was a member, and respected both at home and abroad as one of the first literary characters of the age, he might have justly hoped to be free from any of the darker misfortunes of life. This exemption, however, was not to be his lot, serving under a despotic government, of which the head, Charles IV., was one of the weakest-minded of mortals, guided by a favourite such as Godoy. When Jovellanos fell under this favourite's resentment, to make the blow inflicted on that illustrious individual more poignant, it was extended to others, whose only fault was that they shared his esteem. Melendez was ordered away from Madrid within twenty-four hours, though his friends procured for him soon after a commission from the government as inspector of barracks at Medina del Campo, where he gave himself up again to study and such duties as were assigned him. Beyond these, however, he particularly exerted himself, it is recorded, in attending to the sick at the hospitals, providing that they should not be sent out into the world, as had often been previously the case, imperfectly cured or clothed, and unable to effect their livelihood.

In this humble occupation he might have been supposed exempt at least from further malignity, but unfortunately some sycophant of power thought it would be pleasing to the favourite to have a frivolous accusation forwarded against him, which had the effect of his being sent on half salary to Zamora. There he was fortunate enough to have the intrigues against him made known, and in June 1802, he received a royal order to have his full salary allowed, with liberty to reside where he pleased. He would have preferred Madrid, but he found it most prudent to return to Salamanca, and there, arranging his house and library, began to enjoy a more peaceful life than what he had passed since he left the University.

The literary world might now have hoped for further efforts of genius in this asylum, and perhaps some superior work worthy of his talents and fame; but his spirits had been broken down by adversity and injustice, and his attention was distracted by hopes and fears, from which he could never free himself. A poem on Creation, and a translation of the Æneid, were the fruits of six years' retirement from the world; and he proposed another edition of his works, which however he did not accomplish, on the rapid succession of events which again called him forth to a short period of active life, and subsequent years of suffering.

The revolution of Aranjuez brought Melendez to Madrid, in the hopes of recovering his former employments; but in the troubled state of the country, he soon wished to return to his house, without being able to effect it. The French had now made themselves masters of the capital, and Melendez was unfortunately induced to take office under them. This conduct was contrary, not only to the course taken by Jovellanos and his other friends, but also to the whole tenor of his former life and opinions. His easy temper, which had at all times led him submissive to the wishes of those who had his confidence, no doubt on this occasion had been influenced by persons near him, and he might have thought it a hopeless struggle to contend with Napoleon.

Having however engaged in this unpatriotic service, he was sent as a commissioner, on the part of the intrusive government, to the Asturias, where the people had already risen in vindication of the national independence. Melendez and his colleague were seized by the populace, notwithstanding the efforts of the local authorities, who had placed them for security in the prison, the doors of which were forced, and they were led out to be put to death. All entreaties were in vain. Melendez protested his attachment to the national cause, and even began reciting some patriotic verses he had been writing, but the excited multitude would not hear him. They added insults to menaces, and as a great favour only permitted them to confess before they should be executed. Thus a little time was gained; but this was at length concluded and they were tied to a tree, and the party prepared to shoot them, when a dispute arose whether they should be shot from in front or behind as traitors, a piece of etiquette in such cases considered of importance. The latter counsel prevailed, and the prisoners had to be loosened and tied again accordingly, when the authorities and religious orders of the place, with a particular Cross famous among them, appeared approaching for their rescue. The people hereon became calmed, and Melendez and his colleague were taken back to the prison, whence they were soon permitted to return to Madrid.

On the success of the Spanish army at Bailen, the French retired from the capital, and Melendez remained at Madrid, hoping, through the influence of Jovellanos, to be taken into favour with the constitutional party. But fortune again seemed to side with the French, and they returned to Madrid, when Melendez was again induced to join them, and accepted office as Councillor of State and President of a Board of Public Instruction. Thus he inevitably compromised himself in a cause which was not that of his heart or principles, and whose apparently irresistible strength could only have excused his adhesion to it. This supposition, however, also proved erroneous; and when the French armies had to abandon Spain, Melendez, with their other principal adherents, had to fly with them also, having had the further misfortune to have his house plundered, and his valuable library destroyed, by the very marauders for whose sake he had lost all his hopes of the future at home.

Before entering France, Melendez, kneeling down, kissed the Spanish soil, saying, "I shall not return to tread thee again." His apprehensions, notwithstanding his anxiety to do so, proved correct. He passed four years in France, residing at Toulouse, Montpelier, Nismes and Alaix, as circumstances compelled him, in great privation and with bodily sufferings, the more aggravating, in his advanced age, the bitter remembrances of the past. A paralytic affection first incapacitated him from all exertion, and finally, an apoplectic attack terminated his existence, at Montpelier, on the 24th May, 1817, in the arms of his wife, who had followed him through all the vicissitudes of life, and surrounded by the companions of his exile. A monument was afterwards placed to his memory in the cemetery by the Duke de Frias.

Notwithstanding the indecision of his character in public life, Melendez was in private remarkable for laborious application to his studies and duties. His reading was immense, and his desire unceasing to be useful, and to contribute, by all the means in his power, to the well-being of his fellows. His kindness of heart is conspicuous in all his writings, which also portray the diffidence of his own powers, ascribed to him by his biographer.

His principal objects of veneration seem to have been the writings of Newton and Locke. The former, as the "Great Newton," is often named by him. Pope he took for his model avowedly in poetry, and he strove to imitate the moral and philosophic tone of that great poet's writings, whose elegance of style he certainly rivalled. Nothing in Spanish verse had been ever produced to equal the sweetness of his verses, their easy tone, and sparkling thoughts and expression. He was much attached to drawing, but had no inclination for music, not even to the charms of song, the more singular in one whose ear for the melody of verse appears to have been so sensitive. To the very last he seems to have been endeavouring to improve his poems, which have been thus observed to have often lost in strength and expression what they gained in cadence.

"The principles of his philosophy were benevolence and toleration; and he belonged to that race of philanthropists who hope for the progressive amelioration of the human race, and the advent of a period, when civilization, or the empire of the understanding, extended over the earth, will give men that grade of perfection and felicity compatible with the faculties and the existence of each individual. Such are the manifestations of his philosophic poems, and such a state he endeavoured to aid in producing by his talents and labours."

His influence as a poet has certainly been very great. All the writers in Spain, who immediately succeeded him, especially Quintana, showed evident proofs of having profited by the lessons his example gave them, and those lessons seem to have sunk deeply into the minds of successive generations, so as to leave no doubt of their continuing in the same course.

After his arrival in France, Melendez wrote a few short

poems, which, notwithstanding his age and failing health, showed his spirit was still the same, and his imagination as lively as ever. At Nismes he prepared an edition of his works, which the Spanish government published at their cost after his death, when they also gave his widow the pension allotted for her, as according to her husband's former rank. This edition has been the one subsequently several times reprinted, with a biography by the eminent Quintana, worthy of himself and of his master. The prologue to it, by Melendez, is very interestiug, and from it we learn, with regret, that upon the destruction of his library, "the most choice and varied he had ever seen belonging to a private individual, in the formation of which he had expended a great part of his patrimony and all his literary life," he had lost what he considered some of his best poems, and some tracts, in prose, which he had prepared for the press, on Legislation, on Civil Economy, the Criminal Laws, on Prisons, Mendicancy and other subjects.

The misfortunes of Melendez were certainly much to be lamented, but throughout them he could unquestionably console himself with the conviction of having been actuated ever by upright motives, and of leaving to his country an imperishable name. His literary career had been an eminently successful one, and he had felt the full enjoyment of fame. In the prologue, above mentioned, he refers very feelingly to the reverses to which he had been subjected, but also with apparent satisfaction to the various editions and notices of his works, published both in Spain and abroad.

In leaving revised his works, published afterwards by the government, Madrid 1820, Melendez left also this positive direction: "Although I have composed many other poems, these appear to me the least imperfect, and I therefore forbid the others to be reprinted under any pretext. I earnestly request this of the editor, and expect it of his probity and good feeling, that he will fulfil this, my will, in every respect." In accordance with this request, many of his earlier works have been, with much propriety, omitted, and the remainder have been considerably corrected; at the same time that a great number of poems are added, that had not been previously published. The best edition of his works is that by Salva, Paris 1832.

Melendez enjoyed in his day a higher reputation than readers at present are willing to concede him, comparing him with the other poets that have since appeared in Spain. But the merits of writers should be considered, in justice, relatively only to those who have preceded them, and by this standard he is certainly fully entitled to the eulogiums which his contemporaries awarded him.

MELENDEZ VALDES.

JUVENILITIES.

When I was yet a child,
  A child Dorila too,
To gather there the flowerets wild,
  We roved the forest through.

And gaily garlands then,
  With passing skill display'd,
To crown us both, in childish vein,
  Her little fingers made.

And thus our joys to share,
  In such our thoughts and play,
We pass'd along, a happy pair,
  The hours and days away.

But ev'n in sports like these,
  Soon age came hurrying by!
And of our innocence the ease
  Malicious seem'd to fly.

I knew not how it was,
    To see me she would smile;
And but to speak to her would cause
    Me pleasure strange the while.

Then beat my heart the more,
    When flowers to her I brought;
And she, to wreathe them as before,
    Seem'd silent, lost in thought.

One evening after this
    We saw two turtle-doves,
With trembling throat, who, wrapt in bliss,
    Were wooing in their loves.

In manifest delight,
    With wings and feathers bow'd,
Their eyes fix'd on each other bright,
    They languish'd, moaning loud.

The example made us bold,
    And with a pure caress,
The troubles we had felt we told,
    Our pains and happiness.

And at once from our view
    Then, like a shadow, fled
Our childhood and its joys, but new,
    Love gave us his instead.

THE TIMID LOVER.

In the sharp pains the tyrant Love
  Since first I saw thee made me feel,
To thee a thousand times above,
  I come those pains to heal,
My village girl! but soon as nigh
  To thee I find my way,
If e'er so bold to be I try,
  I know not what to say.

My voices fail, and mournful sighs,
  Malicious phrenzy watching o'er,
The place of them alone supplies;
  While mocks my efforts more
The traitor god, when anxious by
  My thoughts to speak I pray;
If e'er so bold to be I try,
  I know not what to say.

Then feels his fire so strong my soul,
  Meseems to die my only fate,
My tears in torrents freely roll,
  And with deep groanings wait,

To move thy feeling heart's reply;
　But vainly, all astray,
If e'er so bold to be I try,
　I know not what to say.

I know not what, in trembling fear,
　That seals my lips, as yet to learn
A foolish hope, thou mayst ev'n here
　My hapless love discern.
I feel I must for ever fly
　From thy side far away;
If e'er so bold to be I try,
　I know not what to say.

Alas! if thou couldst, my adored!
　But hear those sighs, and thoughts express'd,
What happiness 'twould me afford!
　I should be, Phyllis, blest.
But woe is me! beneath thine eye,
　To sink in mock'd dismay,
If e'er so bold to be I try,
　I know not what to say.

MY VILLAGE LIFE.

When able happily am I
   To my poor village to escape,
From all the city's noise to fly,
   And cares of every shape;

Like a new man my spirits give
   Me then to feel, in joyous link;
For only then I seem to live,
   And only then to think.

The insufferable hours that there
   In weariness to me return'd,
Now on a course so gently bear,
   Their flight is scarce discern'd.

The nights that there in sloth and play
   Alone their occupations keep,
Here with choice books I pass away,
   And in untroubled sleep.

With the first dawn I wake, to change
   Rejoiced the soft bed's balmy rest,
Through the life-giving air to range,
   That free dilates the breast.

It pleases me the heavens to view,
    O'erspread with red and golden glows,
When first his lustres to renew,
    His splendours Phœbus shows.

It pleases me, when bright his rays,
    Above the zenith fiery shine,
To lose me in the thick wood's maze,
    And in their shade recline.

When languidly he hides his head,
    In last reflection, even then
The mountain heights I eager tread,
    To follow him again.

And when the night its mantle wide
    Extends around of beaming lights,
Their motions, measuring as they glide,
    My watchful eye recites.

Then to my books return'd, with awe,
    My wondering thoughts, to trace, rehearse
The course of that portentous law,
    That rules the universe.

From them, and from the lofty height
    Of such my thoughts, I then descend
To where my rustic friends await,
    My leisure to attend.

And with them taking up the part,
   They give me in their toils and cares
To share, with jokes that merry start,
   Away the evening wears.

About his crops one tells me all,
   Another all about his vines,
And what their neighbours may befall
   Each many a tale combines.

I ponder o'er each sage advice;
   Their proverbs carefully I store;
Their doubts and quarrels judge concise,
   As arbitrator o'er.

My judgements all extol they free,
   And all together talking loud;
For innocent equality
   Reigns in their breasts avow'd.

Then soon the servant comes to bring
   The brimming jugs, and next with these
The mirthful girl supplies the ring
   With chestnuts, and the cheese.

And all, in brotherly content,
   Draw nearer round, to pass untold
The sparkling cups, that wine present
   Of more than three years old.

And thus my pleasant days to pass,
  In peace and happiness supreme,
(For so our tastes our pleasures class,)
  But like a moment seem.

REMEMBRANCES OF YOUTH.

Like a clear little stream,
  That with scarcely a sound,
Through the plain among flowers,
  Glides whirling around,

So the fugitive years
  Of my easy life sped,
Amidst laughter and play,
  Like a dream have fled.

On that dream to look back,
  Oft in wonder I dwell;
Nor to tear me have power
  From its pleasing spell.

On each side in soft ease,
  With friends cherish'd and gay,
In diversions and dance,
  In banquets and play,

With roses Cytheran
   Sweet martyrdoms twine,
Of the blinded ring join'd
   To deliriums of wine.

And hopes so fallacious,
   Bright castles that shone
In the air as upraised,
   By the winds overthrown.

With the Muses to crown
   The grave tasks, that are born
Of wisdom, with laurel
   Their sons to adorn :

Here a thousand retreats
   Of charm'd leafy arcade,
That to slumber beguile,
   In freshness and shade :

There beyond in the bowers
   Of sweet Cnidus arise,
As of fear and desire,
   Half mingled, the sighs :

There the broad river spreads,
   Showing soft its delights,
To oblivion of all
   Whose crystal invites ;

With a gaze of desire
   The fair banks I descend,
And to the false waters
   My thirsty lips bend;

For a full draught I seek,
   But feel suddenly by,
Disenchant me the call
   Of a friendly cry:—

" Where impell'd dost thou go,
   In such blind madness, where?
O, fool! round thy footsteps
   Hid dangers are there!

" The wild fancy restrain,
   Light ill-omen'd is this,
Where but lures thee to whelm
   A fatal abyss.

" Of thy happier years
   Is the verdure dispell'd,
And what were then graces
   Now vices are held.

" Thou art man! it befits
   Thee repenting in truth,
To gild virtuous with toils
   The errors of youth!"

I yield, from the current
   I tremblingly fly:
But with eyes looking back,
   Repeat with a sigh,—

" If to fall be a sin,
   What hast thou, Nature, meant?
The path made so easy,
   So sweet the descent?

" How blest are the creatures,
   With instincts secure,
Whom to swerve from the right
   No perils allure!"

OF THE SCIENCES.

I APPLIED myself to science,
   In its great truths believing,
That from my troubles I hence
   Some ease might be receiving.

O! what a sad delusion!
   What lessons dear I learn'd me!
To verses in conclusion,
   And mirth and dance I turn'd me.

As if it were that life could
   Produce so little trouble,
That we with toils and strife would
   Make each one of them double.

I stand by smiling Bacchus,
   In joys us wont to wrap he;
The wise, Dorila, lack us
   The knowledge to be happy.

What matters it, if even
   In fair as diamond splendour,
The sun is fix'd in heaven?
   Me light he's born to render.

The moon is, so me tell they,
   With living beings swarmy;
"There may be thousands," well they
   Can never come to harm me!

From Danube to the Ganges,
   History tells how did he
The Macedonian launch his
   Proud banner fierce and giddy!

What's that to us, to entice us,
   If only half this valley,
To feed our lambs suffice us,
   With all our wants to tally?

If not, leave all to justice:
   Give me some drink, o'erpower'd
With but to name this goddess,
   I feel myself a coward.

They much who study ever
   Have thousand plagues annoy them;
Which in their best endeavour
   Their peace and joy destroy them:

And then what do they gather?
   A thousand doubts upspringing,
Which other puzzlings farther
   Them other doubts are bringing.

And so through life they haste on,
   One enviable truly!
Disputes and hates to waste on,
   And ne'er agreeing throughly.

My shepherd girl! but bring me
   Then wine abundant very,
And fear not songs I'll sing thee,
   As endlessly and merry.

THE DISDAINFUL SHEPHERDESS.

If, as thou sayst, thou lovest me well,
   Dear girl, those scornfulnesses cease;
For love can ne'er in union dwell
   With such asperities.

Show sharp disdain, to plight if e'er
   Another proffers thee his troth;
To two at once to listen fair
   Is an offence to both.

Let one be chosen, so to prove
   How great your happiness may be;
Thou calmly to enjoy his love,
   And he to love thee free;

Above all maids to extol thee most;
   And thou to tenderness incline,
To yield repaying him the boast
   His love gives forth for thine.

Reserve and rigour to preside
   In love, is like the ice in spring,
That robs fair May of all its pride,
   The flocks of pasturing:

But kindness, like the gentle rain,
    Which April gives to glad the field,
Which makes all flourishing the plain,
    And seeds their stores to yield.

Be not disdainful then, but kind:
    Know not to certain beauteous eyes
Alone all beauty is confined,
    Or locks of golden dyes.

Vain puff'd-up beauty will appear,
    But like some showy ivy stem;
They may surprise, but fruitless, ne'er
    Have any valuing them.

If join'd with kindness, like the vine
    It seems, with fruitful stores array'd;
Where all contentedly recline,
    Beneath its peaceful shade:

And whose green stems, the elm around,
    When twining with adorning grace
Its leaves, will hold it also bound,
    Firm in its fond embrace.

Flower of a day is beauty's bloom;
    Time leaves it soon behind: if e'er
Thou doubt'st my word, let Celia's doom
    The lesson true declare.

Celia, for witching beauty famed
    Once far and wide, so foolish proud,
A thousand captives who contemn'd
    That all before her bow'd,

Now worn by years would blindly try
    Who to her service may be won;
But finds all from her turn to fly,
    To look at her finds none.

For with her snow and rose the beams
    And lustre of her eyes are flown,
And like a wither'd rose-tree seems,
    Sad, wrinkled and alone.

'Tis but ingenuous kindness true,
    The maid that loves in honour's bonds,
Who listens to her lover sue,
    And tenderly responds;

Who at his pleasantries will smile,
    Who dances with him at the feast,
Receives the flowers his gift, the while
    His love with like increased;

Who him her future husband sees,
    Is neither coy nor feels ashamed,
For he as hers, and she as his,
    The village through are named,

That always like the dawn will seem,
    When calm its light shines o'er the plain,
And keeping all beneath her beam
    Bound captive in her chain :

Years without clouding pass away ;
    Care to oppress her ne'er affects ;
Ev'n rivalry forgives her sway,
    And envy's self respects.

Her cheerfulness and happy vein,
    Being to latest age to share,
Delight of all the shepherd train,
    Enchantment of the fair.

Be then, my Amaryllis ! kind ;
    Cease those disdainfulnesses, cease ;
For with thy pleasing grace combined
    Such harshness ill agrees.

The heavens ne'er form'd thee perfect thus,
    Surpassingly of matchless cost,
That such high gifts should ruinous
    Be miserably lost.

Be kind, receive thy lover's vow,
    And all the village thou wilt find,
Who murmur at thy coldness now,
    To praise thee then as kind.

Thus sang Belardo, at her door,
　His shepherd girl to wait upon,
Who scornful, from her casement o'er,
　Bids him be silent and begone.

IV.

LEANDRO FERNANDEZ MORATIN.

SPANISH writers have in general too much overrated the merits of their national dramas, and foreigners have too often repeated the eulogies, as if they were deserved. Like those of antiquity, the Spanish, though they abound in passages of much poetry and feeling, are almost entirely deficient in that delineation of individual character, which constitutes the highest class of the art. Thus all the representations may be observed of the same description of personages and incidents, given often with much ingenuity, but also often in the worst taste, and always betokening a limited power of invention. Of this school Calderon de la Barca was the great type, both as regards his merits and defects. Lopez de Vega too, though his comedies are more representations of manners and every-day life than Calderon's, only showed his capability of something better, if he had allowed his genius to seek a reputation for perfectness, rather than for fecundity. The inferior order of writers mistook the errors of these for excellences, and thus exaggerated them.

There were not, however, wanting in Spain persons of better judgement, who observed those errors with a view to correct them, and among whom the prominent place is due to the two Moratins, father and son. Of these the former seems to have been the first of his countrymen who openly denounced the wrong tendencies of the national dramatists; and the latter, following in the same track, may be pronounced the great reformer of the Spanish stage, to whom it owes some of its best productions.

The elder Moratin was one of the ablest writers of verses in Spain during the last century, before the new æra of poetry arose, and his merits, if not of themselves superior to those of his contemporaries, have had an advantage over them, in connexion with the reputation of the son, who has rendered them more celebrated by a pleasing memoir of his father, prefixed to his works. From this we learn, that if the father did not attain a high rank himself as a poet or dramatist, yet he well deserves to be remembered as a bold and judicious critic, who, both by precept and example, effected much good in his own day, and still more by instilling good lessons into the mind of the son, so as to enable him to attain his merited success.

In the words of this memoir, "Calderon at that time enjoyed so high a reputation, that it appeared a sacrilegious hardihood to notice defects in his comedies or sacramental pieces, which, repeated annually on the stage with every possible pomp and appliance, delighted the vulgar of all classes, and perpetuated the applauses of their famous author. Moratin published three Discourses, which he entitled, 'Exposition of the Misconceptions of the Spanish Theatre,' written with the good judgement of a man of taste, and with the zeal of a citizen interested in the progression and literary glory of his country. In the first he showed the defects in which the old plays abounded; as also the modern, with which poets, without rule or plan, supplied the players, sanctioning every time more irregularity and ignorance. In the two following, he proved that the Autos of Calderon, so admired by the multitude, ought not to be suffered in a country that prided itself as civilized. It is unnecessary to say what opposition these discourses encountered; it is enough to add, that the third was scarcely published when the government prohibited the repetition of what he had condemned:—a memorable epoch in the annals of the Spanish stage, which can never remember, without praise, that judicious and intrepid writer to whom it owed so useful a reform."

Of this able critic, Leandro Moratin was the only son that survived childhood. He was born at Madrid, the 10th of March, 1760, and in his earliest years is described as having been remarkable for infantile grace and vivacity. At four years of age, however, he unfortunately had a severe attack of the smallpox, which not only left its disfiguring marks on his countenance, but also seemed to have changed his character, making him the rest of his life shy and reserved. As he grew up he shunned all playfellows; like Demophilus, he was a man among boys,—Κεῖνος γὰρ ἐν παισὶν νέος—and devoting himself to drawing and making juvenile verses, pursued his favourite studies in secret, so that even the father seemed not to have been ever fully aware of the bent of his son's genius.

The elder Moratin, whose father had been jewel-keeper to Isabel Farnesi, widow of Philip V., had been brought up to the profession of the law, in which he had not acquired any eminence, though he had some as an author. Seeing his son's talent for drawing, he had first intended him to take advantage of it as an artist, but finally placed him with a brother, Miguel de Moratin, who was a jeweller, to learn his occupation. In his earlier years the younger Moratin had been only at an obscure private school in Madrid, but he had good examples and lessons at home, and recourse to his father's library, where he found all the best works in Spanish literature, for secret study, beyond the tasks set in routine for his education. In 1779 the Spanish Academy, in the course of its objects for the promotion of literary pursuits, had offered, as a subject for a prize poem, The Taking of Granada; when the Accessit was awarded to a competitor who had signed himself Efren de Lardnoz y Morante. On this person being called for, Leandro Moratin, to the surprise of his father, presented himself as the author, producing the rough copy of the verses he had sent. This was naturally a source of great delight to the father, who might thus foresee, in hope at least, his son's future success. But he did not live to witness it, having died the following year, at only forty-two years of age, leaving a widow dependent on his son's labours as a working jeweller. At this business he continued, therefore, combining however with it his former studies, as far as his leisure permitted him.

In 1782 he obtained the honour of another Accessit from the Academy for a Satire on the vicious practices introduced into the Spanish language, and a greater feeling thereupon arose in his favour from literary persons who remembered his father, with the respect due to his merits. Hence, also, Leandro Moratin, notwithstanding his natural reserve, was drawn from his retirement into the company of several young men of kindred tastes and pursuits, whose conversation and society had great and good effect on his mind and future efforts.

In 1785 he published an edition of his father's poems, with reflections, which may be considered his first essay on criticism and declaration of opinion on matters of taste, according to the precepts of the purest classicism, then so much in fashion. From his earliest years he had been much attached to the theatre, then sunk to the low state which he so feelingly describes in the preliminary discourse to his Comedies, subsequently published; and having witnessed his father's anxiety to reform its abuses, he felt it a sort of inheritance left him to attempt the task. He had already begun one of his plays, which however he had not sufficient leisure to complete, on account of the demands for his daily labour; but about this time his mother died, and Leandro had then only his own wants to consider.

At the same time the good and great Jovellanos, whose notice he had attracted, proposed him as secretary to the Conde de Cabarrus, then going to Paris on a special mission, where accordingly Leandro went with that able and enlightened statesman, in January 1787, returning to Madrid in the January following. Shortly after the Conde and Jovellanos fell into ill-favour at court, and all their friends were involved in their fall. Moratin took shelter in the obscurity of his original occupation, and so escaped notice. He completed his play, but could not get it represented, and in the course of delays had the license for it withdrawn. He wished to be exempt from labour for maintenance, to give himself up to his favourite studies, but sought in vain for other means of attaining this end than from the favour of the government. A change in the ministry having now occurred, he wrote a petition, in verse, to the Conde de Florida Blanca, in which, humorously depicting his wants, he asked a small benefice in the church. This, though a very small one, was granted him, and thereupon he had to take the first orders of the tonsure. Shortly afterwards, Godoy, Prince of the Peace, came into power, and became a still more effectual patron for Moratin, on whom he conferred other benefices and favours, to the amount of about £600 a year sterling, so that he became at once, for his position in life, wealthy, and enabled to devote himself entirely to literature.

It has been the fashion lately for all parties to decry Godoy, and there can be no doubt that he was guilty of much misconduct in the exercise of power. But he was in this only acting according to the circumstances in which he was placed, and the favourite and minister of a weak-minded and despotic monarch could not be expected to have acted much otherwise than he did. In the memoirs he published in his later years in his justification, Godoy has, in a tone of apparent sincerity and earnestness, sometimes amounting even to eloquence, shown that often he could not have acted otherwise, and that his faults were the faults of his position, while his merits were his own. He declares that he was the first minister in Spain who curbed the power of the Inquisition, and that he had never instituted any prosecution for private opinions. His treatment of Jovellanos he might well excuse to himself, as a return for hostility manifested to him under circumstances that he might consider to warrant it. But of other eminent men of learning and of the arts he was the munificent patron, of Melendez among others, and of Moratin more especially. The former dedicated to him the second edition of his works, and Moratin now one of his plays, which had been received with much favour. From this dedication, a judgement may be formed by the translation, of the spirit of Moratin, that, while under the sense of great obligations, he did not condescend, like other poets, to flatter his Mæcenas's vanity by ascriptions of descent from ancient kings or other fictions; but dwelt only on his personal qualities, and the great power which he undoubtedly possessed, as exercised in his favour. The same spirit Moratin showed in his letter to Jovellanos, in which adulation could less be imputed to him, as that illustrious individual was in disgrace at court, and no longer the dispenser of the favours of the government.

But Moratin showed the independence of his character still more decidedly, in refusing the request made by Godoy that he should write eulogistic verses on a lady of the court; and it is to the honour of Godoy, we are informed, that though he was at first angry at the refusal, he passed it over without subsequent notice.

To another request made by Godoy, for an ode on the Battle of Trafalgar, Moratin acceded, though it is stated with considerable disinclination to the task. He could not, he replied at first, celebrate a lost battle, and as Hermosillia tells us, could not hide from himself the ridiculousness of having to represent a complete defeat as a glorious triumph, though the "dreaded Nelson" had fallen in it. He felt bound, however, to obey the favourite and to reconcile his task to justice, wrote his 'Shade of Nelson,' in imitation of the Prophecy of Nereus, and of the Tagus by Fray Luis de Leon. In this poem, he represents Nelson appearing the same night on the heights of Trafalgar, and foretelling England's approaching ruin, notwithstanding the victory which had been gained "so dearly, as to be in reality a discomfiture." He observes, that "Napoleon, having overcome the Austrians, would now turn all his energies to the conquest of England, while Spain would raise a mightier fleet to join him. He therefore counselled his countrymen to abandon their ambitious projects and make peace, and to create disunion in foreign countries by corrupting their cabinets, for the purpose of maintaining their preponderance." The thoughts are expressed in elegant poetical language, but the whole argument shows how little feeling he had in favour of the subject. In the last edition of his works prepared for publication before his death, he took care to have it omitted, but it has been again inserted in subsequent editions.

Prior to this, however, he had had a full opportunity of judging the character of the English nation. He had obtained permission to go abroad from Godoy, who also munificently gave him the means for that purpose. He first went to Paris, where he had scarcely arrived, in September 1792, when hearing a great tumult in the streets, and looking out for the occasion of it, he saw the head of the Princess de Lamballe borne along by the infuriated multitude on a pike. Horror-struck at the sight, he immediately left Paris for London, as, says his biographer, " anxious to contemplate for the first time true liberty arrayed in popular forms, without the mortal convulsions of licentiousness, or the withering foot-marks of oppression." Here he stayed about a year, taking notes of the lively impressions made on him of the "character, ideas, traditions, legislation, and political and commercial tendency of that singular nation, so worthy of being studied." It may be allowed us to regret that those notes were never published, and perhaps the censor's license for them could not have been obtained. The only fruit of his visit was a translation of Hamlet, which he published in 1798, on his return.

On leaving England, Moratin passed through Flanders and some parts of Germany and Switzerland to Italy, whence, after visiting all the principal cities there, he returned to Spain in December 1796. Previous to his arrival in Madrid, he had been appointed Secretary Interpreter of languages, a valuable appointment in itself, but still more so to him, as it left him sufficient leisure for study. He took advantage of this to proceed with several dramas with which he enriched the Spanish stage, and had projected others which he felt under the necessity of abandoning. In several of his pieces, and especially in the Mogigata, which Maury translates La Femelle Tartuffe, he had offended the clerical party, so that he was denounced to the Inquisition, and though preserved from their power under the protection of Godoy, he was subjected to many and great annoyances. In consequence of these, he determined to give up further writing for the stage, contenting himself with producing afterwards only some translations from the French, and with preparing his most valuable work, 'On the Spanish Theatre.' This work treats the subject historically, and abounds with much interesting information as well as sound criticisms. On it he passed the latter years of his life, so that it was not published until after his death.

Shortly after his return from Italy he was named one of a commission to reform the stage, and on this proving insufficient for the purposes intended, he was appointed Director of Theatres by royal order. No one, it might be thought, could be better adapted for this office, and it would have seemed one agreeable to his inclinations; but he declined it, preferring to effect the reforms he recommended by example rather than by exercise of authority.

The events of the 19th March, 1808, deprived Godoy of his power, and the French armies soon after entered Madrid. Moratin had remained at his post in the execution of the duties of his office, and became involved in the course of proceedings, the final character of which he could not foresee. He was set down as one of the French party, and so exposed to public obloquy, that when the French had to evacuate Madrid, he felt himself under the necessity of going with them. When they returned he returned with them, and was appointed, by Joseph Buonaparte, Chief of the Royal Library, an appointment which was most congenial to his taste, and which would have been exceedingly appropriate for him to accept, had it been only from the national government.

As it was, he had to fly from Madrid a second time with the intruders, and henceforth there was nothing for him in life but privations to endure. Some houses which he had bought had been seized, and one of them sold. Another, which was restored to him, had been much injured, and his books and property destroyed. His benefices were denied him; a merchant, with whom he had entrusted his money, became bankrupt; and a dependent, in whom he had confided, by his defalcation brought a further heavy loss on his means. He had at first retired to France, but having been excepted from the list of the proscribed by Ferdinand VII., he returned to Spain, and for a length of time resided at Barcelona. But the Inquisition was attempting to rise again into power, and Moratin, naturally of a timid disposition, felt himself marked out for a victim. He could not submit to live subject to be watched and kept in constant alarm; and even when this office was finally put down, he felt the frequent recurrence of public commotions more agitating than he could endure. He therefore determined again to retire to France, first to Bayonne, in 1823, and afterwards to Bordeaux, to live with a friend, named Silvela, who had a seminary at that place, and in whose society he felt sure of enjoying domestic happiness.

Through his whole life, Moratin seems to have required the aid of friends on whom to rely for daily needs and attentions; and it was fortunate for him, in his advanced age and under the pressure of infirmities, to possess such a resting-place as in Silvela's establishment. Shortly after this friend removed to Paris, where also Moratin followed him, and there he died, the 21st June, 1828. He was buried in the cemetery of Père la Chaise, in one of the lines to the right of the chapel, between the remains of Molière and Lafontaine, where a simple monument, with a cinerary urn, marks his grave.

"There," says his biographer, "in a foreign land, lies a celebrated Spaniard, to whom his country did not offer sufficient security to allow him to die tranquilly in her bosom. A man averse to all party feeling, obedient to existing authority, whether of fact or of right, absorbed in his studies, teacher from his retirement of the purest morality, incapable of injuring any one, or of exciting disorder even indirectly, he had to wander forth many years, not proscribed, but driven away by apprehensions too justly entertained."

After his death there were several editions of his works published, both in France and Spain: the last one in the collection of Spanish authors by Rivadeneyra, Madrid 1848, as the last seems most correct and complete. This republication is more interesting, as also containing, in the same volume, the works of his father, Nicolas Moratin. It is to be regretted that other works of his, yet existing in manuscript, have not been added, especially the account of his travels.

Moratin was an exceedingly careful writer, and very fastidious in the correction of his verses. His admirers, especially those of the classic school, have praised him as a great lyric poet, even superior to Melendez. This, however, he felt was not just; and without derogating from his merits, we must pronounce him far inferior to that eminent poet, whose works surpassed all that had preceded him in Spanish poetry. The fame of Moratin must rest on his plays, into which, however, it is not the object of this work to enter, confined as it is to lyric poetry. They are only five in number, and, like Sheridan's, are remarkable for neatness and elegance of dialogue, as much as for incident and character. The Spanish theatre owes all its subsequent merit to Moratin; he reformed the taste of the times by giving the stage better works than it had previously possessed, and assuredly was thus one of the greatest public benefactors of his age.

LEANDRO FERNANDEZ MORATIN.

DEDICATION OF THE COMEDY OF THE MOGIGATA TO THE PRINCE OF THE PEACE.

THIS moral fiction, which the facile Muse,
Thalia kind inspired, and which await
The numerous crowds that throng the Spanish scene,
Therein acquiring voice, and life, and form,
To thee I now present, with feelings pure
Of gratitude and love. By other path
The difficult height of Pindus to ascend,
In vain have I aspired, in vain; and oft
Have wept me baffled, o'er the bold attempt.
How often, striking the Aonian chords,
To win her have I sought, so fleeting, coy,
The beauty that in silence I adore!
To imitate the voice and harmony,
Which Echo erst repeated in the woods
Of green Zurgüen: oft as Clio waked

The trumpet that diffuses martial rage,
I wish'd, with her sublimest ardour fired,
To celebrate the lofty deeds of Spain:
From her proud neck as beating, broken off,
The barbarous yoke; the conqueror in turn
Conquer'd on the burning sands of Libya:
Numantia with the miseries appeased,
Proud Rome was doom'd to know, abandon'd prey
To frightful military outrages:
Cortes, in the valley of Otumba,
Lord of the golden standard, at his feet
The sceptre of the West! but angrily,
Menander's muse offended, soon reproved
My error, and the lyre and pastoral pipe
Snatch'd from me, and the clarion of Mars.

" Follow," she said to me, " the only track
Which my voice indicates, if thou wouldst seek
The honour, that despite of silent death,
May make thy name immortal. I in love
A thousand times upon thy infant lip
Have printed a soft kiss, and bade thee sleep
To the repeated heavenly tones I raised.
Thou my delight wast ever, and my care;
And the propitious gifts, which Nature shed
On thee, it was my joy to cultivate.
Now with loud festive acclamation sounds

Thy country's scene in thy just praise, on high
Thy glory to affirm. Thou follow on
To sacred Helicon, which Cynthia bathes
With her immortal light, the Muses' crown
Of ivy and of laurel there to gain."

Be not offended, Sir, if e'er so poor
The tribute that I dedicate; and what
Could worthy be the greatness of thy name?
The gift is humble, the desire is rich;
And not sufficing more my sterile vein,
What I can give I offer. Prostrate thus,
On the rude altars he has raised, is wont
The husbandman to heap the simple fruits
Of his fields gather'd round; and offering them
To the high tutelar deity he adores,
Spreads them forth grateful, incenses and flowers.

EPISTLE TO DON GASPAR DE JOVELLANOS,

SENT FROM ROME.

Yes! the pure friendship, that in kindly bonds
Our souls united, durable exists,
Illustrious Jovino! nor can time,

Nor distance, nor the mountains us between,
Nor stormy seas hoarse roaring, separate
Remembrance of thee from my memory.

The sound of Mars, that now sweet peace awhile
Suspends, has long unhappy silence placed
On my affection. Thou I know content
Livest in obscure delicious quietude,
For ever with untiring zeal inspired
To aid the public weal; of virtue e'er,
And talent, the protector and the friend.

These verses which I frame unpolish'd, free,
Though not corrected with thy learned taste,
In truth announce to thee my constant faith.
And so may Heaven but soon to me return
The hour again to see thee, and relate
Familiarly discoursing, to my view
Whatever of its varied scenes the world
Presented. From my native shores to those
Which bathes the Seine, blood-stain'd and turbulent;
The daring Briton's, master of the sea,
To the bold Belgian's; from the deep-flowing Rhine
To the high tops of Apennine snow-crown'd,
And that height further, which in burning smoke
Covers and ashes over Naples wide,
The different nations I have visited,

Acquiring useful knowledge, never gain'd
By learned reading in retired abodes.
For there we cannot see the difference great
Which climate, worship, arts, opinions,
And laws occasion. That is found alone,
If thou wouldst study man, in man himself.

Now the rough Winter, which augments the waves
Of Tiber, on his banks has me detain'd,
Inhabitant of Rome. O! that with thee
'T were granted me to rove through her, to scan
The wonderful remains of glories past,
Which Time, whose force can naught resist, has spared!
Thou nursling of the Muses and the Arts,
Faithful oracle of bright history,
What learning thou wouldst give the affluent lip;
What images sublime, by genius fired,
In the great empire's ruin thou wouldst find!
Fell the great city, which had triumph'd o'er
The nations the most warlike, and with her
Ended the Latin valour and renown.
And she who to the Betis from the Nile
Her eagles proudly bore, the child of Mars,
The Capitol with barbarous trophies deck'd,
Conducting to her car of ivory bound
Great kings subdued, amid the hoarse applause
Of wide-throng'd forums, and the trumpet's sounds,

Who to the world gave laws, now horrible
Night covers her.   She perish'd, nor expect
More tokens of her ancient worth to find.

Those mouldering edifices, which the plough
Breaks through in shapeless masses, once they were
Circuses, strong palaces, and theatres;
Proud arches, costly baths, and sepulchres;
Where thou mayst hear perchance, for so 't is said,
In the deep silence of the gloomy shade,
A funeral lament, they only tell
The glory of the people of Quirinus.
And this to future races but remains
The mistress of the world, illustrious Rome!
This and no more remain'd? of all her arts
And dreaded power? What could not aught avail
Her virtue, wisdom, valour, all conjoin'd,
With such her opulence, the law severe
To mitigate, or stay the blows of fate?

Alas! if all is mortal—if to Time
Alike the strong wall and the tender flower
Must yield—if that will bronze and porphyry break,
Destroying them and burying in dust,
For whom so guards unhappy Avarice
His treasuries untouch'd? for whom foretells
Immortal fame, the adulation vile

That crimes and violence traitorous exalts?
For what so hastening to the tomb runs on
The human race, revengeful, envious,
And haughty? Why, if all that e'er exists,
And what man sees is all but ruins? all.
For never to return the hours fly past
Precipitate, and to their end but lead,
Of the most lofty empires of the earth,
The perishable splendour. The Deity,
That hidden animates the universe,
Alone eternal lives, and He alone
Is powerful and great.

V.

JUAN BAUTISTA DE ARRIAZA.

In the history of the literature of every country, it is interesting to observe with what noiseless steps true genius generally proceeds to win popular favour, compared with the means to which mediocrity resorts for whatever share of notice it can attain. There are some writers who, with great talent, have some counterbalancing deficiency, respecting whose merits more discussion will be consequently excited, than respecting the superior qualities of others, not liable to the same observations. To obtain that kind of notoriety, it is often requisite to belong to some school or party, whose praise will give a temporary importance to works written, according to their taste or system, while those out of their pale will be passed over with at best only cold commendations. In Spain, as elsewhere, poetry has had its classical and romantic schools, and the merits of all writers, belonging to one or the other of them, were fully set forth by their respective partisans; while, if there happened to be one who could not be claimed by either, like Arriaza, he was allowed to pass comparatively unnoticed by the critics of the day.

Of this very pleasing author no detailed biography has

been published; and his claims to be considered one of the first modern poets of Spain seem to be scarcely recognized by his countrymen, who read with surprise the commendations passed on him abroad. Thus they have allowed seven editions of his works to be circulated and exhausted, without satisfying our curiosity by any of those particulars of private life, with which we love to consider the characters of worth and genius. All we are informed of him, in the short notices given of Arriaza by Wolf, Maury and Ochoa, is, that he was born at Madrid, in the year 1770, where the last-mentioned writer also says he died, in 1837.

From his name, it would seem that he was of Basque descent, and his family connections must have been "noble" and influential, from his career through life, though we have no account given of them. We learn, however, that he was educated at the Seminary of Nobles at Madrid, whence he was afterwards sent a cadet to the Military College at Segovia, and that he finally entered the navy. In one of his Epistles, in verse, he informs us that he was engaged in the expedition to Oran, and thence sailed to Constantinople, of which he gives a poetical description.

In 1798 he had to quit this service, on account of a disease of the eyes; and he then published the first edition of his poems. In 1802 he was appointed Secretary of Legation at London, and there wrote his principal poem, 'Emilia,' which was published at Madrid in the year following. The subject was the wish of a lady of fortune to bring up orphan children and others to the study of the fine arts; and it contains many fine passages, but was left unfinished.

In 1805 he went to Paris, where also he resided some time. On his return to Spain, he took part in the struggles against the French, having entered the ranks as a soldier, and having by his verses also vehemently instigated his countrymen to rise against the invaders. Of all the poets of the day, he seems to have been the most prolific in those patriotic effusions, which, no doubt, agreeing so well with the national temperament, had no small effect in keeping up the spirit of the Spanish people throughout the war. When the French entered Madrid, Arriaza, while engaged in resisting them, had a brother killed by his side, fighting in the same cause, to whose memory he has given a tribute of affection accordingly among his verses.

In the subsequent discussions in Spain respecting the government, Arriaza took part with those who advocated the rights of the absolute king. For this advocacy, on the return of Ferdinand VII. to full power, he received his reward, having been appointed Knight of the Order of Charles III., and Secretary of Decrees, besides receiving several other minor favours and offices. Henceforth Arriaza seems to have passed his life at court, in the quiet enjoyment of literary pursuits. He might be considered the Poet Laureate of Spain, as he seems to have allowed scarcely any opportunity to pass by unhonoured, of paying homage to the court in celebration of birthdays and other such occasions. His works abound with these loyal effusions, though they might generally have been better omitted.

It must, however, be said, in justice, that he was evidently sincere in those principles, to which he adhered under all circumstances, even when the Constitutionalists were in the ascendent. Once only he was betrayed into an eulogium of the other line of opinions, which had an effect rather ludicrous, so far as he was concerned in it. In 1820, when the constitution of 1812 had been anew promulgated, a friend of his, Don Luis de Onis, was appointed minister from Spain to Naples, and a banquet having been given him on his departure, Arriaza was induced to write verses on the occasion, which, full of apparent enthusiasm, abounded in spirit and beautiful images, beyond his usual facility and fulness of expression. Carried away, no doubt, by the contagion of the company, he gave way to what, in soberer mood, he would have thought most dangerous doctrines. He painted the envoy as going "to Parthenope to announce our revolution;" adding, "To Parthenope that is now groaning beneath flowery chains, and to whom, though her syrens celebrate her in songs of slavery, thou wilt be the Spanish Tyrtæus, and raise them to the high employ to sing of country and virtue;" praising the heroism of Riego as to be offered as an example, "to throw down the holds of oppression." The Neapolitan government obtained notice of this composition, and actually used it as sufficient cause for objecting to receive Don Luis as Spanish minister, "because he was coming to inculcate revolutionary principles." Arriaza heard with horror that he was stigmatized as a liberal, and was urgent to disclaim such opinions, notwithstanding what he had written. Don Luis meanwhile was detained at Rome, until, by a strange coincidence, the revolution broke out at Naples also, and he entered the city almost as in fulfilment of the prophecy, that he was to be the harbinger of it.

The best edition of Arriaza's works is that of 1829, printed at the Royal Press of Madrid, of which the one of Paris, 1834, is a reprint. They consist of almost all varieties of song, and are almost all equally charming. His satirical pieces even are light and pleasing, as well as his anacreontic and erotic effusions, while his patriotic songs and odes breathe a spirit well suited to the subjects.

Maury, who has made him better known abroad by his praises than others, his contemporaries, seems to have regarded him with especial favour. He says of him:—"Depuis Lope de Vega, M. d'Arriaza est le seul de nos poëtes qui nous semble penser en vers. La nature le fit poëte, les évènements l'ont fait auteur. Il était arrivé à sa réputation littéraire sans y prétendre, il l'accrue pour ainsi dire à son corps défendant." In truth he seems to have poured forth his verses without effort, as a bird does its song, with a simplicity and truthfulness which went to the heart of the hearer, and left in it a sensation of their being only the echoes of its own. As Maury has well observed, "parlent à la raison et à l'esprit, comme au cœur et à l'imagination, elles offrent en même temps aux amateurs de la langue Castillane les sons harmonieux et les tournures piquantes qui la distinguent avec une grande élégance de diction et une clarté rare chez la plupart de nos écrivains."

It is true that his style is exceedingly easy, and the expression generally very clear, but it must also be acknowledged, on the part of the translator, that obscurities are frequently to be found in his lines, when he must discover a meaning for himself. It was Arriaza's own doctrine in the prologue to his works, "that there can be no true expression of ideas where there does not reign the utmost clearness of diction; that what the reader does not conceive at the first simple reading, cannot make in his imagination the prompt effect required, and much less move his heart in any way. This clearness," he observes, "should also be associated with a constant elegance of expression; though he does not consider this elegance to consist in a succession of grammatical inversions, or revolving adjectives, or metaphor on metaphor, but the mode most select and noble of saying things becomingly to the style in which they are written."

Arriaza was eminently what the French call a *poëte de société*; and thus his verses were favourites with the higher classes particularly. He abjured the practices of the Romanticists who affected to despise the shackles of metre, as if the melody of verse, being merely mechanism, were of inferior consideration. On the contrary, he intimates that he considers it of primary importance, as if "whether a statue should be made of wax or marble." Thus he made cadence a principal study, and his verses becoming thereby better adapted for music, obtained greater vogue in the higher circles by means of accompaniments. Some even seem to have been expressly written for that purpose; for instance, among other pieces of a domestic character, one, a very pleasing Recitative, in which his wife and daughter join him in thanksgiving for his recovery from a dangerous illness. Though generally far from being impassioned, some of his verses are full of tender feeling, as the 'Young Sailor's Farewell.' This may be pronounced the most popular piece of modern poetry in Spain, being most in the memories of those whom he himself calls "the natural judges in these matters, the youth of both sexes, in whose lively imagination and sensible hearts may find better acceptation, the only two gifts with which I may rejoice to have endowed my verses, naturalness and harmony."

Arriaza must have acquired in his youth the rudiments of a sound education, and he was distinguished in later life for a knowledge of the French, Italian and English languages. Still he was not considered by his contemporaries as a person of extensive reading; and thus we do not find in his works any allusions or illustrations of a classical character, though it is almost ludicrous to observe with what pertinacity he introduces the personages of the heathen mythology, on all occasions where he can do so. Some of his ideas also run into the ridiculous, as in one of his best pieces, 'La Profecia del Pirineo,' he says, that on the heroic defenders of Zaragoza "there were at once on their faithful brows raining bombs and laurels."

The Ode to Trafalgar, notwithstanding its being liable to

the observation above made, of too frequent invocations of the Muses, is an admirable exemplification of an appropriate poem on such a subject. This battle, no doubt on account of its decisive effect, has been more celebrated than others. But it must be acknowledged to have been an unequal fight between the British and the Spanish portion of the allied fleet, as the former were in a high state of discipline, and the latter were newly levied and hurried out of port, before the officers and men had become sufficiently acquainted with one another to take their respective parts, with the precision necessary for such an occasion. Yet it is well known that the Spaniards fought with desperate and unswerving courage throughout, and their poets were therefore well warranted in taking the subject, as one doing honour to the national bravery.

The circumstances of the battle have lately again come into discussion in Spain, with naturally considerable warmth, on M. Thiers, in his History of the Consulate and the Empire, having been guilty of the extraordinary error to allege that the Spanish fleet fled, the greater part of them, from the battle, when, in fact, it was only the division of the French Admiral Dumanoir that had done so. This he did "for the purpose of preserving a naval division for France," as Dumanoir himself afterwards stated, in his justification, though he was disappointed in that patriotic wish, having been met a few days after by Sir Robert Calder's squadron, when all his four ships were taken in a less renowned combat.

The translation of the Ode has been made as nearly into the same metre with the original, as the forms of verse used in the two languages would admit. That of the 'Farewell' may be considered in the same light also, though the original has the first and fourth lines rhyming together, and the second with the third. This is an old and common form in Spanish poetry, and agrees well with our alternate lines of eight and six syllables, which Johnson considered "the most soft and pleasing of our lyric measures." In the Ode, it is interesting to observe not only the manly style of sentiment throughout, but also the absence of any ungenerous feeling against the English. Arriaza had, however, both as a seaman and a diplomatist, while resident in England, had sufficient opportunities of learning to think more justly of the English character than some other writers of the Continent.

Beyond his poems, Arriaza wrote several political pamphlets. The first was published at Seville in 1809, after the battle of Talavera, when the English, notwithstanding the victory, had to retreat into Portugal, giving occasion to the French party in Spain to allege that they were about to abandon the country to the French, and keep possession of the principal ports. In this pamphlet, which he entitled the 'Pharos of Public Opinion,' Arriaza combated these suspicions, and by a strenuous assertion of the good faith of the English, succeeded in disabusing the minds of his countrymen of what he termed "such malignant insinuations."

The second pamphlet he termed 'Virtue of Necessity,' shortly after the disastrous battle of Ocania; and its object was to stimulate the English government and nation to give more assistance than they had yet done, by money and otherwise. He proposed in return to give the English free right of commerce with the Spanish colonies in America, at least for a stated period, observing that they already had extensive dealings with them by contraband, and that the free commerce would make the English neutral, at least, in the question of the colonies wishing to declare themselves independent, while otherwise it would be their interest to have them independent. This pamphlet especially is full of sound statesmanlike ideas, and proves how well he was acquainted with the state of public feeling in England, on the several particulars respecting which he was writing.

A third pamphlet he wrote in English, and published it in London in 1810, where he was then sent on the part of the Spanish government. This he entitled 'Observations on the system of war of the Allies in the Peninsula;' and he endeavoured in it to urge the English to send more troops to the Peninsula, at certain points, where he considered they would be of most avail in disconcerting the plans of the French, and assisting the Guerrilla warfare the Spaniards were carrying on. He explained the determined fidelity of the Spaniards to the cause of their independence, but showed they would be insufficient to effect it, without the assistance he came to seek. This pamphlet was favourably received in England, and was noticed in Parliament; and the author had the good fortune to hope that his efforts had been successful, as he says, "The English government then sent greater reinforcements to their army, which emerging from its inaction, acquired the superiority preserved until the happy conclusion of the war."

For these and other writings, Arriaza received the thanks of the Regency in the name of the king, and had just cause to consider that a sufficient counterbalance to the misrepresentations made of his conduct in France, and elsewhere, by the opposite party. In a note affixed to the last edition of his poems, he complains that in a work published in France, 'Biography of Contemporary Characters,' there was an article respecting him "full of errors, even regarding the most public circumstances of his life," which he seems to have considered written from party feeling. If his surmises were correct, it is the more to be regretted that he did not take the best means of correcting those misrepresentations, by giving an authentic biographical account of his career in reply. He might thus not only have done justice to himself, but also have satisfied the desires of his admirers, who would naturally have felt sufficient interest in his fame to have rejoiced in those details. Whatever may be the course which a man of genius takes in public life from honest principles, he may always rely on finding in literature a neutral harbour where he may retire in confidence from all turmoils, and expect full justice awarded to his motives and memory. In the midst of political contentions, where so much always depends on circumstances with which we are little acquainted, it is often difficult at the time to know what is the proper course to follow. It is enough for us that those we admire have ever been distinguished for their sincerity and uprightness in the conduct they pursued.

With regard to Arriaza, our greatest regret must be that, with his apparently extreme facility of versification, and capability of elevating his mind to the conception of nobler subjects, he confined his genius so much to trivial events of the day, and thus wrote for his contemporaries instead of for posterity.

JUAN BAUTISTA DE ARRIAZA.

TEMPEST AND WAR,

OR

THE BATTLE OF TRAFALGAR.

ODE.

I FAIN would sing of victory;
But know, the God of harmony,
   Dispenser of renown,
For fortune's turn has little care,
And bids superior valour bear,
   Alone, the immortal crown.

See in his temple, shining yet,
Those at Thermopylæ who set
   Of manly fortitude
Examples rare, or 'neath thy wall
Who, sad Numantia, shared thy fall,
   But falling unsubdued.

There are to whom has fate bestow'd
The lot, that always on the road
   Of docile laurels borne,
Success should fly their steps before,
And in their hands events in store
   Should lose each cruel thorn.

As heroes these the vulgar choose,
If not as gods, but I refuse
   Such homage for the mind;
And in Bellona's doubtful strife,
Where fortune's angry frowns are rife,
   There heroes seek to find.

O! true of heart, and brave as true!
Illustrious Clio, turn thy view
   Afar the vast seas o'er;
For deeds, in spite of fate abhorr'd,
Than these more worthy to record
   Ne'er pass'd thy view before.

To abase the wealthy Gades, see,
From haunts of deep obscurity,
   The fellest Fury rise!
And from her direful hand launch'd forth,
Transform'd the forests of the North,
   She floating walls supplies.

Her envy is the city fair
Of Hercules, so proudly there,
   Couch'd on the Atlantic gates;
Girt by the sea, that from the west
Comes fraught with gold, and her behest
   Before her bending waits.

With venal aid of hate assists
Unfruitful England, throne of mists,
   Whose fields no sun behold;
Which Flora with false smile has clad
In sterile green, where flowers look sad,
   And love itself is cold.

Greedy the poison gold to seize,
They with the monster Avarice,
   The peace of Spain abhor;
And by their horrid arts increased,
Turn ev'n the treasures of the East
   To instruments of war.

Their proud Armada, which the main
Tosses to heaven, or threats in vain
   To engulf, they mustering show:
Ye suffer it not, ye pupils brave
Of the Basans, and to the wave
   Launch yours to meet the foe.

As by conflicting winds close driven,
The dark clouds o'er the vault of heaven
   Across each other fly;
And troubling mortals with the roar,
The electric fluids flashing o'er
   Dispute the sway on high,

So from both sides the battle roll'd,
The sails their wings of flame unfold,
   And ship to ship they close;
Combined, O! day of hapless fame,
Four elements with man proclaim
   The unequal war that rose.

Who in the whirlwind of dense smoke,
To Mars that in fit incense woke,
   From hollow ordnance sent,
With iron flames, a countless host,
Sounds that unhinging shaking cross'd
   The eternal firmament,—

Who in that lake of fire and blood,
Midst crashing masts and raging flood
   Of havoc and its train,—
Who by the light the picture shows,
May not your blood-stain'd brows disclose,
   O! noble chiefs of Spain?

With crimson dyed, or with the brand
Of sulphurous powder, firm ye stand,
   As in the conflict dire,
The sacrilegious giants rear'd,
Serene the shining gods appear'd,
   Midst rolling clouds of fire.

Shouts forth your courage hoarsely high
Bellona's metal roar, the cry
   The combat to inflame;
Nor fear ye mortals, when ye view
The streams of blood the waves imbue,
   Your prowess that proclaim.

With iron clogg'd the air, the breath
Is drawn each with a dart of Death,
   Whose skeleton immense
Rises exulting o'er the scene,
To see such fury rage, and glean
   His devastation thence.

O! how he crops youth's fairest flowers,
Or grief o'er life for ever lowers!
   See there for vengeance strains
One arm for one that off is torn,
Or when away the head is borne,
   Erect the trunk remains.

But, ah! what fiery column broke
There to the wind, and mid dense smoke
   Then to the abyss down threw
Heads, bodies, arms and woods confused,
And hands yet with the swords unloosed
   They for their country drew!

Struck by the sound groans Trafalgar;
Olympus shakes as in the war
   The savage Titans waged,
When through the waves their forges roll'd
Ætna, Vesuvius, and untold
   Volcanoes burning raged.

Trembling the monsters of the deep
Against each other beating, sweep
   Off to the Herculean Strait;
In horror heaven is clouded o'er,
Lashing the seas the north winds roar,
   In shame infuriate.

Of its own rage, the foaming brine,
Is born the tempest, fearful sign
   Of more disastrous night;
Mars at the view restrains his cry;
Bark Scylla and Charybdis high,
   The fiends whom wrecks delight.

Swift as a thunderbolt ye come,
The unhappy relics to consume
   Of fire, ye winds and waves!
O, Night! who may thy fearfulness,
Thy vast amount of woes express,
   Without the tear it craves!

Yield to the cruel element
At length the ships, that long unbent
   Its haughtiest rage defied;
Men sink yet living, and for e'er
Closes o'er them their sepulchre,
   The insatiable tide.

Save him, Minerva! who around
From East to West, the earth's wide bound,
   Was happier once thy care!
Urania, this thy votary save!
O, Love! how many fond hearts crave
   That one's last sigh to share!

Some to their much-loved country swim,
That horror-struck retires, and dim
   In quicksands seems to fly;
Hid by the waves them death unveils,
And to the wreck'd-worn seamen's wails
   They only fierce reply.

Never may Time, in his long flight,
Join day more terrible and night:
   But who in such a strife,
Who constant overcame such fate,
Where may we danger find so great
   For dauntless heart in life?

O, Clio! where? yet midst that rage,
With golden pen and deathless page,
   Thou lovest the brave to greet;
Gravina, Alava, each name
Write, and Escanio's, echoes fame
   Olympic will repeat.

And others, but my voice repels
The love that in my memory dwells;
   O, Cosmo! hard thy lot!
O, Muses! him the laurels give,
Whose friend is only left to live,
   And weep him unforgot.

Tried adverse fortune to endure,
Your valour proved sublime and pure,
   O, Mariners of Spain!
Your life your country's shield and strength,
Defended and avenged at length,
   She will be yet again.

The Lion and the Eagle yet
May have them Neptune's arm abet,
   Now England's slave and boast;
Who from her lofty poops shall view
Your troops resistless pouring through
   In torrents on her coast.

Suffice it now, as tribute paid,
Her great Chief's death; the Thames to shade,
   Doubling with grief her gloom:
That cover'd thus with honour'd scars,
She sees you wait, in happier wars,
   The combat to resume.

Ye go, as on the Libyan shore
The lion walks, that fiercely tore
   The hunter's cunning snare;
That not ingloriously o'erborne,
Calmly and fear'd, though bleeding, worn—
   Regains his sandy lair.

THE PARTING.

Sylvia! the cruel moment's near,
   When I must say farewell!
For hark! the cannon's sounds we hear
   Of my departure tell.
Thy lover comes to give thee now
   The last adieu, and part!
With sorrow overcast his brow,
   And sorrowful his heart.

Come, object of my love divine!
   Reach me those beauteous arms:
Would fate my happy lot assign
   My home and rest thy charms,
The blow that threatens its decree
   To give, I should not meet;
For sooner then than part, 't would see
   Me dying at thy feet.

O! had our passion equal force,
   Or been of equal growth,
The grief of absence might its course
   Divide between us both!

But thou a face indifferent,
   Or pleased, dost give to view,
Whilst I have not ev'n breath content
   To say to thee, Adieu.

A gentle river murmuring by,
   In calmness bathes the plain,
And of its waters the supply
   Sees beauteous flowers attain;
In silence thou, my lonely grief,
   Dost bathe my wretched breast,
And Sylvia's pity in relief
   For me canst not arrest.

But what, my Sylvia, dost thou say?
   What means that tender sigh?
Why do I see, mid tears that stray,
   Shine forth thy beaming eye?
As opens to the sun opposed
   On some clear day the cloud,
And his rays make the drops disclosed
   To sparkle as they flow'd.

On me dost thou those languid eyes
   Turn with that tender gaze?
Loses thy cheek its rosy dyes,
   Nor beauty less displays?

Thy ruby lips a moment brief
    Thou opest, and sorrow seals!
How fair the very show of grief
    Itself in thee reveals!

Insensate! how I wildly thought
    My bitter griefs would gain
Some ease, if thou wert also taught
    A portion of my pain!
Pardon the error that deceived,
    O, Sylvia! I implore;
Me more thy sorrow now has grieved,
    Than thy disdain before.

My bliss! I pray no more to swerve!
    Calm those heart-breaking pains:
Thy grief to have, does not deserve
    All that the world contains.
May all life's hours, in calm serene,
    Be ever pass'd by thee;
And all that darker intervene
    Reserved alone for me!

For me, whose lonely wretched doom
    By heaven has been decreed
To bear fate's cruelty and gloom,
    Wherever it may lead.

But not on thee, so lovely born,
    Form'd of a power divine,
To hold ev'n fate a subject sworn
    To every will of thine.

Whilst thou my absence mayst lament,
    Thy comfort mayst descry,
By fate a thousand lovers sent
    More to thy choice than I.
Some one she pleases me above
    To favour chance may show;
But one to love thee as I love,
    That none can ever know.

'T was not thy graces won my heart,
    Nor yet thy faultless face;
But 't was some sympathy apart
    I might from birth retrace.
I long a picture loved to draw
    Of charms I fancied true,
And thy perfections when I saw,
    The original I knew.

No traveller upon the ground
    By sudden lightning thrown,
The blow could more at once confound,
    Left helpless and alone,

Than I to see that beauteous brow,
  In hapless love was lost;
At thy feet forced at once to bow,
  To adore whate'er the cost.

But I depart, alas! the pain
  No words can e'er express;
Heaven only knows it that can scan
  The inmost heart's recess;
And saw the hours of deep delight,
  So full now long pass'd by,
That all my wishes' utmost height
  Heap'd up could satisfy.

Now while the breezes fair avail,
  The waves are gently stirr'd,
And of the mariners the hail
  Confused afar is heard:
Now from the deep's tenacious hold
  The anchor's fangs they heave,
And all conspiring are enroll'd
  Me swifter death to give.

Now with a vacillating foot
  The slender boat I tread,
Soon destined from the bank to shoot,
  As to the great bark sped.

Sylvia, in this sad moment's pause,
    O! what a mournful crowd
Of thoughts around thy lover close,
    To assault him and o'ercloud!

The sweet requital in return
    Thou givest my love I know;
And kind remembrances discern
    All thy affections show;
Whilst here each proof assures me well
    That naught thy heart can move;
But in my absence, who can tell
    If thou wilt faithful prove?

For those divine attractions whence
    Now all my joys arise,
Perhaps may fate the cause dispense
    Of all my miseries;
And whilst I absent and forlorn
    My pledges lost deplore,
Some rival gains of me in scorn
    The enchantments I adore!

But no, my bliss, my glory! ne'er
    Were given the winds in vain
Those vows, which envied me to share
    The universe my gain.

Let us time's tyranny defy,
    And distance, constant thus
Remaining in that changeless tie,
    That then united us.

When rises first the beamy sun,
    When sets his beauteous ray,
When moon and stars their courses run,
    On thee my thoughts will stay.
From that enchanting form my heart
    No moment will be free;
And traitress thou, when I depart
    Wilt ne'er ev'n think of me!

At lonely hours across my thought
    Gulf'd in the ocean vast,
The scenes to memory will be brought
    With thee I saw and pass'd.
Then will my sorrows make me feel
    My lot more dark to be,
And thou more cruel than the steel
    Wilt ne'er ev'n think of me!

"There first her matchless form I saw;
    There first my faith I swore;
And from her flattering lips could draw
    The happy 'Yes' they wore!"

As these reflections by me file,
    Rise griefs in like degree;
And thou, who knows, if thou the while
    Wilt e'er ev'n think of me?

Then as I hours of glory call
    Those when I thee beheld;
And of my griefs the sources all
    When from thy sight repell'd;
A thousand times the thoughts enhance
    The doom 't is mine to see,
Meanwhile who knows, if thou perchance
    Wilt e'er ev'n think of me?

When in the heavens I view unfurl'd
    The awful signs arise,
With which the Ruler of the world
    Poor mortals terrifies;
When sounds are in the deepest caves
    Of horrid thunderings nigh,
And of the seas the troubled waves
    Rage furiously on high;

When by the south wind is impell'd
    The proud Tyrrhenian main,
As if from its deep bosom swell'd
    To assault the starry train;

When the despairing steersman turns
   To prayer, instead of skill,
Seeing his bark the ocean spurns
   The plaything of its will;

Amid the hoarse and troubled cries
   The people raise around,
While shines the sword before their eyes
   Of death, to strike them bound;
Ev'n then will I my love's farewell
   In that dark hour renew,
And to the winds my sighs shall tell—
   Sylvia! my life, Adieu!

VI.

MANUEL JOSÈ QUINTANA.

CONNECTING the present age of modern Spanish poetry with that of the past generation, by a happily protracted existence, as well as by the style and tone of his writings, the venerable subject of this memoir still survives, to close a life of active usefulness in a healthy and honoured old age.

Quintana was born at Madrid, the 11th April, 1772, of a respectable family of Estremadura. He received his primary education in classical learning at Cordova, whence he proceeded to Salamanca, and graduated there in canon and civil law. In this university he had the advantage of studying under Melendez Valdes, by whom he was soon favourably noticed, and was made known to the illustrious Jovellanos, by whose counsels also he had the good fortune to be assisted. Thus his natural disposition for the study of elegant literature was encouraged, both by precept and example, under two such able directors, to take a higher course than the mere study of law, for which profession he was destined.

Having been admitted an Advocate of the Supreme Court, he has held various appointments, as fiscal of the tribunal of commerce, and censor of theatres; afterwards chief clerk of the Secretary-General to the Central Junta of Government, secretary of decrees and interpretation of languages, member of the censorship to the Cortes, and of the commission for the formation of a new plan of education. In the last, he was charged with the duty of drawing up a report of all the works on the subject presented to the government, which was, in 1835, approved of by the Cortes.

In the two former of these employments he was interrupted by the French invasion, when he took an active part against the invaders. Receiving afterwards the other offices mentioned, he wrote many of the proclamations and other addresses which were put forth on the part of the national government, during the struggle for independence. Throughout those eventful times, he was in the most advanced rank of the party that advocated constitutional rights, so that when Ferdinand VII. returned to the possession of absolute power, in 1814, he was, amongst the proscribed, made a prisoner, and confined in the castle of Pamplona.

There he was kept six years, without being allowed to communicate with his friends, or make use of his pen. On the constitutional government becoming re-established, he was released, and restored to his offices as secretary for the interpretation of languages, and member of the board of censors. In 1821, the directorship-general of public education having been formed, he was made president, until 1823, when the constitution was again set aside, and he was again deprived of his employments.

Hereupon Quintana retired to Estremadura to his family, and lived there till the end of 1828, when he was permitted to return to Madrid, to continue his labours and literary studies. The following year he was named member of the board for the museum of natural sciences, and in 1833 was re-established in his former employment, as secretary for interpretations, for which his knowledge of the French, English and other languages rendered him qualified, and also reappointed president of the council of public instruction. He was shortly after appointed preceptor to her present Majesty, Queen Isabel II., and although ever maintaining strong liberal principles, has been since, under the administration of Narvaez, named a senator of the kingdom.

Quintana first appeared as an author in 1795, when he published a small volume of poems, among which was an Ode to the Sea, considered one of his best compositions. The greater part, however, of them were of unequal merit, and those have been omitted in subsequent editions: the next one was published in 1802, and it has been reprinted with additions several times. The best and most complete edition of his poetical works was published at Madrid, in 1820, in two volumes, entitled, ' Poems, including the patriotic odes and tragedies, the Duke of Viseo, and Pelayo.' Of this edition five or six surreptitious reprints have been made at Bordeaux and elsewhere, the laws regarding copyright having only lately been made accordant with justice in Spain as regards authors, though they do not yet extend them protection against piratical republications from abroad.

The tragedy of the ' Duke of Viseo,' imitated from the English, the ' Castle Spectre ' of Lewis, was brought forward in 1801, and that of ' Pelayo ' in 1805. The latter, on a favourite subject of their ancient history, was received with much favour by his countrymen, as were also many of his patriotic odes and poems, written in a spirit accordant with the national feeling. Most of these were at the time inserted in two periodical works he had under his direction; the first, ' Variedades de Ciencias, Literatura y Artes,' and the second, the ' Seminario Patriotico,' which was of a political character, and established to promote, and sustain the spirit of independence, against the French invasion.

Beyond his original poems, Quintana has done an important service to Spanish literature by publishing 'A Collection of select Spanish Poetry,' altogether in six volumes, Madrid, 1830–33, with critical and biographical notices, reprinted in Paris by Baudry, 1838. These notices are written in a tone of great impartiality and fairness, and are preceded by a Dissertation, as an Introduction, on the History of Spanish Poetry, which, written as it is with eminent ability, Mr. Wiffen has shown great judgement in translating, prefixed to his very correct and elegant version of the works of Garcilasso de la Vega, London, 1823. Besides this valuable collection of Spanish poetry, Quintana has favoured the public with a work in three volumes,—' Lives of celebrated Spaniards,' of which the first volume was published in 1807, the other two in 1830 and 1833 respectively.

The first volume, which has been translated into English by Mr. Preston, London, 1823, contains the lives of the earlier heroes of Spanish history,—the Cid Campeador, Guzman the Good, Roger de Lauria, the Prince of Viana, and Gonzalo de Cordova; all bearing impressions of the enthusiastic and poetic feelings, characteristic of the comparatively youthful period of life at which they were written. It was Quintana's intention to have proceeded with a series of like biographies; but the subsequent public events, in which he had to take so active a part, interrupted the task, and when he resumed it, after the lapse of twenty years, it was under the influence of other feelings. He then proceeded principally with the lives of persons distinguished in American history; the second volume containing those of Vasco Nunez de Balboa and Francisco Pizarro; and the third volume those of Alvaro de Luna, and Bartolome de las Casas. Of these two volumes, the former has been translated into English by Mrs. Hobson, Edinburgh, 1832; and of the third a translation has been announced, London, 1851; both, and the latter especially, well deserving of study.

In the first volume, treating of heroes, whose history, almost lost in the obscurity of remote times, might be considered among the fabulous legends prevailing everywhere in the first formations of society, it seemed only appropriate to give a colouring of poetry, to characters of whose actions nothing could be judged, except by their outward bearing. But in the others he could write as a philosophic historian, inquiring into the motives of actions, and teaching lessons of public morality by individual examples. The life of Alvaro is thus particularly interesting, depicting the caprices of fortune, as they affect

> The wish indulged in courts to shine,
> And power too great to keep or to resign.

In the other lives he maintains the high tone of feeling shown in his beautiful Ode to Balmis, the philanthropic introducer of vaccination into America, where the ravages of the disease, so graphically described by Humboldt, had made this benefit more peculiarly desirable.

The generous sentiments expressed in this ode are such as to do honour not only to Quintana, but also to the nation, where they are in the present generation adopted, as we find them repeated emphatically by so popular a writer as Larra. More than thirty years had elapsed after writing that ode, when Quintana, in the Life of the enthusiastic Las Casas, proved his consistency of character and principles, by maintaining them in a work of historical character, as he had done in poetry in his youth.

In the prologue to the third volume he says, "The author

will be accused of little regard for the honour of his country, when he so frankly adopts the sentiments and principles of the Protector of the Indians, whose imprudent writings have been the occasion of so much opprobrium, and of subministering such arms to the detractors of Spanish glories. But neither the extravagance or fanatical exaggerations of Las Casas, nor the abuse which the malignity of strangers have made of them, can erase from deeds their nature and character. The author has not gone to imbibe them from suspicious fountains; nor to judge them as he has done, has he regarded other principles than those of natural equity, or other feelings than those of his own heart. Documents carefully appended for this purpose, and the attentive perusal of Herrera, Oviedo, and others our own writers as impartial and judicious as those, give the same result in events and opinions. What then was to be done? To deny the impressions received, and repel the decision which humanity and justice dictate, on account of not compromising what is called the honour of the country? But the honour of a country consists in actions truly great, noble and virtuous of its inhabitants; not in gilding with justifications, or insufficient exculpations, those that unfortunately bear on themselves the seal of being iniquitous and cruel. To strangers who to depress us, accuse us of cruelty and barbarity in our discoveries and conquests of the New World, we might reply with other examples on their own part, as or more atrocious than ours, and in times and under circumstances sufficiently less excusable. . . . . . .

"The great glories and usefulnesses, which result from extended conquests and dominations, are always bought at a great price, whether of blood, or violence, or reputation and fame: unhappy tribute to be paid even by nations the most civilized, when the impulse of destiny bears them to the same situation. Glorious, without doubt, was for us the discovery of the New World! But at what cost was it bought! For myself what affects me, leaving apart as not required here the question of the advantages which Europe has derived from that singular event, I will say, that wherever I find, whether in the past or the present, aggressors and aggrieved, oppressors and oppressed, on no account of ulterior utility, nor even of national consideration, am I able to incline myself to the former, or to fail in sympathizing with the latter. I may have put therefore into this historical question more entireness and candour than is commonly expected, when referring to our own conduct, but no odious prejudices, nor an inclination to injure or detract. Let us everywhere give some place in books to justice, now that unfortunately it is wont to have so little left it in the affairs of the world."

Holding such high opinions in all his writings, it may be seen that the youth of Spain cannot have a better guide to take for private study than those writings, the best preparatives for honourable exertion in life; and Quintana's own history shows, that whatever misfortunes may befall any one individually, he does not labour or suffer in vain, who labours or suffers honestly in a just cause. In another part of the same prologue, Quintana says of his own lot, "Of this variety of circumstances and continued alternations, from good to ill, and from ill to good, not small has been the part fallen to the author of this work. Drawn by the force of events from his study and domestic lares, flattered and excessively exalted now, afterwards borne down and contemned, falling into imprisonment and proceeded against capitally, destined to a long and perhaps indefinite detention, deprived during it of communications and even of his pen, released from it, when he least hoped, to rise and prosper, and descending again soon to be endangered, he has experienced all, and nothing now can be to him new. Let it not be supposed from this that he puts it forth here as a merit, and less, that he presents it in complaint. For of whom should I complain? Of men? These in the midst of my greatest calamities, with very few exceptions, have shown themselves constantly regardful, benevolent, and even respectful towards me. Of fortune? And what pledges had she given me to moderate for me the rigour with which she treated the rest? Were they not of as much or more value than I? Political and moral turbulences are the same as the great physical disorders, in which the elements becoming excited, no one is sheltered from their fury."

Resigning himself thus to his fate, Quintana seems to have learned the philosophical secret of preserving his equanimity in all the vicissitudes of life, to the enjoyment of a tranquil old age. The privilege of attaining this is a favour to every one, to whom it is granted; but its highest enjoyments must be consequent only on a life of active usefulness, with a conscience void of offence. The man of cultivated mind, who has been called upon to do or to suffer more than others his fellows in the turmoils of the world, may then be supposed to receive his greater reward in the remembrances of scenes, happier perhaps in the retrospect than in the reality, which may have given them even the semblance of a longer existence. As perspectives appear lengthened, according to the number and variety of objects that intervene to the view, so life itself may appear to have been longer or shorter, according to the memory and character of events witnessed in its course. Described as a person of athletic form, yet unbowed by the burden of fourscore years, Quintana, as before observed, still survives, to receive the honour justly due to him for his honourable exertions through life, the remembrances of which may thus give him more pleasurable enjoyments, than can be supposed to fall to the lot of ordinary mortals.

As a poet, if a foreigner may be allowed to express an opinion, for which he has no native authority to adduce, Quintana may be said to be more eloquent than poetical. As Quintilian said of Lucan, both also natives of Spain, "ut dicam quod sentio, magis oratoribus quam poetis annumerandus." Quintana's eloquence consists in earnestness more than in flights of fancy. His favourite subjects were the glories of his country; and his patriotic odes, in which he endeavoured to incite his countrymen to imitate the examples of their forefathers, have been pronounced his best compositions. He has as a poet paid his tribute of admiration to beauty and the arts; but his whole soul seems to be poured forth when pathetically mourning over the dimmed glories of his country, as when at the thought "of our miserable squadrons flying before the British," he turns to the Padillias and Guzmans of former days, "when the Spaniard was master of half of Europe, and threw himself upon unknown and immense seas to give a new world to men."

As a patriotic poet Quintana has been compared to Beranger, and is said to have had the same power over the minds of his countrymen. If the parallel be correct, it may be curious to consider how characteristically these two poets appeal to the feelings of their admirers; one by songs and incidents, which though often trivial, yet speak to the heart in its most sensitive points, while the other proceeds to the same object by martial odes of commanding austerity. Besides the Ode to Balmis, the other one in this work, on the Battle of Trafalgar, has been chosen for translation, as most likely to interest the English reader, though it may not be in itself so much to be admired as some others of his poems. The reader will perhaps observe a constrained style in it, even beyond that of translation,—sentiments forced, as if the subject had not been taken voluntarily. It must not therefore be looked upon as a favourable specimen of Quintana's genius, like the Ode to Balmis, which more fully shows the character of his mind.

Quintana, more than other poets of his time, has written in one style of verse, as in imitation of the Pindaric ode, or of our Gray and Dryden. Thus with free metres and often unfettered by rhyme, he has a staid measured tone, well suited to the subjects he has generally adopted. They are considered in Spain as of an elegiac character; and as accordant with them, they have fallen in the translation into the form of our elegies, or the heroic lines with alternate rhymes, the style of verse which Dryden, a high authority on such a question, pronounced "the most magnificent of all the measures which our language affords."

Much as Quintana has published, both of his own works and of the works of others, for the advancement of sound learning and moral instruction, we have still great cause to regret that the circumstances of the times in which he has lived have prevented him from publishing more. Not only has he been interrupted in the course of those instructive biographies, of which we have such valuable beginnings, but we might have hoped, if he had lived in more peaceful times, that he would have given the world some work, of a character more distinctively his own, to place his name still higher in the history of elegant literature. It was one of the maxims of the wise Jovellanos, "that it was not sufficient for the purposes of good government to keep the people quiet, but that they ought to be kept contented." Without this condition the other cannot be expected; and for all public commotions, therefore, the rulers are always most responsible, as unmindful of this truth. The greatest evil is, when the whole literary world has thus also further cause to complain of their misdeeds, as affecting those who were endowed with talents of a higher order, such as to make all men interested in their well-being. It is to be hoped that we are now, under the benignant reign of Isabel the Second, entitled to expect a more liberal government, and the advent of a still brighter æra for the literature of Spain.

Taking the space of eighty years, as comprehending the period during which modern Spanish poetry has been peculiarly distinguished for superior excellence, we may now make a further division of this period, into the former and latter parts of it. All the poets, whose lives we have hitherto traced, wrote their principal works previously to the year 1810; after which time we have a succession of writers, whose genius may perhaps be found to take a yet wider range of thought and feeling, consequent on the extended field of knowledge, which later events presented to their observation.

MANUEL JOSÈ QUINTANA.

TO THE SPANISH EXPEDITION FOR THE PROMOTION OF VACCINATION IN AMERICA,

UNDER DON FRANCISCO BALMIS.

FAIR Virgin of the world, America!
   Thou who so innocent to heaven display'st
Thy bosom stored with plenty's rich array,
   And brow of gentle youth! Thou, who so graced
The tenderest and most lovely of the zones
   Of mother Earth to shine, shouldst be of fate
The sweet delight and favour'd love it owns,
   That but pursues thee with relentless hate,
Hear me! If ever was a time mine eyes,
   When scanning thy eventful history,
Did not burst forth in tears; if could thy cries
   My heart e'er hear unmoved, from pity free

And indignation; then let me disclaim'd
  Of virtue be eternally as held,
And barbarous and wicked be one named
  As those who with such ruin thee assail'd.

In the eternal book of life are borne,
  Written in blood, those cries, which then sent forth
Thy lips to Heaven, such fury doom'd to mourn,
  And yet against my country call in wrath.
Forbidding glory and success attend
  The fatal field of crimes. Will they ne'er cease?
Will not the bitter expiation end
  Sufficed of three eventful centuries?
We are not now those who on daring's wing,
  Before the world, the Atlantic's depths disdain'd,
And from the silence found thee covering,
  That fiercely tore thee, bleeding and enchain'd!

"No, ye are not the same. But my lament
  Is not for this to cease: I could forget
The rigours which my conquerors relent,
  Their avarice with cruelties beset:
The crime was of the age, and not of Spain.
  But when can I forget the evils sore
Which I must miserably yet sustain?
  Among them one, come, see what I deplore,

If horror will not you deter. From you,
  Your fatal ships first launch'd, the mortal pest,
The poison that now desolates me flew.
  As in doom'd plains by ruthless foes oppress'd,
As serpent that incessantly devours,
  So ever from your coming, to consume
Has it raged o'er me. See here, how it lowers!
  And in the hidden place of death and gloom,
Buries my children and my loves. Affords
  Your skill no remedy? O! ye, who call
Yourselves as of America the lords,
  Have pity on my agony. See, fall
Beneath your insane fury, not sufficed
  One generation, but a hundred slain!
And I expiring, desolate, unprized,
  Beseech assistance, and beseech in vain."

Such were the cries that to Olympus rose,
  When in the fields of Albion found remote,
Variola's fell havocs to oppose,
  Kind Nature show'd the happy antidote.
The docile mother of the herd was found
  Enrich'd with this great gift; there stored attent
Where from her copious milky founts around
  She gives so many life and aliment.
Jenner to mortals first the gift reveal'd:
  Thenceforward mothers to their hearts could press

Their children without fear to lose them heal'd;
   Nor fear'd thenceforward in her loveliness
The maiden, lest the fatal venom spoil
   Her cheek of roses, or her brow of snow.
All Europe then is join'd in grateful toil,
   For gift so precious and immense to know,
In praises loud to echo Jenner's name;
   And altars to his skill to raise decrees,
There to long ages hallowing his fame,
   Beside their tutelar divinities.

Of such a glory at the radiant light,
   With noble emulation fill'd his breast,
A Spaniard rose,—" Let not my country slight,"
   He cried, " on such a great occasion's test,
Her ancient magnanimity to employ.
   'T is fortune's gift discovering it alone;
That let an Englishman his right enjoy.
   Let Spain's sublime and generous heart be shown,
Giving her majesty more honour true,
   By carrying this treasure to the lands
Which most the evil's dire oppressions knew.
   There, for I feel a deity commands,
There will I fly, and of the raging wave
   Will brave in bearing it the furious strife;
America's infested plains to save
   From death, as planting there the tree of life."

He spoke, and scarcely from his burning lip
   These echoes had beneficently flow'd,
When floating in the port, prepared the ship,
   To give commencement to so blest a road,
Moved spreading her white canvas to the air.
   On his fate launch'd himself the aëronaut.
Waves of the sea, in favouring calmness bear,
   As sacred, this deposit to be brought
Through your serene and liquid fields.   There goes
   Of thousand generations long the hope;
Nor whelm it, nor let thunder it oppose;
   Arrest the lightning, with no storms to cope,
Stay them until that from those fertile shores
   Come forth the prows, triumphant in their pride,
That fraught remote with all their golden stores,
   With vice and curses also come allied.

Honour to Balmis! O, heroic soul!
   That in such noble toil devotest thy breath,
Go fearless to thy end.   The dreadful roll
   Of ocean always hoarse, and threatening death;
The fearful whirlpool's all-devouring throat,
   The cavern'd rock's black face, where dash'd by fate,
Break the wreck'd barks, the dangers they denote
   Greatest are not most cruel thee that wait.
From man expect them!   Impious, envious man,
   In error wrapp'd and blind, will prove him bent,

When hush'd against thee is the hurricane,
  To combat rough the generous intent.
But firmly and secure press forward on;
  And hold in mind, when comes for strife the day,
That without constant, anxious toil, can none
  Hope glory's palms to seize, and bear away.

At length thou comest; America salutes
  Her benefactor, and at once her veins
The destined balm to purify deputes.
  A further generous ardour then regains
Thy breast; and thou, obedient to the hand
  Divine that leads thee, turn'st the sounding prow
Where Ganges rolls, and every Eastern land
  The gift may take. The Southern Ocean now
Astonish'd sees thee, o'er her mighty breast
  Untiring passing. Luzon thee admires,
Good always sowing on thy road impress'd:
  And as it China's toilsome shore acquires,
Confucius from his tomb of honour'd fame,
  If could his venerable form arise,
To see it in glad wonder might exclaim,
  " 'T was worthy of my virtue, this emprise! "

Right worthy was it of thee, mighty sage!
  Worthy of that divine and highest light,

Which reason and which virtue erst array'd
　　To shine in happier days, now quench'd in night.
Thou, Balmis! never mayst return; nor grows
　　In Europe now the sacred laurel meet
With which to crown thee.　There in calm repose,
　　Where peace and independence a retreat
May find, there rest thee! where thou mayst receive
　　At length the august reward of deeds so blest.
Nations immense shall come for thee to grieve,
　　Raising in grateful hymns to Heaven address'd
Thy name with fervorous zeal.　And though now laid
　　In the cold tomb's dark precincts thou refuse
To hear them, listen to them thus convey'd
　　At least, as in the accents of my Muse.

ON THE BATTLE OF TRAFALGAR.

Not with an easy hand wills Fate to give
　　Nations, or heroes, power and renown:
Triumphant Rome, whose empire to receive
　　A hemisphere submissively bow'd down,

Yielding itself in silent servitude,
    How often did she vanquish'd groan? repell'd
As she her course of loftiness pursued!
    Her ground to Hannibal she scarcely held;
Italian blood of Trevia the sands,
    And wavy Thrasymenus deeply dyed,
And Roman matrons the victorious bands
    Of Cannæ nigh approaching them descried,
As some portentous comet fearful lower.
    Who drove them thence? Who from the Capitol
Turn'd on the throne, that founded Dido's power,
    The clouds that threaten'd then o'er them to roll?
Who in the fields of Zama, from the yoke
    They fear'd, with direful slaughter to set free,
At length the sceptre of great Carthage broke,
    With which she held her sovereignty, the sea?

Unswerving courage! that alone the shield
    That turns adversity's sharp knife aside:
To joy turns sorrow; bids despair to yield
    To glory, and of fortune learns to guide
The dubious whirlwind, victory in its train;
    For a high-minded race commands its fate.
O, Spain! my country! covering thy domain,
    The mourning shows how great thy suffering state;
But still hope on, and with undaunted brow,
    From base dejection free, behold the walls

Of thy own lofty Gades, which avow
    Thy strength, though fate them now awhile appals;
Which though affrighted, blushing in their shame,
    As bathing them around the waves extend,
Yet loud thy sons' heroic deeds proclaim,
    Far on the sounding billows they defend.

From the proud castled poop that crowns his high
    Indomitable ship, the Briton round
Look'd, on his power and glory to rely,
    And boastful cried, "Companions renown'd!
See, there they come: new trophies to attain
    Wait your unconquer'd arms; the feeble pines
That Spain prepares for her defence in vain:
    Fate from our yoke exemption none assigns.
We are the sons of Neptune. Do they dare
    To plough the waves before us? Call to mind
Aboukir's memorable day! to share
    Another such a triumph: let us find
One moment as sufficing us to come,
    To conquer, and destroy them. Grant it me,
Kind fate! and let us crown'd with laurels home
    Our wealthy Thames again returning see."

He spoke, and spread his sails. With swimming prows
    Opening the waves, they follow him elate,

Conquerors of winds and waves. With dauntless brow
  The Spaniards view them, and in calmness wait,
Contemning their fierce arrogance, and high
  Their bosoms beating with indignant rage.
Just anger! sacred ardour! "There come nigh
  Those cruel foes, who hasten war to wage,
And spill our blood, when we reposed secure
  Beneath the wings of peace. They who are led
By avarice vile; who friendship's laws abjure;
  Who in their endless tyranny o'erspread
Would hold condemn'd the seas; who to unite,
  As brothers, pride and insolence of power
With treachery and rapacity delight;
  Who "—but with mantle dark night brings the hour
To enwrap the world. Wandering round the shrouds
  Are frightful shades, dire slaughter that portend
And fearful expectations raise. Through opening clouds
  The day displays the field, where wildly blend
Fury and death; and horrid Mars the scene
  Swells loud with shouts of war, upraised in air
His standard high. To answer intervene
  From hollow brass the mortal roarings glare.
The echo thunders, and the waves resound,
  Dashing themselves in rage to Afric's shore :
In conflict fly the ships to ships around,
  By rancour moved. Less violent its store

M

Of heap'd-up ice in mountains, the South Pole
 Emits immense, loud thundering through the waves
To glide, and on the adventurous seaman roll.
 Nor with less clamour loosen'd from their caves
Rush the black tempests, when the East and North,
 Troubling the heavens enraged in furious war,
And dire encounter, all their strength put forth,
 And shake the centre of the globe afar.

Thrice the fierce islander advanced to break
 Our squadron's wall, confiding in his might:
Thrice by the Spanish force repulsed, to shake
 His hopes of victory he sees the fight.
Who shall depict his fury and his rage,
 When with that flag before so proud he saw
The flag of Spain invincible engage?
 'T is not to skill or valour to o'erawe,
Solely he trusts to fortune for success.
 Doubling his ships, redoubling them again,
From poop to prow, from side to side to press,
 In an unequal fight is made sustain
Each Spanish ship a thousand, thousand fires;
 And they with equal breath that death receive
So send it back. No, not to my desires,
 If heaven would grant it me, could I achieve
The task that day's heroic deeds to tell,
 Not with a hundred tongues; hid from the sun

By smoke, Fame's trumpet shall their praises swell,
   And bronze and marble for their names be won.

At length the moment comes, when Death extends
   His pale and horrid hand, to signalize
Great victims.   Brave Alcedo to him bends,
   And nobly Moyua, with Castanios, dies.
And Alcalà, Churruca, also ye!
   Of Betis and Guipuzcoa the pride.
O! if Fate knew to spare, would it not be
   Enough to soothe, upon your brows allied
Minerva's olive with Mars' laurels seen?
   From your illustrious and inquiring mind
What could the world, or stars, their mysteries screen?
   Of your great course the traces left behind
The Cyclades are full, nor less the seas
   Of far America.   How seeks to mourn,
New tears from her sad heart her grief to appease,
   The widow'd land such heroes from her torn;
And still she sheds them o'er your cruel fate.
   O! that ye two could live, and I in place
Of grief, of sorrowing song, to consecrate
   To you the funeral accents that I raise,
Might have opposed my bosom to the stroke,
   And thus my useless life my country give!
That I might thus your cruel lot revoke,
   To bear the wounds, so that ye two might live!

And she might proudly raise her front anew,
  Victorious crown'd with rays of glory bright,
Her course 'gainst arduous fortune to pursue,
  Triumphant in your wisdom and your might.

Yet fell ye not, ye generous squadrons! there,
  Without revenge and slaughter. Spreading wide,
Rivers of English blood your powers declare.
  And Albion also horror-struck descried
Mountains of bodies weigh, a heavy pile,
  On her so proud Armada. Nelson, too!
Terrible shade! O, think not, no, that vile
  My voice to name thee, e'er an insult threw
On thy last sigh. As English I abhor,
  But hero I admire thee. O, thy fate!
Of captive ships a crowd, the spoils of war,
  The Thames awaits, and now exults elate
To hail with shouts the conqueror's return!
  But only pale and cold beholds her Chief!
Great lesson left for human pride to learn,
  And worthy holocaust for Spanish grief.

Yet still the rage of Mars impels the arm
  Of destiny; mow'd down unnumber'd lives.
By fury launch'd, voracious flames alarm;
  On every side planks burning. Loosely drives

Each ship a fierce volcano; blazing high
    Through the wide air 't is raised, and thrown again
With horrid bursting in the seas to lie,
    Engulf'd. Do other havocs yet remain?
Yes, for that Heaven, displeased to see such foes,
    Bids the inclement north winds rise to part
The furious combatants, and day to close
    In stormy night. 'T is order'd, and athwart
They throw themselves the miserable barks,
    Lashing the waves on high with cruel wings.
As each this new unequal combat marks
    For ruin, falls the mast, and over swings
Trembling beneath the assault. The hulls divide,
    And where the gaping seams the waves invite,
They enter, while the dying Spaniards cried,
    "O! that we were to perish, but in fight!"

In that remorseless conflict, high in air,
    Then shining forth their glorious forms display'd
The mighty champions, who of old to bear
    The trident and the spear, supreme had made
Before the Iberian flag the nations bow.
    There Lauria, Trovar, and Bazan were seen,
And Aviles, their brother heroes now
    Of Spain to welcome, and in death convene.
"Come among us," they cried, "among the brave
    You emulate. Already you have gain'd

Your fair reward. The example that you gave
   Of valour, Spain in constancy sustain'd
Her warriors shows, inciting to prepare
   For other conflicts they undaunted greet.
Look to the city of Alcides! there
   Gravina, Alavà and Escanio meet!
Cisneros and a hundred more combine
   There in firm column, with proud hopes to bless
Our native land. Come, fly ye here, and shine
   In heaven their stars of glory, and success."

MODERN POETS

AND

POETRY OF SPAIN.

PART II.

VII.

FRANCISCO MARTINEZ DE LA ROSA.

THROUGHOUT the civilized world, and even beyond it, this eminent statesman has long been heard of, as one who, while devoting his life faithfully to promote the welfare of his own country, had exerted himself no less assiduously for the general interests of mankind. As an orator, a statesman and a political writer, he has thus obtained a deservedly high European reputation, due to his services and merits. In Spain he is further known as one of the first literary characters of whom his country has to boast, and as a dramatist and lyric poet of a very superior order.

Martinez de la Rosa was born the 10th March, 1789, at Granada, where also he received his education, completing it at the University in that city. Before the age of twenty he had gone through the usual course of study in the ancient and some of the modern languages, in philosophy, mathematics, canon and civil law, with such success as to have been enabled to undertake a professorship of philosophy there, perfecting himself in the art of oratory, in which his natural talents already had become manifest, as they soon afterwards gave him the means of greater distinction. From those pursuits he was called away, in 1808, on the occurrence of the French invasion, to take an active part in the struggle for national independence, into which he entered with youthful ardour, by public declamations, and by writing in a periodical instituted to maintain it.

As the French arms advanced victoriously, Martinez de la Rosa, with others of the party who had been most conspicuous in their opposition to them, had to take refuge in Cadiz. He was first employed to proceed to Gibraltar, as his future colleague, the Conde de Toreno, had been sent to London, to obtain a cessation of hostilities, in the war then yet existing between England and Spain, and concert measures of alliance against the French. In this mission he had the desired success, having further obtained from the governor of Gibraltar arms and ammunition, which enabled the Spanish forces under Castanios to march and obtain, at Bailen, the memorable triumph of the 19th July, 1808. In consequence of this victory, the French had to evacuate Madrid, and the Central Junta was formed, superseding the first actors in the conflict. On this, Martinez de la Rosa took advantage of the circumstances to go to England, and observe there himself, says his biographer, the celebrated Pacheco, "in its birthplace, where it was natural, complete and necessary, that representative system, which the spirit of reform wished to bring over for the people of the Continent." Wolf says he had there a diplomatic commission, adding, that he took advantage of it "to familiarize himself with the English constitution, for which he always had a great predilection."

Whether he had public duties entrusted to him or not, Martinez de la Rosa seems then to have stayed some time in London, studying the workings of the parliamentary system, the good fruits of which he, as Mirabeau had before him, found in his legislative career. There he printed, in 1811, his poem, Zaragoza, written in competition for the prize offered by the Central Junta, in celebration of the defence of that city in 1809, and there also he wrote several other poems. The one of Zaragoza seems not to have been reprinted in Spain till the publication of his collected poems in Madrid in 1833, and no adjudication ever was made on the compositions prepared at the suggestion of the Junta, but it is stated that the judges had unanimously agreed to confer on him the premium offered in the name of the nation.

In 1811 the French armies had driven the assertors of national independence from all the other principal parts of Spain to Cadiz, and there the Cortes were convoked to meet. There then, Martinez de la Rosa returned, and though not yet of the age required by law to be chosen a Deputy, he took part in all the deliberations of the national councils, and was appointed Secretary to the commission on the freedom of the press. Meanwhile the siege of Cadiz was commenced by the French and pressed unremittingly; but the spirit of the defenders did not fail them. Martinez de la Rosa and Quintana continued their literary labours, and the former produced a comedy and a tragedy, both of which were received with much favour. The latter continues a favourite on the stage, on a subject well chosen from Spanish history, and entitled the 'Widow of Padillia.' To use his own words, "It was represented, for the first time, in July 1812, and in days so unfortunate, that it could not be produced even in the theatre at Cadiz, on account of the great danger from the bombs of the enemy, which had nearly caused, a little before, the destruction of the building, crowded at the time with a numerous audience. For this reason they had to erect a theatre of wood in another part of the city, at a distance from where the French artillery had directed their aim."

Shortly after this the siege was raised, and the French

having again evacuated Madrid, the Cortes were convoked to assemble there, when Martinez de la Rosa was elected Deputy for his native city. He had throughout the struggle joined the most active members of the liberal party, Arguelles, Quintana and others, who, all honourable and patriotic characters, had acted in perfect sincerity in forming the Constitution of 1812, as it was called, which they hoped would secure the future freedom of the country.

In this, however, they found themselves mistaken; the representative system had scarcely time to develope its advantages, when it was overthrown entirely on the return of Ferdinand to Spain, who, by his decree of the 4th of May, 1814, annulled the Constitution, and dissolved the Cortes. Had he been contented with this, as in re-assumption of the regal authority exercised by his predecessors, the liberal party might have had only to lament the abrupt termination of their hopes. But, unfortunately, proceedings still more arbitrary were commenced against their leaders individually, of a nature unknown, even in Spain, till then, and in comparison with which the rule of the Prince of the Peace was a pattern of toleration. As those leaders had not been guilty of any act which could make them amenable to any legal tribunal, Ferdinand VII. took on himself to pass the sentences he chose to inflict on them for the opinions they had held, and the conduct they had pursued, in the momentous struggle for national independence, resulting in his restoration. The partisans of the Absolute King wished to extort from Martinez de la Rosa a retractation of the opinions he had maintained; but they miscalculated his character. He refused to listen to their overtures, and he was sentenced to ten years' imprisonment in the penal settlement of Gomera in Africa.

In 1820 a reaction took place, and the constitutional party again obtained possession of the government. Martinez de la Rosa had then passed six years of unjust imprisonment, when he was recalled to Spain, and was received, in his native city, with triumphal arches erected to welcome him, and other tokens of public respect and rejoicing. At the first election of deputies afterwards for the Cortes, he was sent with that character from Granada, but his sentiments on public affairs had become considerably modified. Others of the liberal party had returned from exile or imprisonment with exasperated feelings; but Martinez de la Rosa had employed his time more philosophically, in considering the means that should be adopted, to use his own expression, "for resolving the problem, most important for the human race, how to unite order with liberty." Avoiding all extreme opinions, he gave his support to the ministry he found existing and their successors, as the means of preserving order, until they fell under the combination of unworthy jealousies among their own party, and the constant attacks of those holding the extreme opinions of democracy and absolutism.

On the 1st March, 1821, Martinez de la Rosa was called on to form a ministry, which duty he finally undertook, though he had at first strenuously declined it. He had good reason to decline it, as the king himself was throughout that period plotting against his own ministers and government, to re-establish himself in absolute power. At the end of June, Martinez de la Rosa found himself under the necessity of tendering his resignation, and insisting upon its being accepted, though both the king and the council at first refused to do so. The moderate course which he wished to follow pleased neither party; and even he, who had suffered six years of unjust imprisonment in the popular cause, was now looked on as a traitor by the people, and ran great risk of being murdered in a public commotion raised in the city. Had he chosen to take a more decisive part, either on the one side or the other, the weight of his character would no doubt have given it the preponderance. As it was, the question was decided by the invasion of the French under the Duc d'Angoulême, who restored Ferdinand VII. to his former authority.

When the French entered Spain, the constitutionalist government had retired to Seville; but Martinez de la Rosa had been obliged, from illness, to remain at Madrid. There being called upon to give in his adhesion to the authority imposed by foreign arms on the nation, he declined to do so, and thought himself fortunate in having no severer penalty to suffer thereupon, than to have his passport given him to go from Spain, while others had to suffer so much more severely. He then retired to Paris, where he resided eight years, paying occasional visits to Italy, and though not proscribed directly as an exile, yet he was not allowed to return to his country.

During those eight years he devoted his leisure to literary pursuits, and composed most of those works on which his fame must permanently rest; such as his poem, 'Arte Poetica;' his very beautiful 'Ode on the Death of the Duchess de Frias,' and several plays; among them the 'Tragedy of the Conspiracy of Venice,' considered the best of all he had written. Thus occupied in endeavouring to make future generations wiser and better, Martinez de la Rosa gained increased respect at home with his increased reputation abroad; and on the moderating of the first angry party-feelings in Spain, was at the end of eight years allowed to return to Granada.

The events of 1830 had produced the effect in Spain of milder councils being adopted in the government, which prevailed still more on the Queen Christina assuming power, first on the illness of the king, and afterwards as Regent on his death in 1833. Martinez de la Rosa had then been permitted to return to Madrid, and in this latter year he published the first collection of his poems, dedicating himself to writing at the same time his 'Life of Perez del Pulgar,' one of the old warriors of Spain, and other works. From these labours he was then called to undertake again the duties of government. The existing ministry formed under a former line of policy, was not suitable to the exigences of the times, rendered still more pressing now by the pretensions of Don Carlos to the throne. It was necessary to oppose those pretensions, by obtaining the zealous aid of the constitutional party; and Martinez de la Rosa was chosen as the leader, embodying in himself the characteristics of moderation and just principles, to form a ministry.

It does not become a foreigner, least of all in a purely literary work, to enter in judgement on any questions of a political nature. The best-intentioned persons in the world may take different views of the same question, under the same emergences, and the wisdom of any particular measure is not always to be judged of by the result. In the conflicts of contending parties, the most unscrupulous and daring may often succeed, where wiser and better men may fail. Of Martinez de la Rosa, his biographer has observed, that "he was one of those men who would not conspire even for good ends unlawfully; and that if he could not obtain what he wished by just means, he would cross his arms, and leave the rest to Providence." The events of those years present much ground for regret for all parties, and it is a truly honourable consideration for such a one as Martinez de la Rosa, that, acting according to the best of his judgement on many very difficult occasions, he might have been compelled to yield to force and violence, without any imputation on his probity or statesmanship.

But if it be beyond our consideration of duty to enter on

questions of internal polity, there are two others, connected with his administration, to which we may venture to refer, as to be judged of by those great principles of right and justice, which are applicable to all times and all countries, and become thus fairly subject to commendation or censure, as affecting the general interests of mankind.

Though Martinez de la Rosa had been one of the principal actors among those who had established the Constitution of 1812, for which also he suffered as a prisoner and an exile, he learned soon to perceive that it required considerable modifications in a country like Spain, where the people were not fully prepared to receive it. One of his first measures then was to promulgate what might be termed a new Constitution, called the Estatuto Real, the general wisdom and propriety of which may be admitted, or at least not disputed, while one part of it may be pronounced indefensible. This was in the design to subvert the ancient rights of the Basque people, by amalgamating their provinces into the kingdom, without obtaining or asking their assent. This was a measure unjust in itself; and because unjust, also impolitic; leading to a long-protracted struggle, in which the whole force of Spain being employed, army after army was destroyed, and general after general disgraced, by a comparatively inconsiderable number of undisciplined peasantry. When England sought to incorporate the Parliaments of Scotland and Ireland into that of the United Kingdom, it was sought by what might be called legal, though not always honourable means. On the same principle, the consent of the Basques ought to have been obtained by the Spanish government, rather than the attempt made, furtively or forcibly, to deprive them of their ancient privileges.

On another great question affecting humanity, it is pleasing to consider Martinez de la Rosa among the foremost characters of the age, in attempting the suppression of the slave trade with Africa. In 1817 a treaty was made between England and Spain to suppress this traffic, which, after the experience of a few years, it was found necessary to make more stringent. Propositions to this effect were therefore made year after year to successive Spanish governments by the British, but in vain, until in 1835 Lord Palmerston was successful enough to find in him a minister of Spain, who had the courage to consent to those suggestions. The treaty of that year was then entered into, and signed on the part of the two countries, by Sir George Villiers, now Earl of Clarendon, and Martinez de la Rosa, which has had the desired effect of preventing the trade being protected by the Spanish flag. But this able statesman has done still more, to entitle him to the respect of all who look with interest on this important question. One of the stipulations of the treaty declared that a penal law should be passed in Spain, in accordance with it, to punish all Spanish subjects found infringing it. This stipulation no other Spanish minister could be found to fulfil; and after the lapse of ten years, having again come into power, it was left for him in good faith to accomplish the engagement he had previously undertaken. Accordingly in 1845, he passed a law, answering the purposes required, which received the approbation of the British government, and which seems to have been so far effective in its application.

Great, undoubtedly, is the praise due to those philanthropic statesmen, who, even at the Congress of Vienna, agreed to protect the liberty of Africa. But much greater must be acknowledged due to one who, unsupported almost in his own country, having to oppose himself to a strong colonial interest, and the cry they raised against him of acting in subservience to a foreign power, yet had the moral courage to follow the dictates of justice and humanity, on behalf of an injured race, notwithstanding all the enmity he had to encounter in so doing.

In 1836 Martinez de la Rosa had to yield his place in the government to other hands; and in 1840 he thought proper to retire again to Paris, engaging himself in those literary pursuits from which he had latterly been estranged. It is not our province to follow his political course, through the different public questions on which he had to act. During the four intermediate years various ministries were formed, to some of which he had to give an honourable support, to others as honourable an opposition; but the Regency of Espartero he avoided to acknowledge. When this fell under the attack of Narvaez, he came forward again into public life, and accepted office for a short time in the government; but seemed resolved to take the first opportunity of giving up the post of active exertion for one of more private character, though of no less public utility. Accordingly, on the accession of Pius IX. to the Papacy, he was appointed Ambassador to Rome, which important office he still continues to hold, for the advantage of the Roman Catholic church itself, as well as of his own country, in the several questions that have come since under discussion, subject to his intervention.

As a politician, Martinez de la Rosa has been conspicuous for constant rectitude and consistency of principles. "Not even in moments of the utmost defamation," says his biographer, "has a word been ever raised against his purity of conduct, nor have his greatest enemies ever permitted themselves to impugn in the least his intentions." As an orator, he has had few to equal him in his time, none to surpass him; but his eloquence has been modelled by his character to persuade and defend rather than attack; and thus, if not abounding in brilliant sallies, it has been found of more essential service to the cause of good government.

Beyond the 'History of Perez del Pulgar,' Martinez de la Rosa has written several other works in prose, one of which, the latest, entitled 'Spirit of the Age,' is in fact, so far as yet published, a History of the French Revolution, preceded by a few general observations on political questions. It has already advanced to six volumes, and becoming a political and philosophical history of contemporaneous events, may be extended to the utmost limits. A novel which he wrote earlier in life, 'Donna de Solis,' is acknowledged a failure, as showing "that no man, however eminent, can write successfully on all kinds of subjects."

The principal literary success which Martinez de la Rosa has had, seems to have been as a dramatist; but into those works it would be impossible to enter, to treat them with justice, except by making them a prominent subject of consideration. His poems, published as before stated in 1833, contain compositions in various styles, from the light Anacreontic to the project of an Epic Poem on the Wars of Granada, of which, however, he has only published fragments. Besides a translation of Horace's 'Art of Poetry,' he has also given the world an 'Ars Poetica,' for the benefit of his own countrymen, which he has enriched with many excellent notes and criticisms.

Some of the rules laid down in this 'Ars Poetica' are well worthy of study, as giving room for reflection, for carrying their suggestions even further than he has done. Thus, while insisting on the young poet depending on the excellency of his ear for the melody of verse, instead of having to count the syllables for the requisite purpose, he observes, that as the ancients regulated their metres by time, making so many long or short feet of equivalent measure, of which the judgement must depend on the cadence, so in the verses of the best Spanish poets, there are often some lines containing three or four more syllables than others, to which they form the counterpart, and which are read in the same measure, with increased pleasure for the variation.

The same observation may apply to English verse, though perhaps not so fully. Many of our syllables containing shortly sounded vowels, such as a Hebrew scholar might call Sheva and its compounds, pronounced distinctly, but two in the time of an ordinary syllable, may be found to give an elegance to the line, which would sound faulty with only one of them. But we may go further, and observe, that as in music the melody may be continued by the pause, instead of a note in the bar, so in a line, a pause with one or more long syllables may have the effect of a syllable, instead of the sound or foot to make up the measure. Readers of poetry will not require to be reminded of instances of this adaptation of sounds, and if they notice any such lines in these translations, they will perceive that they have been written in accordance with the precepts referred to.

It must be acknowledged, that in the generality of his poems, Martinez de la Rosa has not risen to any such height of sublimity or fancy as to give him a place in the superior class of poets. But one of the latest critical writers, Ferrer del Rio, who has given a more disparaging estimate of his poetical talents than justice might award, pronounces the 'Epistle to the Duke de Frias' as a composition for which "judges the most grave and least complaisant might place him on the top of Parnassus." The 'Remembrance of Spain,' Del Rio declares to be poor in images, without feeling or depth, but with much of pastoral innocency. The 'Return to Spain' is, according to him, a mere itinerary of his travels, more than an expression of pleasure on escaping from past evil. But in the 'Epistle to the Duke de Frias,' he finds " true-felt inspiration, an appropriate expression, and a plan well traced out,"—"without vagueness or artificial labour, but with phrases that soften and ideas that satisfy the mind," becoming the subject.

Another anonymous critic finds the writer dwelling too much on the remembrance of his own sorrows, instead of offering consolation to the mourner, and some incongruity in felicitating him on having witnessed the last pangs of mortality. But these topics, on such an occasion, are true to nature. Grief is apt to be egotistical, and the mind cannot but dwell on the subject in which it is absorbed. Nor is the other a less natural suggestion; and thus we may observe, that the great master of antiquity represents the sweetest of his characters lamenting that she had not been by the side of her lord at such a time, as the height of her misfortune, to receive his last embrace, and his last word to be remembered ever after:—

> Ἕκτορ, ἐμοὶ δὲ μάλιστα λελείψεται ἄλγεα λυγρά.
> Οὐ γάρ μοι θνῄσκων λεχέων ἐκ χεῖρας ὄρεξας·
> Οὐ δὲ τί μοι εἶπες πυκινὸν ἔπος, οὗ τέ κεν αἰεὶ
> Μεμνῄμην νύκτας τε καὶ ἤματα δακρυχέουσα.

In this 'Epistle to the Duke de Frias,' Martinez de la Rosa has also introduced, as a fit consideration in his grief, the same topic of the instability of earthly things, which "the Roman friend of Rome's least mortal mind" offered him on a similar occasion of sympathy. But it also seems a favourite subject of our poet's thoughts at all times, as befitting the philosopher and the scholar, to dwell on the passing nature of worldly greatness, and so lead the mind to higher suggestions than those of the present moment. These ideas he has carried further in another work he has published, 'Book for Children,' in which, like many other eminent characters, who have given the aid of their talents to the development of juvenile minds, he has inculcated lessons of virtue, and the instinct of good taste, with the feelings of patriotism and religion, as the basis of moral well-being.

Martinez de la Rosa published his works in a collected form first, in five volumes, 1827–30, at Paris, where they have been again lately reprinted. Besides these, there have been two editions in Spain, one at Madrid and the other at Barcelona. From Her Catholic Majesty he has received the decoration of the Golden Fleece, the highest order of Spain, besides other similar honours. But the world at large will consider his greatest honour to consist in having raised himself from mediocrity of station, by his talents and exertions, to the high position he has attained "without stain or reproach," while, by his literary works, he has enabled all mankind to become benefited by his genius, and interested in his fame.

FRANCISCO MARTINEZ DE LA ROSA.

REMEMBRANCE OF SPAIN,

WRITTEN IN LONDON IN 1811.

I saw upon the shady Thames
  Unnumber'd ships with riches fraught;
I saw the power the nation claims
  Immense, the greatness it has wrought,
  And arts that such renown have brought.

But the afflicted mind exhaled
  A thousand sighs; again to view
The flowery banks the wish prevail'd,
  Where glides the Douro calmly through,
  Or Henil's streams their course pursue.

I saw the proud Court's ladies forth
  Their wealth and grandeur gaily show;
I saw the beauties of the North,
  Their bright complexions white as snow,
  Commingling with the rose's glow.

Their eyes appear'd of heavenly blue,
    Their tresses of the purest gold;
Their stately forms arose to view,
    Beneath the veil's transparent fold,
    As white and lovely to behold.

But what avail the gay brocade,
    The city's silks, and jewels' pride;
Or charms in rosy smiles array'd,
    With brilliant gaiety supplied,
    That all to beauty are allied?

When but is seen my country girl,
    Clad in her robe of simple white,
Shamed are the needless silk and pearl;
    And by her pure and blooming light
    Confused hides beauty at the sight.

Where shall I find in icy clime
    Her black and beaming eyes of fire?
That whether scornfully the time,
    To look, or kindly they desire,
    To rob me of my peace conspire?

Where the black hair that may like hers
    In hue with ebony compare?
Where the light foot that never stirs,
    When bounding o'er the meadows fair,
    The lowly flowers that blossom there?

Maids of the Henil! dark ye be;
   But ne'er would I exchanged resign
Your charms for all that here I see,
   Proud Albion shows, of brows that fine
   Ev'n as the polish'd ivory shine.

O, father Douro! gentle stream,
   Whose sands a golden store supply,
Deign of my heart the wish supreme
   To hear, thy sacred margins by,
   That it may be my lot to die!

RETURN TO GRANADA,

OCTOBER 27, 1831.

My loved country! thee again
   I come at length return'd to see;
Thy beauteous soil, thy fields where reign
   Plenty and joy unceasingly!
Thy radiant sun, thy peaceful skies,
   Yes! there extended o'er the plain,
From hill to hill, I see arise

The far-famed city! Noble towers,
  Midst groves of ever-blooming flowers;
Kissing her walls are crystal streams,
  Her valley lofty heights surround,
And the snow-topp'd Sierra gleams,
  Crowning the far horizon's bound.

Not vain thy memory me pursued
  Where'er I stray'd; with that imbued,
Troubling my hopes, my joys, my rest,
  The thoughts my heart and soul oppress'd.
On the cold margin of the Thames,
  Or Seine, I thought of thee, and sigh'd
Again to view the bank that gems
  Thy Henil's or thy Douro's tide.
And if perchance my voice essay'd
  Some gayer song, for short relief,
Soon for lament the attempts I made
  Were check'd, and doubled was my grief.

Vain the delicious Arno show'd,
  Offering to me her fruitful shore,
Of peace and loves the soft abode,
  With flowers enamell'd o'er.
" More blooming are the plains where flows
  The gentle Henil through,

And lovelier still Granada shows
   Her pleasant site to view!"
Murmuring such words in mournful thought,
   I oft with tearful eyes repined,
Upraised to Heaven, as memory brought
   My fathers' homes and hearths to mind.
At times the solitary view
   Of rural scenes more seem'd to soothe;
From cities terror-struck I flew,
   And breathless, anxious, o'er the uncouth
Rough Alps I took my way.
   But not so pure, so vivid show'd
Their snowy tops the sun's bright ray,
   As from our snow Sierra glow'd
The streams of light, the god of day
   O'er earth and heaven bestow'd.

   My griefs Pompeii flatter'd more:
Its fearful ruins, silent streets,
Deserted porticos, retreats
   Of men with grass run o'er.
And in my troubled mind began
   Grave thoughts to rise, how vain is all
The power of miserable man.
   To abase his fame, his pride to gall,
How fate delights! and works that vast

He rears, and dares eternal call,
   Throws over with a blast!
Today the traveller, as he roves
    Along the Tiber, has to trace
Through ruins, where that was high Jove's
    Triumphant city had its place!
The plough breaks up the fruitful mould,
    The sacred relics now we see
Of Herculaneum that enfold,
    As in a darksome tomb! If be
Pompeii's walls still standing, yet
   Are their foundations undermined
By age, and as the rude winds threat,
    They tremble to their fall inclined.

Thus in my youth I saw the tower
Of the superb Alhambra lower,
Broken, and imminent appal
   The Douro threatening with its fall.
Each rapid moment of my life
   Hasten'd the term with ruin rife;
And of the Alcazar's sovereign pride,
   Where once the Moorish power enchain'd
Their fame as left to ages wide,
   Mine eyes may soon not find descried
    Its ruins ev'n remain'd.

As that dark image o'er me glooms,
  My heart sinks heavy in my breast;
I bow myself before the tombs,
  In tears with grief oppress'd.

What is thy magic? what may be
  The ineffable enchantment found,
O, country! O, sweet name, in thee?
  Ever so dear to man the sound!
The sunburnt African will sigh
For his parch'd sands and burning sky,
Perchance afar, and round the plains
However blooming he disdains.
  Ev'n the rude Laplander, if fate
In luckless hour him off has torn
  From his own soil, disconsolate
Will to return there longing mourn;
Envying the eternal night's repose,
His icebound shores and endless snows.

And I, to whom kind fate assign'd
  My birth within thy happy fold,
Granada! and my growth as kind
  Within thy blissful bounds to mould,
Far from my country, and beset
With griefs, how could I thee forget?

On Africa's inhuman shore,
To the wreck'd seaman rough and drear,
Thy sacred name I o'er and o'er
Repeated, which the waves to hear
Back to the Spanish regions bore.
On the far Pole's dark furious sea,
By the Batavian's energy
Bridled, again thy name was heard:
Heard it the Rhone, the foamy Rhine,
The Pyrenæan heights the word
Repeated with the Apennine,
And in Vesuvius' burning cave
Then first the sound the echos gave.

EPISTLE TO THE DUQUE DE FRIAS,

ON THE DEATH OF THE DUQUESA.

From the dark gloomy borders of the Seine,
  Where with black clouds around the heaven extends,
The earth o'erwhelm'd with snow, the heart with pain,
  Thee thy unhappy friend his greeting sends;

To thee still more unhappy! nor deters
  Him ev'n the fear to touch the wounds unheal'd,
Yet bleeding sore, or see thee how it stirs
  Fresh tears to bathe thine eyes thy sorrows yield.

What would he be, if man were not to weep?
  A thousand times I've thank'd our God, who gave
The heart to soothe its griefs in tears to steep;
  As rain we see subdue the raging wave.

Weep then, ay, weep! others, and abler friends
  As faithful, with success may in thine ears
Make heard the voice that stoic virtue lends;
  But I, who in the world my cup of tears

Oft to the dregs have drain'd, no cure could find
  For grief, but what from grief I might derive;
When with vain struggling tired, the powerless mind
  Submissive ceased beneath the weight to strive.

Dear friend! wilt thou believe me? time will come,
  When the sharp edge of sorrow worn away,
That grief and anguish now so burdensome,
  At length a placid sadness will allay;

In which absorb'd, as yet o'erwhelm'd, the soul
  Folds itself up all silently to bear;
Nor seeks nor envies, as around they roll,
  The world's delights or pleasures more to share.

Thou doubt'st perchance; and once there was a time
   I also doubted it; and endless thought
My deep affliction, and insulting crime
   To tell me to an end it could be brought.

And yet it was! for so from God to man
   That is another mercy, which alone,
Amidst so many woes 't is his to scan,
   Aids him this weary life to suffer on.

Hope then, believe my words, and trust in me:
   Who in this world the unhappy privilege
Has bought so dear to speak of misery?
   These many years that saw it me assiege,

Saw me no day but as the plaything vile
   Of a dire fate, that like a shrub amain
The hurricane tears up, and raised awhile
   It fiercely dashes to the earth again.

I know it true, against the blows of fate,
   When that against ourselves they only glance,
The firm heart shielded can withstand its hate;
   But so it is not oft: and thou, perchance,

Mayst think I never one have lost I loved
   More than my life. If sorrow will give truce
Thee for a moment, turn thine eyes disproved
   To an unhappy orphan, weak, recluse,

And sorrowing solitary in the world,
   Without scarce one to whom to weep his woe;
For to the grave relentless death had hurl'd,
   One after one, all he was born to know.

In the same season, thou wilt see sufficed
   Thy loss to open forth the wounds I bear,
I lost a mother kind, and idolized,
   My joy, and comforter in every care;

On her steps my reaved father to the grave
   Soon follow'd, and both sank o'erwhelm'd in tears,
Calling my name afar; the cries they gave
   Fell on my heart, but not upon my ears.

I ran, I flew, I came, but all in vain:
   Both now beneath the fatal stone reposed,
And I my height of anguish to attain,
   But found the covering earth yet newly closed.

Thou in thy grave affliction more hast found
   Thee to console, if possible; (how turn
Rebels against me thy own woes around!
   From my rude voice perforce thou hast to learn

That he who fortune flatter'd not before,
   Will neither flatter grief) thou in thy loss
Hast found a thousand comforts, which forbore
   My cruel fate to grant my path across;

Thou soothing saw'st thy wife in her last pains;
    Her last sigh couldst receive; couldst press her hands,
Her arms raised to thee, and her pledge remains
    In thine, her daughter still thy love demands.

But I, not wishing it, am in thy breast
    A dagger striking, thus again to view
That fatal night's dark image to suggest,
    When life with death its fearful struggles drew.

Now ended are her pains, for ever o'er!
    Herself she pray'd for it, with pious eyes
To heaven, and hope, amidst the pangs she bore,
    Shone on her brow serene in death to rise.

O! were it given us to penetrate
    The secrets of the tomb, how oft our grief
Would it not soften down, however great!
    In this same moment who of the belief

Could not assure thee, while thou dost lament,
    Unhappy, thy lost wife's untimely doom,
That she is there enjoying permanent
    A lot more happy than this side the tomb?

Thou, silent, lowly bendest down thy head;
    But thou mayst not be silent; answer me;
Sound, if thou darest it, the abyss to tread,
    That separates thy lost loved wife from thee.

Take through eternity thy course, and then
    Tell me of where she is, what is her state?
Happy or miserable? or again,
    We should rejoice in, or lament her fate?

To thee I may repeat it, others gay
    Will laugh at my dark fancy; not long past
The time I was by that enchanting bay
    Of the Tyrrhenian sea; the city vast,

Mother of pleasures, I forsook, and bent,
    Absorb'd, my feeble steps, where lowly lies
Pompeii; palaces with gardens blent
    And fountains brilliant, shone before my eyes;

But deeper penetrates the mind, and sad,
    Slowly along I went with heavy heart:
Flowers amid lava grew! and rich, and glad
    Today the scenes on every side impart

The towns and villages, which others hide
    That stood as happy there a former day;
Those now that flourish built up by the side
    Of some forgotten that have pass'd away.

At length I came where we the walls descry
    Of the deserted city, which the abode
Proclaim'd it was of men in times gone by;
    Their sepulchres stood bordering the road!

There for a resting-place the traveller stays,
   For shade and for repose: the gate now gain'd,
Awhile the vacillating foot delays
   To enter, as if fearing it profaned

Too bold the mansions of the dead. No word,
   No sound, no murmur. It would seem that there
Ev'n Echo's self is mute, no answer heard!
   Slowly I through the narrow streets repair

Without a human footstep! Porticos
   And plazas by no living beings trod,
Walls with deserted hearths, and temples rose
   And altars, without victims or a god.

How little, mean and miserable seem'd
   The world before mine eyes, when there I stood!
A bitter smile upon my features gleam'd,
   To think of man's ambition, schemes of blood,

And projects without end, when by a blast,
   Like smoke, their good and evil are represt;
Ashes a mighty city overcast,
   As light dust covers o'er some poor ants' nest!

Thus wrapp'd in mournful thoughts, I paced along
   That vast and silent precinct, as behind
Roves some unbodied shade the tombs among;
   The ties me yet to this low earth that bind

I felt to loosen, and the soul set free
    Launch'd itself forth, ev'n into endless space,
Leaving behind it ages.—Couldst thou see
    What is this wretched life, compared its trace

With that immensity, most surely, friend,
    In thine eyes would remain congeal'd those tears,
Which now profuse thou shedd'st, and thou wouldst bend
    Down on the earth thy gaze, where soon appears,

Thyself must see, the end of all our toil;
    The rest that she enjoys beyond the sky,
For whom thou weep'st, whilst o'er this care-worn soil
    Dragging life's heavy burden, as do I.

Yet till 't is granted thee to meet again
    Thy lost adored, the moments consecrate
Of absence to her memory that remain:
    Thy heart let her remembrance animate;

Let thy lips ever her dear name repeat:
    Nor how forget that clear ingenuous mind,
That heavenly beauty, generous soul, to meet
    So rare! the world admired such gifts combined.

But now I see thee to the dusky grove
    Of cypress and rose-bay trees take thy way;
On thy right hand a crown is hanging, wove
    Of mournful everlastings; nor astray

Thine eyes scarce raising, fearing to behold
    The monument of thine eternal grief,
That guards her ashes! Different she consoled,
    Hastening in charity, as for relief

The poor unhappy and the orphans knew!
    For whom she ever show'd a parent's care:
They who partook her gifts and kindness true,
    Now in long files and slow, thy griefs to share

Silent and mournful on thy steps attend,
    Around her tomb; dost thou not hear them? theirs,
Theirs are the tearful sobbings that ascend,
    And cries that interrupt the funeral prayers.

Not ev'n a flower to deck her sepulchre,
    Have I to send thee! flowers may not be grown
To bud in beds of ice; or if they were,
    They soon would wither at my touch alone.

ANACREONTIC.

Let the thunder burst,
   Pour out and drink the wine!
Thou never saw'st a thunderbolt
   Strike the tender vine.

Vesuvius himself
   To Bacchus tribute pays,
And spares the vineyard flourishing,
   Where his lava sways.

In Italy in vain
   I hero sought or sage;
Mine eyes but dusty ruins found,
   Mouldering with age.

Of Rome the image scarce
   Remains to be portray'd;
A tomb is Herculaneum,
   Pompeii is a shade.

But I found Falernum,
   His nectar rich remain'd,
And in memory of Horace,
   A bottleful I drain'd.

BACCHANALIAN.

In chorus we sing, of wine, sweet wine,
Its power benign, and its flavour divine.

 Against power so sweet
  No guard is secure,
 Nor gate, nor yet wall,
  Nor will castle endure,
 Nor doubtings, nor watchings,
  How strict or demure.
        Chorus.

 With thee the fair maiden
  Shows herself fairer,
 With thee has the matron
  New beauty to glare her;
 Ev'n the sad widow
  Finds love an ensnarer.
        Chorus.

 With thee the poor captive,
  Though heavy his chains,
 Ne'er feels in his feasting
  Or torments or pains,
 But a place with his lord
  As an equal he gains.
        Chorus.

With thee the worn seaman
    The south wind defies,
While echoes the thunder
    He singing replies,
And of winds and the waves
    Will the fury despise.
                          Chorus.

Thou hast power o'er the lip
    Of the fool and the sage,
From the breast to root out
    Gall, venom and rage,
What rancour and envy
    Would hide, to assuage.
                          Chorus.

With thee will the coward
    Of courage make show,
The niggard so vile
    Learn bounteous to grow,
And the feeble and old
    Fresh vigour to know.
                          Chorus.

Thy colour so pure
    Outrivals the flowers,
Thy odorous essence
    The rich myrrh's showers,
The rosemary honey
    Thy taste overpowers.
                          Chorus.

Oblivion thou givest
    To troubles and sorrow,
Joys fleeting a show
    Of eternal to borrow,
And robb'st of its horrors
    The fate of tomorrow.

In chorus we sing, of wine, sweet wine,
Its power benign, and its flavour divine.

VIII.

ANGEL DE SAAVEDRA,

DUKE DE RIVAS.

THERE are few persons to whom Fortune can be said to have "come with both hands full," more truly than to the illustrious subject of this notice; even the very reverses of life, which have fallen to his lot, have come like favours; as they have been incurred honourably, and have proved the harbingers of many advantages.

Angel de Saavedra was born at Cordova, the 1st March, 1791, the second son of Don Juan Martin de Saavedra, Duke de Rivas, and Donna Maria Ramirez, Marchioness of Andia, Grandees of Spain, both persons not less eminent for private virtues than for their exalted rank. He received his primary education under his father's care; but he dying in 1802, Angel was then removed to the College of Nobles at Madrid. In accordance with the privileges then enjoyed by youths of noble birth, he was, while yet a child of ten months, nominated a cornet of cavalry, and held a commission as captain when but seven years old. At that age, pursuing his studies, it was observed that he did not show much application or inclination for abstruser subjects; but his quickness of apprehension, and felicity of memory gave him a superiority over his companions, many of whom were distinguished for much greater industry. History and poetry were, from his earliest years, his favourite subjects of study; and in original compositions and translations from the classics, he then already began to show the bent of his genius. At the same time he also began to show his great talent for drawing, in which art, no less than in poetry, he has so much excelled; and it is recorded that for the greatest punishment to be awarded him for juvenile delinquencies, it was found sufficient to take away his pencils, and forbid his taking his drawing lesson for the day.

In 1806 the regiment, to which he was attached, had orders to join Napoleon's army in Germany, with the Spanish contingent; whereupon the Duchess de Rivas, as her son's guardian, procured his exchange into the Royal Guard, by which he lost rank, having now only that of a sub-lieutenant, in the rank as a guardsman. Having joined this corps in the beginning of 1807, it was the lot of Don Angel to witness the scenes which then occurred in the palace, little creditable to any of the parties, including the arrest of the Prince of the Asturias, afterwards Ferdinand VII., and the proceedings against him. It was perhaps fortunate for the young guardsman that he was so soon called into active service. A privileged corps is always a dangerous trial for a young man entering into life; though, in addition to his own right-mindedness, he had the good fortune to be joined to the Flemish battalion of the guard, where he became intimate with a young Belgian officer of kindred tastes and character, who, by example and association, confirmed him in his inclinations. He also became acquainted with some other young men who had the conducting of a literary periodical, to which he contributed several articles, both in prose and verse. For a young man of sixteen, desirous of distinction, this was a privilege which could not fail of producing good results in subsequent improvement, if his early efforts were found to be approved, as an encouragement to continue them.

From such occupations was Saavedra called away soon, to engage in the important events, upon which the future fate of his country was to depend. Napoleon's troops had crossed the Pyrenees, and under pretence of marching through the country to Portugal, had seized upon the principal fortresses of Spain. The Court of Madrid, aware too late of the treachery intended, was thrown into irremediable confusion, heightened by the internal dissensions of the royal family. The troops at Madrid were summoned in haste to the king at Aranjuez, when Saavedra among them witnessed the pitiable scenes, which ended in the abdication of Charles IV. and the declaration of Ferdinand VII., in whose escort he returned to Madrid. But the French armies were already in possession of the country, and had the royal family in their power. They soon had further possession of Madrid, and the guards, in which Saavedra's elder brother, the Duke de Rivas, was also serving with him, were ordered away to the Escurial, as the French leaders were aware of the part they had taken at Aranjuez, and were fearful of their influence with the people, in the course of resistance then widely spreading against the invaders.

Murat, then chief of the French forces, and of the provisional government, had good reason to fear that so influential a body as the Royal Guards, all composed of individuals of rank, might be induced to take part with the insurrectionists in the rising struggle; and he therefore sent to them to the Escurial, one of the principal Spanish officers, also one of the Royal Guard, who had attached himself to the French interest, to persuade the others to join the same cause. This officer having accordingly come to the Escurial, called together the members of the guard, and stating to them that the students of the Military College at Segovia were in a state of rebellion against the authorities, expressed Murat's wish that the guards should join the French troops to suppress the movement, to prevent further ill-consequences. The assembly received the proposal at first in silence and perplexity. But it was one of those occasions when a right mind and strong heart availed more than conventional dignity; and thus, though perhaps the youngest person present, Angel de Saavedra rose up, and with all the impetuosity of youth, declared in impassioned language, that "none of the guard would do treason to their country, or become an instrument of foreign tyranny, for the oppression and punishment of their companions in arms." He therefore, in the name of his comrades, gave a positive refusal to the mandate.

In this, his first harangue, the spirit was as noble, as the sentiments were bold and patriotic. The manner in which it was received showed that it was also in unison with the feelings of the rest of the guard, and Murat's messenger was obliged to content himself with attempting to reprove the young officer, who had ventured to speak before others, so much his superiors in rank and service. But his efforts were of no avail, and he had to return to Madrid, with the information that the guards were also apparently about to join the national party. These passed the night in watch, with their arms and horses prepared, for whatever might be the result. In the morning they received orders to return to Madrid, and obeying the order, at halting for the night, came to deliberate on the course they should adopt. Some thought it would be better to disperse, and go to their respective provinces, to join the several parties already armed in resistance against the invaders. Others, among whom were the two brothers, Saavedra and the Duke de Rivas, thought it would be better for them to keep united, and join as a body, with their standards, the first effective Spanish force they could meet. Unfortunately there was no one of sufficient authority present to command; and the first suggestion, where most of them naturally wished to share the fates of their families, prevailed. Accordingly they dispersed, and the two brothers entered Madrid secretly, finding that those who remained together were too few to remain as a body, against the numerous bands of the enemy spread over the country.

The first wish of the brothers was to join Palafox at Zaragoza, and they started for that purpose with false passports; but found the road too closely beset by the French. In one place, however, they met with a mischance on the other side; where the people, now risen against the invaders, fancied that the travellers who were going armed so mysteriously, were emissaries of the French, and would listen to no declaration to the contrary. Fortunately there happened to be in the town a comrade of the guard, well known there, who hearing the uproar, came and recognized the prisoners, and assuring the multitude of their true character, made them be received with as much enthusiastic welcome, as they had just before been with violence.

Turning from this course, the two brothers then hastened back to join the forces under Castanios, flushed with their triumph at Bailen; and at Sepulveda, Angel Saavedra had his first encounter in fight with the French. With the army he joined, he found about 200 of his comrades of the guards, and these, as a body, now effected much service in the various skirmishes and actions that took place. They had these with varied success at Ucles, Tudela, and other places, where the two brothers distinguished themselves by their activity and bravery. At Tudela the Duke had his horse killed, and received several contusions, which resulted in a fever, on account of which his brother had to take him to their mother's care at Cordova.

Having recovered from this, they again joined the army, and were present at "the memorable battle of Talavera," after which they had to share in the several encounters of Caminias, Madrilejos and Herencia. But now a severer trial awaited them. On the 18th of November, 1809, on the eve of the disastrous battle of Ocania, the French and Spanish forces had an encounter at Antigola, when the Royal Guards, under the Duke de Rivas, though pressed by superior numbers, charged three times on the enemy, before they retired, with the loss of one-third of their number, to Ocania.

In this skirmish, Angel Saavedra had his horse killed at the beginning of the affray, and then had to fight hand to hand at a disadvantage. Thus he soon received two wounds in the head, and another in the breast from a lance which prostrated him, and left him insensible, while the combatants were riding over him and others laid in the same state. About the middle of the night he recovered his sensibility, and found he had been robbed of his clothes. He attempted to rise, but fell down again, unable to move. Happily for him he had sufficient strength to call to a man he saw near, who proved to be a Spanish soldier seeking for spoils, and he, learning the name of the wounded officer, put him on his horse, and took him to his brother. The Duke, who had already been searching for him, and had sent others out for the same purpose unavailingly, now hastened to procure for him medical assistance. With much difficulty he found a surgeon, who, on seeing the patient, declared the case hopeless, and left him to attend to others. The cold air had arrested the bleeding, which now burst forth from the motion of the horse and the warmth of the room used for the hospital, so as to leave him apparently dying. The Duke was in despair, when the people about him brought the barber of the place to dress the wounds, which he did with great skill, giving him hopes of success in saving his brother's life.

As the morning broke, the drums were heard beating for action, announcing the advance of the enemy. The Duke had barely time to procure a common cart of the country into which to place his brother, who was found to have no fewer than eleven wounds upon him, and send him away with seven other wounded companions, before he had to join his troop. Going slowly along, the seven died by his side one after another, and in a few hours they were overtaken by fugitives, whose flight showed the ill-fortune of the day. Saavedra might have shared this ill-fortune further; but one of the escort knew the country well and took him along by-paths to a retired place, where his wounds were again dressed, and afterwards to Baeza, in which city he found better attendance. There, after three weeks, all his wounds were healed, except the one in the breast, and one in the hip, from which he was lame for some years afterwards. He then was enabled to proceed to his mother at Cordova, and there was received, in his native place, with marks of public respect, which could not fail of being very gratifying to his feelings, though at the expense of so much suffering.

In the beginning of 1810 the French came marching towards Cordova, and Saavedra and his mother fled to Malaga. He had frequent bleeding, apparently from the lungs, and his medical advisers were fearful that any extraordinary exertion would have a fatal result. Before they could embark at Malaga for any other place, the French had got possession of the city, and Saavedra and the Duchess had to take refuge, disguised, in a fisherman's hut. In this extremity they were found by a Spanish officer in the French interest, who had formerly shared their hospitality at Cordova, and he repaid it now by procuring for them passports and giving them the means to get to Gibraltar, whence they passed over to Cadiz, then the last hope of Spain.

Arrived at Cadiz, Saavedra was received with the consideration due to his merits. He was put into active service, as far as his strength would allow, and on the staff his talents for drawing as well as for ready composition were found of great value. Many of the military reports were written by him; and he also wrote a defence of the military establishments against a pamphlet which had been published, conducting at the same time a military periodical, published weekly, at Cadiz, throughout 1811. Thrown into association with such men as the Conde de Noronia, Arriaza, Quintana, and Martinez de la Rosa, his love for poetry was further excited, and he composed verses like them, some of which have been preserved among his later works, while he has allowed others to be forgotten. He continued also cultivating his taste for drawing, attending the schools at Cadiz to draw from life as well as from the models; while at leisure moments on duty he amused himself with sketching portraits of his comrades, or of the scenes presented to their view.

But his military duties did not cease at Cadiz. Having been sent out on important commissions with orders, he was led away by his ardour to join in the encounter which took place with the French at Chiclana, in forgetfulness of the commission with which he was charged. Afterwards a division of the army being found in a state of resistance to the orders of the Regency, on account of their general refusing to acknowledge the Duke of Wellington as commander-in-chief, Saavedra was sent with full powers to arrest the disorder. This he did effectually, drawing the division out of Cordova in good order, after deposing the general and other chiefs of the insurrection, who but for this might have brought further reverses on the Spanish arms, such as so many other incapable officers had done previously, influenced in like manner by their presumption and self-conceit.

Saavedra, so far from joining in the vanity and folly of those of his countrymen, who fancied themselves competent to act independently of the British commander, on the contrary, sought to be employed on the staff under the immediate orders of Lord Wellington, but he could not effect it. The wound in his breast again occasioned large effusions of blood from the mouth, and he was obliged to return to Seville, and ultimately was quartered at Cordova. When the war came to an end, he, under these circumstances, retired from military service with the rank of lieutenant-colonel.

While at Cadiz, Saavedra had joined, unreservedly, in the councils of those who framed and attempted to establish in Spain the constitution of 1812. When Ferdinand VII. returned and set it aside, he therefore fully expected that he would be included in the proscription directed against Martinez de la Rosa and others who had distinguished themselves in the assertion of liberal opinions. But instead of this, the king, who probably considered him more of a military than a political character, received him favourably, and gave him the rank of colonel, assigning him Seville for his residence. There accordingly he retired, and while Spain was subjected to the rule of absolutism, employed himself in literary pursuits and drawing, for which the magnificent paintings of Murillo and other Spanish masters in that city gave one of his inclinations so great an incentive. In 1813 he published a volume of poems, and in the following six years brought forward several plays, some of which were represented at Seville with considerable applause, and one had the " marked honour of being prohibited by the censorship." These he republished in a second edition of his works at Madrid in 1821, but though favourably received at the time, they are all acknowledged now to be of little merit. In fact, at that time, having studied principally the later poets of the classical school as it was termed, his mind had not yet attained that expansiveness and vigour which subsequent years of study were destined to give it.

In 1820 Saavedra happened to be in Madrid, probably engaged in superintending this edition of his works, when the events of that year brought into power the party with whom he had been associated at Cadiz at the time of the siege. With characteristic ardour he entered again into close alliance with them, resuming the principles he had previously maintained with them. But though now those friends were in office, he sought nothing for himself further than leave to travel into neighbouring countries, which permission he had sought in vain from the previous government. This favour he now obtained, with full salary allowed, and a commission to examine the military establishments of other nations, and to report to the government on their advances and improvements. He went accordingly to Paris, and after a careful attention to the duties entrusted to him, was about proceeding to Italy, when he was called back to Spain to engage in a new career of public importance.

Before going to Paris, Saavedra had paid a short visit to his native city, and there formed a close intimacy with Alcala Galiano, one of the most learned and talented men of his age, who, with Don Javier Isturitz (the present respected Minister of her Catholic Majesty at London), was now at the head of the government. Galiano, by the fascination of his eloquence, had completely won the good feelings of the young poet, and inspired by the desire of having so able and popular a follower in the legislature, had procured his election as Deputy to the Cortes from Cordova. Flattered by the favour shown him by his fellow-townsmen, Saavedra entered with his accustomed ardour on his duties, and was appointed Secretary to the Cortes, where he came forward as one of the most vehement speakers in the maintenance of liberal opinions. But those opinions were not responded to by the great mass of the people, and were opposed by the foreign courts of Europe. Saavedra had voted for the removal of the court to Seville, and there further voted for the suspension of the king and his transference to Cadiz, when the entry of the French army re-established Ferdinand on his throne. On the 1st October, 1822, Saavedra and Galiano had to take flight from Cadiz to Gibraltar, where he remained till the following May, when he proceeded to London to join the other emigrants there, Isturitz, Galiano, the celebrated Arguelles, whom his countrymen, on account of his remarkable eloquence, have termed the divine, and others.

Even during his short political career, Saavedra had continued his literary pursuits, and now in London he renewed them, writing his poem 'Florinda' and minor pieces, as well as continuing his recreative art of drawing. For his participation in the proceedings against the king, he had been sentenced to death, and his property had been sequestrated. This same measure had been visited on his brother, the Duke de Rivas, who had taken part also in the proceedings, and thus Saavedra had become reduced to very straitened circumstances. Their mother, with natural feeling, forwarded him all the supplies in her power; but these were scanty, and it was necessary for him to seek means of subsistence for himself. He therefore determined on going to Italy to perfect himself in the art of painting, as the best means of employment left him, finding the climate of England also too rigorous for his constitution.

As the Spanish emigrants were forbidden to go to Italy, the Duchess de Rivas besought the Pope's Nuncio at Madrid to grant her son a passport and obtain for him permission to go there for the purposes specified. The Nuncio having communicated with Rome, was enabled to reply, that "as Don Angel Saavedra engaged neither to speak nor to write on political subjects in Italy, nor to frequent English society, his passport would be granted him, assuring him he would there find hospitality and protection." The required securities having been given, and the Nuncio's authorization obtained, on which he had himself written, "Given by express order of His Holiness," Saavedra left London in December, 1824, for Gibraltar, where he remained till the June following. In the meantime he there married, according to previous arrangement, Donna Maria de la Encarnacion Cueto, daughter of a distinguished colonel of artillery, and then, with his young wife, proceeded to Leghorn. Arrived at this city, and presenting his passport to the Roman consul, he was told that, notwithstanding the assurances given him, he was now forbidden to go to Rome; besides which he received an order from the Tuscan government to leave their territorities within three days. Finding all remonstrances useless, Saavedra now, in right of a passport from Gibraltar, applied for aid to the British consul, who took him to his house, and as the only means of putting him in safety, embarked him on board a small Maltese vessel then about to sail for that island. After a protracted voyage, with wretched accommodations and subjected to great peril in a storm, when the men abandoned their tasks, and the captain and Saavedra had to compel them by blows even to resume their labours, they at length reached Malta. Here Saavedra intended to have remained only until he could obtain the means of returning to Gibraltar; but the advantages of climate, of cheapness of living, and the reception he met with from the English authorities, induced him to continue there, until his stay at length extended to five years' residence.

Fortunately for him, there happened then to be residing at Malta Mr. J. H. Frere, formerly British Minister at Madrid, who, in addition to a highly cultivated taste and great general knowledge, was well conversant with the Spanish language and literature also in particular. With this gentleman Saavedra soon entered into terms of intimate friendship, and was taught by him to turn his thoughts from the tame class of poetry he had copied from the French school, and elevate his mind to the high tone of the older poets of Spain, as well as to the study of English literature. These lessons he followed, and thus proved another instance of the remark of Plutarch, that the Muses often suggest the best and most approved productions of genius, taking exile as their means to aid them: Καὶ γὰρ τοῖς παλαιοῖς (ὥς ἔοικεν) αἱ Μοῦσαι τὰ κάλλιστα τῶν συνταγμάτων καὶ δοκιμώτατα, φυγὴν λάβουσαι σύνεργον, ἐπετέλεσαν.

At first Saavedra continued his former style of writing, but after a short time his mind seemed suddenly to expand, and to act under the influence of another genius. He finished, after his arrival at Malta, his poem of 'Florinda,' and wrote there several plays, of the same character as those he had formerly written, but at the same time showed that a change was coming over his mind, by an 'Ode to the Lighthouse at Malta,' known to the reader by Mr. Frere's translation of it, which for spirit and range of thought proved itself the offspring of another and truer inspiration. The expectations thus raised were destined to be fully realized, and the poem he then began, and published subsequently, the 'Moro

Esposito,' or 'Foundling Moor,' proved one of a class entirely unknown to Spanish literature, but quite in accordance with the national genius, so as to be at once accepted by the Spanish public, as entitled to their unqualified admiration. To use the words of his biographer, Pastor Diaz, himself a writer of considerable reputation, "This work, which had no model, nor has yet had a rival, is one of the most precious jewels of our literature, and in our judgement the most beautiful flower of his poetic crown."

But it was not to poetry alone that Saavedra gave his attention at Malta. He continued also his application to painting, not having forgotten his original intention of adopting this art professionally. Notwithstanding the advantages he enjoyed there, however, he was anxious to be nearer his own country, and sought permission to go to France, for which purpose he had an English vessel of war assigned to take him to Marseilles. On arriving there, instead of being allowed to go to Paris as he desired, he was directed to fix his residence at Orleans, where, having exhausted the means afforded him for subsistence, he found it necessary to establish a school for drawing. In this he met with some success, having obtained various pupils and commissions for portraits, and a painting which he had finished with care and ability having been bought at a high price for the museum of the city. Four others of his paintings are in the choir of the cathedral at Seville.

After a few months' residence at Orleans, the revolution of July, 1830, allowed him to go to Paris, where he found his valued friends Isturitz and Galiano, both, like himself, having moderated the warmth of early opinions by the effect of observation as well as of time. Instead of interfering in political questions therefore, he continued his artistic labours. Several portraits he had painted appeared in the Exhibition of

1831 at the Louvre, and his name is to be found in the list for that year of professional artists established in Paris. In consequence of the cholera having broken out there, Saavedra soon after retired to Tours, where he finished his poem, the 'Moro Esposito,' and the Tragedy, 'Don Alvaro,' publishing the former at Paris in two volumes, in 1833.

On the death of Ferdinand VII., under the milder sway of Queen Christina, the emigrants hitherto excluded from Spain were allowed to return to their country. Angel Saavedra hastened to take advantage of the amnesty, and arrived in Spain the 1st of January, 1834, to take the oaths required; after which he took up his residence at Madrid, and gave his adhesion to the government over which Martinez de la Rosa then presided. Now, however, an important change came over his fortunes, which brought him still more prominently before the world, and involved him again in the vicissitudes of public life.

On the 15th of May, 1834, his elder brother died without children; and Angel Saavedra thereupon succeeded to his honours as Duke de Rivas, and to the family estates entailed with the title. As a Grandee of Spain, the new Duke had to take his place in the Chamber of Peers, where he was chosen, on the 24th of July following, second Secretary, and shortly after, first Secretary of the Chamber and Vice-President. Here again, as formerly in the Cortes, he then took his part in the public debates, having on several occasions shown himself to possess great oratorical abilities. One speech he made on the exclusion of Don Carlos and his descendants from the Spanish throne, has been particularly mentioned as combining much eloquence with high political considerations.

But notwithstanding his elevation and parliamentary duties, he still continued his literary pursuits. Having finished the

Tragedy of 'Don Alvaro,' he now brought it forward, and it is not too much to say that never had a drama been produced in Spain of so high a character, or that was attended with such success. At first it was received with wonder, then with long and loud applause; it was repeated at every theatre in Spain, and still continues to excite the admiration of audiences, casting into the shade all his former dramatic productions, and in fact causing a revolution in the dramatic art of the Spanish stage. The old worn-out characters and constantly recurring self-same incidents that had encumbered the scenes have since been swept away, and a higher tone has been in consequence adopted by later writers, though still this remarkable production remains without a rival on the Spanish stage. Yet it is not without faults, and it has been subjected to severe criticisms; but on the representation, so absorbing is the interest which it is said to excite, that all faults are lost sight of in admiration. The subject of the drama is that of the old Greek tragedy, Fatality. Don Alvaro is an Œdipus, destined for misfortune, and not even religion can save him from his mission of crime. "It is a character which belongs to no determinate epoch, perhaps more universal in this as it belongs to all, like the heroes of Shakespeare." There can be no question but that it was the study of Shakespeare which elevated his genius to the production of this masterpiece of the modern Spanish theatre, as had the study of Walter Scott and Byron enabled him to give the world the great poem of the 'Moro Esposito.'

On the 15th of May, 1836, the Duke de Rivas was called on to join the government formed by his friends Isturitz and Galiano, to which he consented with much reluctance. But this ministry was doomed to be of short duration, and was overthrown in the midst of popular commotions. The Duke had to take refuge in the house of the British Minister, the present Earl of Clarendon, where he remained twenty-four days, refusing to emigrate as others of his colleagues had done, though at last he felt himself compelled to do so. With much difficulty he then escaped, and after many perils, passing through Portugal, arrived at Gibraltar.

The moderate counsels of the Isturitz ministry were not agreeable to the temper of the public, and thus the Duke de Rivas was now driven into banishment by his former friends the liberals, as he had formerly been by their mutual enemies the Absolutists. At Gibraltar he thereupon remained a year, dedicating himself again to poetry and painting, having then composed much of his next, and perhaps most popular work, 'Historical Romances.' On the promulgation of the constitution of 1837, accepted by the Queen, the Duke gave in his adhesion to it, and was thus enabled to return to his family from his second exile, on the 1st of August of that year.

In the ensuing elections, the Duke was elected Senator for Cadiz, when, in consonance with his principles, he gave his general support to the ministry, and distinguished himself by several animated discourses he pronounced in the Chamber; particularly one in favour of returning to the nunneries their sequestrated properties, and another for maintaining to the Basque provinces their ancient privileges and rights. For this just and disinterested advocacy of their interests, the constituents inhabiting the two provinces of Biscay and Alava respectively elected him to the Senate in 1840, though the government which then existed did not think proper to sanction their choice.

Shortly after this, another change occurred in the government, and under the administration of Narvaez, the Duke de Rivas was appointed Minister from Her Catholic Majesty to the Court at Naples, in which city he continued upwards of five years in that mission; during also the residence of Pius IX. there, while a fugitive from Rome. On the marriage of the Conde de Montemolin, eldest son of Don Carlos, with a sister of the King of the two Sicilies, he demanded his passport, leaving his post, for which he received the approbation of his sovereign. Since his return to Spain, the Duke has been again appointed Vice-President of the Senate, but seems to have taken little part in public affairs.

Mr. Borrow, in his very amusing work, 'The Bible in Spain,' describes the Duke de Rivas, in 1836, as "a very handsome man;" and so his portraits represent him, agreeing with all the accounts of his personal appearance and courtly manners. Favoured by fortune with the possession of high rank and ample means, he has been still further favoured in his domestic relations, and with a large family, the solace of his age. We have thus traced him through life, distinguished, in every stage in which he has had to exert himself, for eminent ability as well as honourable conduct. As a soldier, engaged in the noblest of causes, the defence of his country, he showed himself conspicuous among the most active and bravest of her defenders. In public life, as an orator, a diplomatist and a statesman, he has proved equally eminent. In private life, he has been no less exemplary for the exercise of the domestic virtues, having in his needs exerted himself to discharge his duty to his family, by the practice of the talents with which he had been endowed, as an artist of superior proficiency. As a dramatist, his works have in that most difficult department gained the fullest success; and in poetry he is the only modern writer in Spain who has given the world a poem of the highest class, combining varied incidents with well-drawn characters and a sustained interest. Our greatest poet of modern days felt constrained to say,

> I twine
> My hopes of being remember'd in my line
> With my land's language;

and in such aspirations may the Duke de Rivas indulge in the retrospect of his past labours to ensure for him a like future remembrance.

Passing by the poems written under the influence of an adhesion to the rules of the classical school, we find the poem of the 'Moro Esposito,' or 'Cordova and Burgos in the fifteenth century,' well-deserving of being classed with the poetical romances of Sir Walter Scott, on the model of which it was written. The subject is the History of the Seven Infantes of Lara, made known to the English reader by Southey and Lockhart, and it contains many passages of extraordinary merit, though severe criticism would point out many faults. "To make felt," says his biographer, "or to record all the beauties of this book, a book as large would be necessary, and they may well compensate for the defects, notwithstanding that at times those same beauties make us see at what small cost the author might have sent forth his work more finished." As in every-day life, he has joined in his narration scenes of the most opposite character, the most magnificent descriptions with what is most ludicrous, and the tenderest with what is oppressing to sensibility. The passages referring to his native city of Cordova are peculiarly beautiful, and show the feelings of the exile, as they lean to his country, in all ages and under all circumstances,—to "sweet Argos" or sacred Athens—

> γενοίμαν,
> ἵν᾽ ὑλᾶεν ἔπεστι πόντου
> πρόβλημ᾽ ἁλίκλυστον, ἄκραν
> ὑπὸ πλάκα Σουνίου,
> τὰς ἱερὰς ὅπως προσεί-
> ποιμ᾽ ἂν 'Αθάνας.

The dedication to Mr. Frere has the singularity of being written in the English language.

The 'Ode to the Lighthouse at Malta' is another exemplification of the Duke's patriotic feeling, as well as the poem of 'The Exile,' which has been translated into English by Mr. Reade. One of his latest works is in the form of a drama, but, like those of Lord Byron, it is not intended for the stage. It is entitled, 'Undeception in a Dream,' and represents the life of man, contrasting its vicissitudes and events with his hopes and desires. Like the tragedy of 'Alvaro,' it is a highly poetical conception, and worthy of the reputation of the noble writer.

It has already been intimated that the most popular of the Duke's works is one published at Madrid in 1841, 'Historical Romances,' from which has been taken, for translation, the 'Alcazar of Seville.' These romances are, in fact, ballads on various subjects in Spanish history, written in the ballad measure of octosyllabic lines, with asonante rhymes for the second and fourth of each quatrain, similar to our own ballads. In the prologue to this work the Duke has written a defence of this measure, which required no defence beyond his own adoption of it, with the example of such writers in it as Melendez and Arriaza in modern times, and almost all the best writers in the language previously. Ochoa has praised "above all" the romance of the Conde de Villa Mediana, and readers generally find most interesting the 'Tale of a Veteran,' so that it may require an explanation for the choice of the one taken, that the character of Pedro, surnamed the Cruel, was best known to the English public, as associated with English history. That of the Conde de Villa Mediana is a lively description of some scenes which led to his assassination by order of the king, who was influenced by jealousy; the 'Tale of the Veteran' gives an account of an adventure in a nunnery, where a nun invites an officer to her cell and poisons him in revenge for his slight to her sister. She then shows him the corpse of a brother officer, who had already fallen a victim to her arts for the like wrong to herself, and she tells him the whole history of her motives and conduct, while she induces him to dig a grave for the first victim, with whom, she tells her second, that he is also to be placed.

Few writers have given the world so many works of a superior order, distinguishable separately for varied excellence, as the Duke de Rivas. He has concentrated in his later productions all the chief merits of a poet, in the choice of his subjects, in the delineation of character and the power of maintaining throughout the interest of the narrative. If he has failed too often in the mechanical execution, in attending to the harmony of verse or poetic expression of the thoughts, these are faults which we may hope will be corrected in subsequent editions, so as to leave him still greater claims on the admiration of his readers.

THE DUKE DE RIVAS.

THE ALCAZAR OF SEVILLE.

I.

Magnificent is the Alcazar,
  For which Seville is renown'd,
Delicious are its gardens,
  With its lofty portals crown'd.
With woods all carved elaborate,
  In a thousand forms about,
It raises high its noble front
  With cornice jutting out;
And there in ancient characters
  A tablet may be seen,
𝔇on 𝔓edro built these palaces,
  The sculptures placed between.
But ill beseem in its saloons
  The modern triflings rear'd,
And in its proud courts men without
  The antique vest or beard.

How many a soft and balmy eve,
   In pleasant converse there,
Have I with Seville's mirthful sons,
   And Seville's daughters fair,
Traversed those blooming bowers along,
   On entering which are rude
Gigantic shapes in myrtles cut,
   Of various attitude;
And rose-bay trees, in long arcades,
   With oranges unite,
And shady labyrinths form, the which
   To thefts of love invite;
And hidden jets of water spring
   All sudden from the floor,
When trod the painted pebbles laid
   In rich mosaic o'er,
That sprinkle on the stranger there,
   While shouts of laughter rise,
From those who warn'd by former fate
   Now shun such pleasantries!

In summer time, at close of day,
   When mid the light cloud's fold,
The sun declines, encircling them
   With scarlet and with gold,
That bright transparent heaven above,
   With purple mists o'erspread,

Cut in a thousand varied hues,
  By softest zephyrs led,
That glowing atmosphere, in which
  One seems to breathe of fire,
How temper they the languid frame,
  And soul divine inspire!
The view too of those baths, that gain
  From all who know them praise,
And that proud edifice which Moors
  And Goths combined to raise,
In some parts harsh, in some more light,
  Here ruins, there repair'd,
The different dominations pass'd
  Are thus by each declared;
With records, and remembrances
  Of ages long pass'd by,
And of more modern years alike
  To arrest the fantasy.
The lemon's and the jasmine's flowers,
  While they the eyes enchant,
Embalm the circumambient air
  With sweets they lavish grant.
The fountains' murmurs, and afar
  The city's varied cries,
With those that from the river near,
  Or Alameda rise,
From Triana, and from the bridge,
  All lost, confused amain,

With sound of bells vibrating loud
    In high Hiralda's fane;—
A scene that never is forgot
    Enchanted forms the whole,
The thoughts of which unceasing cause
    To beat my heart and soul.

Many delicious nights, when yet
    My now all-frozen breast
Beat warmly, have I seen those halls
    By youthful footsteps press'd;
Fill'd with a chosen concourse gay
    In country dance to meet,
Or light quadrille, while festive sounds
    The orchestras repeat:
And from the gilded roofs rebound
    The steps, the laugh perchance
And talk of happy pairs, by love
    United in the dance;
With sound of music mix'd the while,
    Confused and blended o'er,
As sent according echos forth
    From the enamell'd floor.

Yet, ah! those lovely bowers along
    I never once have stray'd,

But saw as in a mental dream
    Padillia's gentle shade,
Flitting before my view to pass,
    Heaving a sigh profound,
Light as a vapour, or a cloud
    That skims the trees around.
Nor ever enter'd I those halls,
    But fancying arise
I saw the founder's phantom, stain'd
    With blood congeal'd the dyes.
Nor in that vestibule obscure,
    Where with the cornice blend
The portraits of the kings, arranged
    In columns to extend,
To that which is blue-tiled below,
    And enamell'd is on high,
Which shows on every side around
    A rich-set balcony,
And gilded lattice roof above
    That crowns it with dark shade,
But thought I saw upon the ground
    A lifeless body laid!
Yet on that pavement may be seen
    A dark stain to this day!
Indelible, which ages pass
    And never wash away:

'T is blood that dark tenacious stain;
   Blood of the murder'd dead:
Alas! how many throng it o'er,
   Nor think on what they tread!

II.

Five hundred years shone younger
   The Alcazar to the day,
Its lofty walls yet lustrous,
   And faultless its array;
And brilliant were the enamels
   Which its gilded roofs reveal,
It show'd itself the mansion fit
   Of the king of proud Castile;
When on one balmy morn it chanced
   Of florid May betide,
In that saloon whose balcony
   Is on the plaza's side,
Two persons of illustrious mien
   In silence deep were there;
One was a Cavalier, and one
   A Lady passing fair.

A Barbary carpet richly wove
   Upon the floor was laid,
The gift or tribute which the Moor
   Granada's king had paid;

A silken curtain, bright with flowers,
　　And ribbons curious wrought,
With various eastern colours deck'd,
　　Which to our Spain had brought
Venetian galleys, as perchance
　　Her Doge's gift of state,
Was thrown across the balcony,
　　The light to moderate.
In the recess in front, with woods
　　Well carved, and richly graced
With mother-o'-pearl inlayings,
　　Was an Oratory placed;
Where of the sovereign Virgin
　　The image stood devout,
The sculpture somewhat rude, but yet
　　Attractions not without;
Which with a plate of silver,
　　For ornament was crown'd,
Its rim reflecting amethysts,
　　And emeralds around.
A manuscript of holy prayers,
　　Which miniatures adorn,
Precious with gold and ivory
　　Upon its coverings borne,
Was seen there placed upon a stand,
　　Form'd of an angel's wings,
The figure badly sculptured,
　　But with neat finishings.

And on the floor of gold brocade
    A cushion one might see,
Which by its sunken pressure show'd
    The marks of bended knee.
And on the pure white walls were hung
    Bright arms along the space,
And interspersed were banners,
    And trophies of the chase.
An ornamental table stood
    In the middle of the floor,
On which a well-tuned lute was placed,
    Though partly cover'd o'er;
A rich-cut board for game of draughts,
    And a coffer by its side
Of silver filigree, and jars
    With chosen flowers supplied.

The Lady near the balcony
    Sat very pensively,
In a great gilded chair of state,
    Whose back was form'd to be
A canopy, or cover o'er,
    And in gay curvings down
Were lions, castles, and the whole
    Surmounted with a crown.
Her dress a silken robe of green,
    Which show'd a various tinge,

In twisted threads, with pearls and gold
    The embroidery and fringe.
Her head-dress than the snow appear'd
    Ev'n whiter to behold,
And covering o'er the fine clear lawn
    Her long dark tresses roll'd.
Her face was heavenly, and her neck
    Divine, but in their hue
Like wax, the colour which fear paints,
    And long-known sorrow too.
Her eyes were like two beaming suns
    Beneath their lashes tall,
Where shone two precious pearly drops
    As ready down to fall.
She was a lily fair, whom death
    Was rudely threatening seen,
For a corroding worm the heart
    Was tearing deep within.
Now in her thin pale hands, convulsed
    It seems with fear or doubt,
Her kerchief white, of border'd lace
    And points, she twists about;
Or with absorb'd distracted mien
    She agitates the air,
With fan, whose feathers Araby
    Had sent, the choicest there.

The Cavalier was slightly form'd,
   And of the middle size,
With reddish beard, a restless mouth,
   And most unquiet eyes.
His visage pale and dry appear'd,
   Nose sharp and of a crook,
Noble his port, but sinister
   And terrible his look.
In a red mantle he was wrapp'd,
   With golden plates o'erspread,
And gracefully his cap was placed
   On one side on his head.
With measured steps, from end to end,
   He paced along the room,
And different passions o'er his face
   Though silent seem'd to come.
At times he reddens, darting round
   Fierce looks, that seem to tell,
As flames cast forth from eyes of fire,
   The very deeds of hell.
And now a fierce and bitter smile
   The extended lip displays,
Or on the gilded roof he fix'd
   A darkly lowering gaze.
Now hastening on his course, from head
   To foot he trembles o'er,
And now proceeds his noble mien
   Of calmness to restore.

Thus have I seen a tiger fierce,
    Now tranquil, now with rage
Revolve himself each side across,
    And round his narrow cage.
Thus pacing o'er the carpet there
    His footsteps are not heard,
But soundless they, yet were distinct
    As ever that he stirr'd,
The crackling of his arms and knees:
    In distant lands, 't is said,
That with like noise has Heaven supplied,
    For man to shun in dread,
O, wonder rare! a serpent, named
    Thence Rattlesnake, that springs
Quick at the moment it comes nigh,
    And kills whome'er it stings.

The Lady was Padillia,
    That sat in mournful strain;
And the stern silent Cavalier
    Don Pedro, King of Spain.

III.

As round some solitary tower,
    At setting of the sun,
Fierce birds of prey are whirling seen,
    Revolving one by one,

Thus with Don Pedro in their turn
    Have various thoughts a trace,
Whose shadows darken as they pass
    The expression of his face.
Now occupies his angry mind
    His brother's power and state,
Of those whose mother he had slain,
    And birth would criminate.
Now of unquietnesses borne,
    Great scorn and insult shown,
Or of his failing treasury,
    Nor means to fill it known.
Now of the fair Aldonza's charms,
    His fortune 't was to gain,
Or of the blood-stain'd forms of those
    He had unjustly slain.
Now some projected enterprise,
    Some treaty to defeat,
Faith-breaking with Granada's Moor,
    Or treason or deceit.
But as the birds the lonely tower,
    The broken heights between,
Are all at length, as one by one,
    Retiring hiding seen;
And constant only one remains,
    Revolving it infest,

The fiercest, strongest on the wing,
    That will admit no rest;
Thus all that multitude confused
    Of passions wild and strange,
Of which Don Pedro for a while
    Was tangled in the range,
At length from breast and head alike
    Fled finding a retreat,
And living left distinct alone,
    With horror great replete,
The image of Fadrique,
    His eldest brother famed,
The pride of knights and Master those
    Of Santiago named.

Now from Humillia's conquer'd walls,
    With matchless courage won,
In triumph had Fadrique come
    O'er vanquish'd Aragon.
Where erst the bars, the castles now
    He floating left abroad,
And to present the keys he brings
    His brother, king and lord.
Well knows the king no rebel he,
    But friend and ally true,
And more than Tello madly hates,
    And more than Henry too.

'T was he Fadrique had the charge
   From France to bring the queen,
The Lady Blanche, but he allow'd
   A year to intervene.
With her in Narbonne he delay'd,
   And rumours thus of those,
Which whether true or false alike
   Are poisonous, arose.
And in Medina's tower the price
   The Lady Blanche now pays,
Of all the palace whisperings,
   And journey's long delays.
And on his shoulders yet untouch'd
   His head Fadrique wears,
Because of his great wealth and power
   And honour'd name he bears.
But, woe for him! the ladies all
   Him as their idol own,
For his gay port and gallant mien,
   And manly courage known.
And if he cause the throne no fear,
   In his fidelity,
He gives what's worse, though that were bad,
   The heart strong jealousy.

Meanwhile the fair Padillia,
   Whose judgement clear and great,

Her royal lover's secret thoughts,
  Though deepest penetrate,
In whom the goodness of her heart
  The enchantment still excels,
That in her beauteous face and form
  So marvellously dwells,
Unhappy victim lives of fears,
  That ever her attend,
Because she loves the king, and sees
  His course in evil end:
She knows that based in blood and grief,
  And persecution's train,
A palace never is secure,
  No throne can fix'd remain.
And she has two young tender girls,
  Who with another sire,
Whate'er their lot, might all have gain'd
  Their hearts could best require;
And in Fadrique's worth she sees
  A stay and partisan.
She knows he comes to Seville now,
  And as from words can scan
Her fierce lord's brow dark lowering,
  In evil hour he came,
And to allay suspicions,
  Or give them higher aim,
At length, though with a trembling lip,
  The silence breaking dared

To speak, and thus the words that pass'd
    Between the two declared:
" Your brother then, Fadrique,
    Triumphant comes today ?"
" And certainly in coming,
    The wretch makes long delay."
" He serves you well, and hero-like,
    As does Humillia show,
Of loyalty gives proofs, and brave
    He is "—" Sufficient so."
" You may be sure, Sire, that his heart
    Will ever true remain."
" Tomorrow still more sure of that."
    Both silent were again.

IV.

With joy the Master to receive,
    Through Seville's streets along,
Great rumour spreads, and arms resound,
    And men and horses throng.
And shouts of welcoming, amidst
    Repeated echoes rise,
Which from Hiralda's lofty tower
    Are scatter'd to the skies.
Now comes the crowd approaching near,
    But less the shouts resound,

And now the palace gates they reach
  Mid silence all around :
As if the Alcazar had enjoy'd
  The privilege to appear,
In sight, and still the enthusiast flow,
  And turn it into fear.
Thus mute and breathless, motionless,
  The people stood in dread,
As if with magical respect
  The plaza's bounds to tread;
And enters there the Master now,
  With but a scanty train,
And of his order some few knights,
  The palace gates to gain.
And forward on his course directs,
  As one without alarms,
Who goes to meet a brother kind,
  With open heart and arms:
Or as some noble chieftain comes,
  For glorious deeds the cause,
From grateful monarch to receive
  Due honours and applause.
Upon a dark and mettled steed,
  That breathes of foam and fire,
And while the bridle scarce restrains,
  Seems proud of its attire,

With a white mantle o'er him cast,
  Flung loosely to the air,
O'er which the collar and red cross
  His dignity declare;
And cap of crimson velvet girt
  His brows, whereon unfold
The winds the feathers' snowy plumes,
  And tassels bound with gold.

All pale as death, the furious King
  His brother saw from far,
When on the plaza entering first,
  And fix'd as statues are,
Awhile he stood upon the floor,
  And from his angry eyes
Seem'd burning horrid lightning thence
  In flashes to arise.
But starting soon, himself around
  He turn'd the room to leave,
As if he would some welcome guest
  Right affably receive.
When thus Padillia saw him turn,
  Her heart beyond relief
Of anguish full, and countenance
  So beauteous mark'd with grief,
She rose, and to the balcony
  Went troubled, by the square,

And to the Master motions wild,
  With gestures to declare,
In evil hour he comes, and waves
  Her kerchief him away,
And by mute signs thus bids him seek
  Safety without delay.
Nothing of this he comprehends,
  But for saluting takes
The warning, and discreetly thus
  A gallant answer makes.
And to the open'd portal comes,
  With guards and bowmen lined,
Who give him passage free, but leave
  His followers behind.

If he knew not Padillia's signs,
  Don Pedro knew them well,
As he before the chamber door
  A moment seem'd to dwell,
In deep suspense o'er his resolve,
  When turning back his eye,
He saw the Lady warn him thus
  By motions thence to fly.
O, heaven! then was that noble act,
  Of pure intent to be
What call'd the executioners forth,
  And seal'd the stern decree.

Follow'd by two esquires alone,
 The Master scarce in haste
Upon the royal vestibule
 His foot confiding placed,
Where various men-at-arms were seen,
 In double iron barr'd,
Pacing along as sentinels
 The entrance stairs to guard,
When over from the balcony,
 Like fiendish shape of ill,
The King looks out, and "Mace-bearers,"
 He shouts, "the Master kill."
Quick as the lightning in a storm
 Comes ere the thunders call,
Six well-appointed maces down
 On Don Fadrique fall.
He raised his hand to grasp his sword,
 But in his tabard's gird
The hilt was bound, impossible
 To draw it at the word.
He fell, a sea of blood around
 Ran from the shatter'd brain,
Raising a cry which reach'd to heaven,
 And doubtless not in vain.
Of deed so horrible the news
 At once around was spread,

And thence the brotherhood and knights
    Together quickly fled.
To hide them in their houses fled
    The people, trembling sore
With horror, and the Alcazar's bounds
    Were desert as before.

V.

'Tis said, the sight of blood so much
    Is wont to infuriate
The tiger, that he still rends on
    With stomach satiate;
Solely because 't is his delight
    With blood the earth to stain,
So doubtless with the King it was
    Such feelings grew amain.
For when he saw Fadrique laid,
    Thus prostrate on the ground,
After the squires in search he ran
    The palace all around;
Who tremblingly and livid fled
    The apartments various o'er,
Nor find they any hiding-place,
    Or whence to fly a door.

One happily at length succeeds,
    To hide or fly outright;
The other, Sancho Villiegas,
    Less happy or adroit,
Seeing the King still follow him,
    Enter'd half dead with fear
Where was Padillia on her couch,
    With her attendants near;
They trembling, as she senseless laid,
    And by her side reclined
Her two young tender girls, who were
    Angels in form and mind.
The unhappy youth still seeing there
    The spectre following nigh,
That even this asylum mocks,
    In his arms quickly high
Snatches the Lady Beatrice,
    Who scarce six years has known,
The child for whom the King has e'er
    The most affection shown.
But, ah! naught serves him this resource,
    As in the desert naught
The holy cross avails, that clasps
    The pilgrim hapless caught;
When roars the south wind, burns the sky,
    And seems as if up-driven

A frightful sea, of waves of sand,
    Commingling earth and heaven;
Thus with the child between his arms,
    And on his knees compress'd,
The furious dagger of the King
    Was planted in his breast.

As if that day had witness'd naught
    The palace new or rare,
The King sat at the table calm
    To eat as usual there;
Play'd afterwards a game of draughts,
    Then went out pacing slow
To see the galleys, arming soon
    To Biscay's shores to go.
And when the night the hemisphere
    Had with its mantle veil'd,
He enters in the Golden Tower,
    Where he shut up has held
The fair Aldonza, whom he took
    From Santa Clara's walls,
And as in blind idolatry
    Who now his heart enthralls.
With Levi then his treasurer,
    Who though a Hebrew vile

Has all his confidence, he goes
    On state affairs awhile;
And very late retires to rest,
    With no attendants nigh,
Only a Moor, a wretch perforce,
    His favourite waiting by.

Enter'd the lofty vestibule,
    The Alcazar's tranquil bound,
One moment paused the King and pass'd
    His gaze in turn around.
A large lamp from the vaulted roof
    Was hanging loose, and cast
Now lights, now shadows, as it swung,
    As by the breezes pass'd.
Between the polish'd columns placed
    Two men in armour were,
But only two dark figures show'd,
    Watching in silence there.
And still was Don Fadrique laid
    Extended on the ground,
With his torn mantle o'er him spread,
    In a lake of blood around.
The King approach'd him, and awhile
    Attentively survey'd,

And seeing that his brother yet
　Was not entirely dead,
Since he perchance as breathing seem'd,
　His breast a heave to make,
He gave him with his foot a push,
　Which made the body shake;
Whereon he, giving to the Moor
　His sharpen'd dagger bare,
Said, "Finish him," and quietly
　To sleep went up the stair.

IX.

MANUEL BRETON DE LOS HERREROS.

IN the country of Lope de Vega and Calderon de la Barca, it was not to be supposed, that on the general revival of the national literature, the drama could be left neglected, in a state unworthy of its ancient reputation. From the time of those great writers until the present, notwithstanding the predilection of the Spanish people for the stage, and the encouragement consequently given for genius to exert itself, no dramas had been produced to equal them in the public admiration. The younger Moratin, who may be justly termed the Spanish Molière, had rather introduced into Spain a new style of drama, that which we call genteel comedy, than followed the track of the ancient masters. It was reserved for a later writer, the subject of this notice, to appear as a rival to them in the exuberance of composition, and possession of popular favour, though it may be a question for future ages to decide on his relative merit.

Breton de los Herreros was born at Quel, a small village in the province of Logronio, the 19th December, 1796. Of his early history, we are only informed that he was educated at the school of San Antonio Abad at Madrid, and that he entered a regiment of infantry as a volunteer, when yet a boy of fourteen. The world at large may be considered to be, with regard to contemporary characters of another nation, in the relation of posterity, making distance have, as Bishop Atterbury remarked to Lord Bolingbroke, the effect of time; and they will thus inquire eagerly into the particulars of the life of one distinguished for genius, however humble his birth, while they will pass heedlessly by the noblest born personage, who has given them no peculiar right of interest in his history. But, as on reading the life of the Duke de Rivas, we feel it a subject of congratulation, that the lance of a French marauder did not cut off one who was destined to be the ornament of his country's literature, so we rejoice again equally that the chance passed away favourably, when a stray ball might have deprived the world of the works of Breton de los Herreros. Serving in his humble line, he was present at various skirmishes with the invaders on their final expulsion from Valencia and Catalonia, at the same time composing patriotic songs on the national triumphs. In 1812, when yet a boy of fifteen, he wrote an Ode to the Constitution, and distinguished himself as an orator among his comrades on the popular subjects of discussion. On the return of Ferdinand VII. to absolute power, he must have been compelled to restrain his tendencies for liberalism, and it may be supposed that his time was at least as well employed in noting the characters of those around him, and the scenes he had to witness, as a storehouse of useful observations for his future writings.

In 1822 he obtained his discharge from the army, and after various attempts made to obtain an eligible employment in the provinces, he went to Madrid, in the summer of 1824, for the same purpose. There again he was equally unsuccessful, and as a last resource, took to the director of the theatre, a comedy which he had written some years previously for pastime. Fortunately for him, the director happened to be in want of a new piece to bring out on the king's birthday, and thinking the one presented would answer his purpose, he undertook its production with more than usual care, on account of the occasion. It was accordingly performed on the 24th October, 1824, and met with such decided success, that the literary fame of the author was at once secured.

The profits accruing from the representation of his comedies were exceedingly trifling; but his natural inclinations led him to writing for the stage, where he now found himself respected as a successful writer; and as he had no other resource for maintenance, he applied himself to this labour with better hopes. A succession of pieces he wrote were equally successful, produced with a rapidity that reminded the world of the fertility that had characterized the genius of Lope de Vega or Calderon. One of his pieces was so much relished, that at the close, the audience insisted on its being repeated all over a second time, with which extraordinary demand the actors had to comply. In 1831 he brought out his comedy of 'Marcela, or Which of the Three?'—the most popular of all his productions, the subject being, which of three lovers, all unworthy of her, the heroine, who is amiability personified, should accept. It was repeated at all the theatres in the kingdom, and went through six editions on publication, besides several surreptitious ones, having some of the verses even passing into "household words," as popular expressions.

In the same year, 1831, he published a small volume of poems, containing lyrical and miscellaneous pieces, and has since written many more of the same character in the different periodicals of Madrid. None of these are, however, deserving of note, except the satirical ones, many of which abound with the wit and humour for which his comedies are remarkable. He is now engaged in publishing at Madrid a collection of all his works, the last volume being intended to contain the miscellaneous poems, which, corrected and collected together from the different papers in which they at first appeared, will no doubt prove to be more worthy of his fame than those published in 1831. In the lyrical poems he is avowedly a follower of the so-called classical school, and rises no higher than those of the same class that had preceded him; their utmost praise being to be characterized as—

Coldly correct and classically dull.

In the satirical pieces, however, he seems in his proper element, playing on words and treating his rhymes with a command of language truly surprising. For this reason, and on account of the numerous local and national allusions contained in them, it is very difficult for a foreigner fully to understand, and almost impossible to be able to translate them. Those pieces attempted in this work may perhaps give some faint image of his style; but they have been chosen as most easy for translation, rather than as the best. Of the Satires published separately after the volume above mentioned, the most applauded have been those entitled, 'Against the Philharmonic Rage;' 'Against the Mania for Writing for the Public;' 'Against the Abuses introduced into Theatrical Declamation;' 'Moral Epistle on the Manners of the Age;' and 'The Rage for Travelling.' With the Spaniards of the present day as with their Roman ancestors, satire is a favourite species of composition, and it has been observed, that a manual of the history of the national dissensions might be composed out of the works of this popular author alone.

Breton, independently of his original writings, has had the

editorship of one of the periodicals of Madrid, and occasional engagements connected with others. He also had at one time an appointment in one of the offices of the government, which he seems to have lost in 1840, on his writing some satirical effusion on the change that had then taken place. Literature has been in every age a grievous exaction, for those who had to follow it as a profession, except under peculiar circumstances. He had only his genius to befriend him, and apparently had not even the virtue of prudence for a counsellor. Thus he has had often to submit to circumstances, which though harassing at the time, he had the wisdom to make subjects of merriment afterwards, to the gain of his literary reputation.

In Spain there can scarcely yet be said to be formed a "reading public," notwithstanding the great number of good works that have been lately published, to supply the demand whenever it shall arise. The most evident and flattering of all the applauses that a literary man can there receive, are those awarded to dramatic successes, and of these, he has had the reward that was certainly due to him. In such a climate as that of Spain, and with such a people, theatrical amusements are more a matter of popular necessity than they are in a colder climate, with people of more domestic requirements; and yet even in England it may be a cause of surprise, considering the honour given to the author of a successful play, that more works of genius have not been produced for the stage. In both countries there is a complaint of the public requiring "novelties;" but the fact is, that in seeking novelties, they are only seeking excellence. When any really good work is presented them, they know how to appreciate it, and in seeking for others even of the same author, they are only expressing their sense of his merits.

In the prospectus of the proposed new edition of his works, he had the satisfaction of stating he had to republish more than sixty original dramas, that had met with a successful reception from the audiences of Madrid. He has besides these produced several that have not been successful, and has translated from the French a great number of others. These have been principally tragedies, and he has adapted them for the Spanish stage, rather than translated them, showing a talent, it has been observed by Del Rio, in so doing equivalent to making them to be counted in the number of his original works. Del Rio cites as a particular example, the translation from Delavigne's Tragedy of 'The Sons of Edward.' Breton's talent is evidently pre-eminent for comedy; but he has written several tragedies also, of which one, the 'Merope,' brought forward in 1835, was received with much favour.

This work, as it has been more than once already intimated, is intended mainly to give an account of the lyrical poetry of Spain as flourishing at present; and, therefore, it would be entering on subjects foreign to our purpose, to inquire at large into the merits of any specific dramatic performances. The Spanish drama may, no doubt, be worthy of especial study, but I confess that I have not felt it deserving of the extravagant praises which some writers have bestowed on it. It would surely be much happier for the people of every country to seek their greatest enjoyments in those of a domestic nature, rather than in those miscellaneous congregations where the quieter virtues can have little exercise. But as human nature is constituted, and public amusements cannot be avoided, it is the duty of every friend of the popular interests to support their being given on the foundation of good taste and moral principles. Though Breton's works do not appear free from all blame in this respect, and though sometimes his witticisms may be observed scarcely fitting even for the stage, yet they show, on the whole, compared with the dramatic productions of other countries, at least equal refinement, as they certainly do more inventive talent than we can point out elsewhere in our age.

Larra, the most discriminating critic of Spain, has observed of Breton, "that in nothing does his peculiar poetical talent shine more than in the simplicity of his plans. In all his comedies it is known that he makes a study and show of forming a plot extremely simple,—little or no action, little or no artifice. This is conceded to talent only, and to superior talent. A comedy, full of incidents, which any one invents, is easy to be passed off on a public always captivated by what interests and excites curiosity. Breton despises these trivial resources, and sustains and carries to a happy conclusion, amid the continual laughter of the audience, and from applause to applause, a comedy based principally on the depicting of some comic characters, in the liveliness and quickness of repartee, in the pureness, flow and harmony of his easy versification. In these gifts he has no rival, though he may have them in regard to intention, profoundness or philosophy."

Ferrer del Rio says of him, "that he has cultivated a style so much his own, that at the first few verses of one of his works, the spectators cry out his name from all parts. Originality is thus one of the qualities that recommend him. He tyrannizes over the public, obliging them to cast away ill-humour, and laugh against their will from the time the curtain rises till the representation ends, and this the same whether in the comedies they applaud, or those they disapprove. He is consequently mirthful and witty in the extreme, and no one can dispute the palm with him under this consideration. None of his scenes fatigue from weariness; none of his verses fail of fullness and harmony; they do not appear made one after another, but at one blow, and as by enchantment. Thus all hail him as a perfect versifier and easy colloquist. Infinite are the matters he has introduced in his comedies, multiplied the characters sketched by his pen, innumerable the situations imagined, and undoubtedly there is due to him the well-founded ascription of a fertile genius. Originality, wit, easy dialogue, sonorous versification, an inexhaustible vein, would not be sufficient to form a good comic writer of manners without the criterion of observation, fit for filling up his pictures with exactness. This criterion also he possesses in a high degree."

High as is this encomium, the writer says of him further, that if it were decreed by Providence that a new race of barbarians should overrun Spain, destroying libraries and other depositaries of human knowledge, yet the name of Breton de los Herreros would survive the disaster, and some vestige of his comedies would remain. "Histories, books of learning, works of legislation, science, philosophy and politics are, no doubt, more profound than his comedies, though from their peculiar nature not so popular. Thus what we have said is to be understood as a means of distinguishing between writings which, that they may not perish in the course of ages, require studious men to adopt them for a test, and learned men to illustrate them by their commentaries, and those compositions that, to succeed in obtaining the honours of immortality, require only a people to recite and transmit them verbally from father to son. The name of Breton may become traditional in Spain, that of other celebrated writers will belong to history."

Breton has been elected a member of the Royal Spanish Academy, and certainly one so highly gifted as he is in his department, is well deserving of every literary honour. The times are gone by when a writer of comedies could be all in all with the public as their favourite author; but probably there is no other existing in Spain who enjoys so much popular regard. As such, notwithstanding the inferior merit of his lyrical and miscellaneous poetry, excepting his satirical writings, it would have been a blameworthy omission to have left his name out of the list of the modern poets of Spain. It was, however, for this reason more advisable to make the selections from those satirical writings; though independently of this consideration, it would have been also desirable, in a work attempting to give a general view of modern Spanish poetry, that so essential and popular a branch of it should not be left unnoticed.

For the poems under this head, Breton has only given the general term "Satirical Letrillias," so that with those translated his numbering only could be adopted for reference. The Letrillia, it may be proper to observe, is what our musical writers call Motetts or small pieces, having generally some well-known proverbial saying for the close of each verse.

MANUEL BRETON DE LOS HERREROS.

SATIRICAL LETRILLIAS.—III.

Such is, dear girl, my tenderness,
  Naught can its equal be!
If thou a dowry didst possess
The charms to rival of thy face,
  I would marry thee.

Thou wert my bliss, my star, my all!
  So kind and fair to see;
And me thy consort to instal,
At once for witness Heaven I call,
  I would marry thee.

Thou dost adore me? yes, and I,
  Thy love so raptures me,
If thou wouldst not so anxious try
To know my pay, and what I buy,
  I would marry thee.

If thou wert not so always coy,
   Ne'er listening to my plea,
But when I, fool! my cash employ
To bring thee sweets, or some fine toy,
   I would marry thee.

If thou must not instructions wait,
   As may mamma agree,
To write or speak to me, or state
When thou wilt meet me at the gate,
   I would marry thee.

If 't were not when to dine, the most
   Thy meagre soup bouillie
Thou givest, as many airs thou show'st,
As Roderic at the hanging-post,
   I would marry thee.

If for my punishment instead
   Of ease and quiet, we
Might not three hungry brothers dread,
And mother too, to keep when wed,
   I would marry thee.

If 't were not when these plagues combine
   With thy tears flowing free,
The virtues of a heavenly sign
I see must solace me, not thine,
   I would marry thee.

Go, get another in thy chain,
    And Heaven for you decree
A thousand joys, for me 't is vain;
I know thee cheat, and tell thee plain,
    I will not marry thee.

SATIRICAL LETRILLIAS.—IV.

Whene'er Don Juan has a feast at home,
I am forgotten as if at Rome;
But he will for funerals me invite,
To kill me with the annoyance quite:
        Well, so be it!

Celeste, with thousand coy excuses,
Will sing the song that set she chooses,
And all about that her environ,
Though like an owl, call her a Siren:
        Well, so be it!

A hundred bees, without reposing,
Work their sweet combs, with skill enclosing;
Alas! for an idle drone they strive,
Who soon will come to devour the hive:
        Well, so be it!

Man to his like moves furious war,
As if were not too numerous far
Alone the medical squadrons straight
The world itself to depopulate!
          Well, so be it!

There are of usurers heaps in Spain,
Of catchpoles, hucksterers, heaps again,
And of vintners too, yet people still
Are talking of robbers on the hill:
          Well, so be it!

In vain may the poor, O Conde! try
Thy door, for the dog makes sole reply;
And yet to spend thou hast extollers,
Over a ball two thousand dollars:
          Well, so be it!

Enough today, my pen, this preaching;
A better time we wait for teaching:
If vices in vain I try to brand,
And find I only write upon sand,
          Well, so be it!

SATIRICAL LETRILLIAS.—VII.

O! what a blockhead is Don Andres,
   So spending his gold without measure,
Who ruins, perhaps, to be a Marquess,
   His house by the waste of his treasure!
A cross on his breast to wear so prim,
Much be the good it will do to him!

Louis is passing the whole long night,
   In the dance, what a fancy to take!
So foolish too, when he easier might
   On his warm soft bed his comfort make;
To stretch as he pleased each weary limb:
Much be the good it will do to him!

O, how short-sighted is Avarice!
   Cenon exposes himself to shame,
For the few pounds more he gains amiss,
   To lose his office and his good name;
For a paltry bribe his fame to dim,
Much be the good it will do to him.

And Clara! what of thee shall I say?
   When slowly along I see thee go,
As if quite lame on the public way,
   And on thy long broad foot bestow

A short narrow shoe for us to see?
Much be the good it will do to thee!

Can it be possibly true, Jerome,
   Though yearly he sees his rents decrease,
When his fat steward shall bring him home
   His bills, will sign them as he may please?
Without any search to scarcely skim?
Much be the good it will do to him!

Fabio wedded with Jane, when above
   A sixpence they neither had, but then
"He loved her so!" Long life to that love,
   Bravo! tomorrow if he seem fain
To hang himself with vexation grim,
Much be the good it will do to him.

Wouldst thou engage with the bulls in fight,
   My friend! thy wish to be gratified,
When to the best champion known will light
   Some luckless thrust give through the right side?
To try thy skill thou art surely free:
Much be the good it will do to thee!

Martin goes a poor rabbit to chase,
   When he could buy for a trifle one
Fully as good in the market-place;
   And he gets fever-struck by the sun!

Well, at the least he has had his whim:
Much be the good it will do to him!

If when such a thing he least expects,
   His house should tumble upon his head,
Because a doubloon Anton neglects
   To give for mending the roof instead,
The hole some rat had made in the rim,
Much be the good it will do to him!

If should some crusty reader exclaim
   Over these lines,—What a wretched style!
What a bad taste to make it his aim!
   My pen more gracefully could the while
Have made the verse go easy and trim,
Much be the good it will do to him!

X.

JOSÈ MARIA HEREDIA.

THE people of Cuba have good cause to be proud of a poet born in their island, whose genius seems always to have found its highest inspiration in expatiating on the charms of the place of his birth.

Heredia was born the 31st December, 1803, at Santiago de Cuba, in which city his family had taken refuge when driven away by the revolution from the island of Santo Domingo, where they had been previously settled. His father, whose profession was that of the law, was shortly afterwards appointed a Judge in Mexico, where he accordingly went with his family, taking his son there for his education under his special superintendence. This duty he had the privilege allowed him to accomplish, when he died in 1820, leaving a reputation for ability and uprightness so eminent as to prove highly advantageous to his son in his subsequent necessities. On his father's death, Heredia returned with his mother and three sisters to Cuba, where he had an uncle and other relations residing, and there he engaged in a course of study for the profession of the law, at the termination of which he was, in 1823, admitted an Advocate in the Supreme Court of the island. From his earliest years he had always shown himself possessed of a very studious disposition, and some of his poems seem to have been written when only eighteen years of age.

In the pursuit of the profession he had adopted, with his talent and energy, Heredia might have hoped soon to acquire a very honourable position; but unfortunately for his future comfort in life, he had imbibed too strongly the principles then prevailing to consider the domination of Spain as an evil which ought to be removed. It is stated, that there was a conspiracy even then formed to declare the independence of the island, in which he was implicated; and that on his being denounced to the government in consequence, he was obliged to fly from the island. Proceedings under this charge were notwithstanding instituted against him, under which he was formally declared banished. He thereupon went, in November 1823, to New York, where he passed the following three years, appearing, from the accounts that reached his friends, to have lived there during that time in great privations. These, and the variableness of the climate, operating severely on his constitution, as a native of the tropics, were no doubt the causes of his becoming a victim to that fatal disease which terminated his existence a few years afterwards.

In New York he acquired soon an accurate knowledge of the English language, which enabled him also to become familiarly acquainted with English literature. Of this he showed no inconsiderable tokens, in a volume of poems which he published there in 1825, having included among them several translations from the English, though he has not acknowledged them generally as such. He continued the same neglect in the edition of his works published subsequently in Mexico in 1832, which was a much superior edition to the former, being more than doubled in regard to its contents, and having the poems formerly published now much corrected and improved.

Not finding his residence in New York offering him any hopes of advancement in life, and despairing of being able to return to his family in Cuba, he determined to go thence to Mexico and seek the assistance of his father's friends in that city. He accordingly went there in 1826, and had scarcely arrived when he was at once appointed to a situation in the office of the Secretary of State. From this minor post he was soon afterwards promoted to discharge various important offices in the provinces, and finally to be named one of the Judges of the Supreme Court of Mexico and a Senator of the Republic. It was while holding one of those appointments as a local judge at Toluca that he published there the second edition of his works just mentioned.

After the death of Ferdinand VII., in 1833, the Regent, Queen Christina, wisely accorded a general amnesty to all expatriated Spaniards, when Heredia, notwithstanding the favourable position he held in Mexico, where also he had married in 1827, wished to take advantage of it to return to his family. On making application, however, for permission to do so, he was refused it by the Captain-General of Cuba, and all he could obtain was permission to go there for two months to visit his aged mother and other relatives, subject to the observation of the police. He went there accordingly in 1836, when, by a singular coincidence, he joined his family again on the same day of the month that thirteen years before he had parted from them.

On his arrival in Cuba, he was subjected to some of those petty annoyances which military governments too often impose on people under their sway. A friend of his who had gone to meet him, found him, notwithstanding his rank in the Mexican republic, or his reputation as a literary character, or his evident state of ill-health, seated on a bench in the court of the government office, to wait his turn at the pleasure of the official, who thought he was showing his dignity by exposing to unnecessary delay those whom he had to note under his inspection. Heredia was so altered that his friend could scarcely recognize him, and his relatives soon had to become apprehensive that his health was seriously endangered. He had given the most solemn assurance to the authorities that he would not in any way during his visit interfere in the public questions of the day, and he fulfilled his promise. If he really had entered in his youth into any plot against the government, the most dangerous conspirator in it could scarcely have been a young man of nineteen, who seems to have been the principal sufferer. But in any case, he had by time and reflection become very altered in sentiment, and his failing strength would not admit of any extraordinary exertion, even if he had remained the same enthusiast for political liberty as he was in his youth. He would have wished to stay the remainder of his life with his family, but it was his duty to return to Mexico after the expiration of the period allowed him, and there he died of consumption on his return, the 6th May, 1839. After his death, his widow and her children came to Cuba, where she died the 16th June, 1844, leaving a son and two daughters in the kindly charge of his relatives.

The Toluca edition of Heredia's poems in two volumes, 1832, does great credit to the Mexican press, being one of the best printed Spanish works to be found. But it is extremely scarce, and therefore deserves a more detailed account of it than might be requisite with works better known. In addition to those contained in the first edition, which is yet comparatively frequently to be met with, it contains his philosophic and patriotic poems, some of which are very spirited, and one, the 'Hymn of the Banished,' an extremely fine one. The copies of the work sent to Havana had these patriotic poems taken out, as otherwise they would have been seized by the authorities; so that most of the copies of the work existing are deficient with regard to them. In the place of the odes thus taken out, another poem, 'On Immortality,' was inserted, which, however, is principally taken from the Seventh Book of Young's Night Thoughts, though not so stated. The other principal poems, in respect of length, are, 'On the Worth of Women,' and 'the Pleasures of Melancholy.' Of another very fine ode, 'To Niagara,' a very excellent translation into English blank verse has appeared in the United States Review.

In the preface to the second edition, he states that he had been induced to undertake it, upon finding that several of the poems in the first had been reprinted in Paris, London, Hamburg and Philadelphia, and had been received with much favour in his own country, where the celebrated Lista had pronounced him "a great poet." There can be no doubt that other editions would have met with very favourable reception, had it not been for the circumstance of his being considered an author obnoxious to the Spanish government. As it is, the Creoles of Cuba have manuscript copies of his poems circulating amongst themselves, generally faulty as dependent on the taste of the individuals who had copied them. The effect of this is apparent in the only edition I am aware of, that has been published in Spain, that of Barcelona, in 1840, acknowledged to be taken from a manuscript copy, in which not only are some of his best compositions omitted, such as the 'Lines to his Horse,' and the poem entitled, 'The Season of the Northers,' but some others, for instance, the 'Ode to the Sun,' are given imperfectly. In return, it gives a poem on receiving the portrait of his mother, which had not appeared in the former editions, and which is not unworthy of being compared with Cowper's on the same subject, though treated differently.

In the prologue to this edition the editor observes, that "in all his productions is seen an excellency of heart and an imagination truly poetical, enabling us to assert with Lista that he is a great poet, and one of the best of our day." He adds, "the poems of Heredia have, in our judgement, the merit of a purity of language, which unfortunately begins to be unknown in Spain. They are of a kind equally apart from the monotony and servileness, ascribed perhaps with reason to the classicists, and from the extravagant aberration of those who affect to be called Romanticists, and believe they are so, because they despise all rules in their compositions, substituting words and phrases unknown to our better writers and poets."

The language of Heredia in his poems is by the concurrent opinion of all Spanish critics very pure, and even strangers can feel its simplicity and nature in connexion with the truly poetical thoughts they contain, free from all conceits or affectations. In his best original compositions, the sentiments expressed are generally of a tender and melancholy character, as might be expected from his history, of one banished from his country and family, while suffering from privations and ill-health, and at length sinking under a fatal disease. Like many other poets, he thus also writes most affectingly when dwelling on his own personal feelings, as if to verify the declaration of Shelley, that

> . . . most men
> Are cradled into poetry by wrong;
> They learn in suffering what they teach in song.

The 'Lines to his Horse' and 'The Season of the

Northers' bear intrinsic evidence of their origin, and also the Ode entitled 'Poesy.' This one bears a strong resemblance in its general tone to the 'Epistle to His Brother' and the poem of 'Sleep and Poetry' by Keats, whose character and fate also were in some degree the same as his. They have the same sentiment, as conscious of fame awaiting them, common to all poets, but peculiarly to those of more sensitive temperament, the 'non omnis moriar,' the hope of immortality,—

'Ελπίδ' ἔχω κλέος εὑ-
ρέσθαι κεν ὑψηλὸν πρόσω.

If the extravagant eulogiums bestowed on the merit of the Sonnet, as a form of verse, by some Italian writers, and echoed by Boileau and others, be at all deserved, Heredia's claims to superiority may be put forward very confidently, in respect of that to 'His Wife' in dedication of the second edition of his works. It contains all the conditions required for a perfect composition of this kind, in the poetical statement of the subject, the application of it, the beautiful simile given as a counterpart, and the strikingly appropriate idea with which it closes. Of this idea, the classical reader will at once perceive the elegance and force; but he cannot do so fully, unless he have also seen in the churches of seaport towns on the continent, as for instance, that of Santa Maria del Socorro, at Cadiz, the votive offerings of gratitude for deliverances from danger.

The 'Ode to Night' might have been considered worthy of equally unqualified commendation, were it not for the circumstance that twelve out of the nineteen stanzas it contains are almost a paraphrase from the Italian of Ippolito Pindemonte. At the time of making the translation hereafter given, I had not read that very pleasing writer, but have since found the source of the poem in his 'Poesie Campestri, Le quattro parti del giorno,' to which, therefore, justice requires the acknowledgement to be given. It is much to be regretted that Heredia did not distinguish his original compositions in all cases from imitations, as there is no statement with regard to this one, of its having been taken from another author. There are other instances of the same neglect, as in a close translation from Campbell of 'The Ode to the Rainbow,' equally unacknowledged. The interests of literature require that such acknowledgements should be uniformly made, that we should know gold from imitations, and give every one his right and place. As the same Italian poet remarked in his 'Opinioni Politiche,'

> Conosco anch'io negli ordini civili
> L'oro dal fango, ed anch'io veggio che altra
> Cosa è il nascere Inglese, ed altra Turco.

Heredia's original poems, many of them written to, or respecting his near relatives or other friends, betoken so much true poetic feeling, as well as flow of poetical ideas, that we cannot suppose the neglect of which we have complained to have been more than an oversight. He might even in some cases have lost remembrance of his obligations, and repeated from memory when he thought he was writing from inspiration. The latter part of his first volume is entirely taken up with "Imitations;" but those we have noticed above are in the second volume, without any distinction from the original poems.

He had, however, in early life so many privations to endure, and so many daily necessities for which to make a daily provision, that we may not be surprised at his inexactness in minor matters. In the preface to the second edition, he says, that "the revolutionary whirlwind had made him traverse over a vast course in a short time, and that with better or worse fortune he had been an advocate, a soldier, a traveller, a teacher of languages, a diplomatist, a journalist, a judge, a writer of history, and a poet at twenty-five years of age. All my writings," he observes, "must partake of the variableness of my lot. The new generation will enjoy serener days, and those who then dedicate themselves to the Muses will be much more happy." On his first going to Mexico, it is to be supposed that he had to enter on military duties in the unsettled state of the country, and that he had some diplomatic commissions entrusted to him by the government, of which, however, we have no other account. This, in fact, may be said to be the first biographical notice of him published, obtained from information given by his relatives, who, having been long separated from him, could not explain the particular references more fully.

As a writer of history, he had published, also in Mexico, a work in four volumes, 8vo. which was chiefly a compilation from Tytler, but with additions in Spanish and Mexican history, suited to the community, for whose benefit it was intended. In this respect, as in so many other parts of his career, the knowledge he had acquired of the English language was of essential assistance to him, while it was no less evident that his knowledge of English literature had improved his taste and strengthened his powers of mind also in his own compositions.

In private life Heredia appears to have been a most amiable character: courteous, generous, and possessed of the most lively sensibility, he made himself beloved by all who had to enter into communication with him. He was also remarkable for the exceeding great ingenuousness of his disposition, which, while it rendered him incapable of vanity in himself, made him at the same time as incapable of dwelling on the faults of others. Several of his poems show further a religious feeling, which no doubt enabled him to bear with becoming equanimity the various trials to which he had been subjected.

Those trials it seemed were appointed to attend him further, even if it had pleased the Almighty to prolong his existence. Shortly before his death, the Mexican legislature passed a law declaring that no one should hold any office under the republic who was not a natural born citizen; and thus he was, among others, deprived of the offices he had held with credit to himself and advantage to the state. If the measure were directed against him personally, it was of short operation, and political intrigues could not avail to deprive him of the consciousness of having fulfilled his duties honourably, or of the claim he had to leave on the remembrance of future ages.

JOSÈ MARIA HEREDIA.

SONNET.
DEDICATION OF THE SECOND EDITION OF HIS POEMS,
TO HIS WIFE.

WHEN yet was burning in my fervid veins
The fieriness of youth, with many a tear
Of grief, 't was mine of all my feelings drear,
  To pour in song the passion and the pains;
  And now to Thee I dedicate the strains,
My Wife! when Love, from youth's illusions freer,
In our pure hearts is glowing deep and clear,
  And calm serene for me the daylight gains.

Thus lost on raging seas, for aid implores
  Of Heaven the unhappy mariner, the mark
  Of tempests bearing on him wild and dark;
And on the altars, when are gain'd the shores,
Faithful to the Deity he adores,
  He consecrates the relics of his bark.

TO HIS HORSE.

Friend of my hours of melancholy gloom,
To soothe me now, come, scouring o'er the plain;
Bear me that I forgetfulness may gain,
    Lost in thy speed from my unhappy doom.

The fond illusions of my love are gone,
Fled never to return! and with them borne
Peace, happiness and hope: the veil is drawn,
    And the bared cheat shows frenzy's end alone.

O! how the memory of pleasures past
Now wearies me! horrible that soul's state,
Of flowers of hope, or freshness desolate!
    What then remains it? Bitterness o'ercast.

This south wind kills me: O! that I could rest
In sweet oblivion, temporary death!
Kind sleep might moderate my feverish breath,
    And my worn soul again with strength be blest.

My Horse, my friend, I do implore thee, fly!
Though with the effort break my frame so weak:
Grant for thy master's brows he thus may seek
    Sleep's balmy wings spread forth benignantly.

Let him from thee gain such refreshment kind;
Though much another day it caused me shame,
In my mad cruelty and frenzy's blame,
  My crimson'd heels, and thy torn flanks to find.

Pardon my fury! beats upon my eye
The sorrowing tear. Friend, when my shouts declare
Impatience, then the biting spur to spare
  Wait not, but toss thy mane, thy head, and fly.

THE SEASON OF THE NORTHERS.

The wearying summer's burning heat
Is now assuaged; for from the North
The winds from frost come shaken forth,
  'Midst clouds o'er Cuba rushing fleet,
  And free us from the fever's wrath.

Deep roars the sea, with breast swell'd high,
And beats the beach with lashing waves;
Zephyr his wings in freshness laves,
  And o'er the sun and shining sky,
  Veil-like, transparent vapours fly.

Hail, happy days! by you o'erthrown
We see the altar, which 'mong flowers
May rear'd to Death: attendant lowers,
   With palid face, vile Fever lone,
   And with sad brilliancy it shone.

Both saw the sons, with anxious brow,
Of milder realms approaching nigh,
Beneath this all-consuming sky:
   With their pale sceptres touch'd, they bow,
   And in the fatal grave are now.

But their reign o'er, on outspread wing,
To purify the poison'd air,
The north winds cold and moisture bear;
   Across our fields they sounding spring,
   And rest from August's rigours bring.

O'er Europe's gloomy climates wide,
Now from the North fierce sweeps the blast;
Verdure and life from earth are past:
   With snow man sees it whelm'd betide,
   And in closed dwellings must abide.

There all is death and grief! but here,
All life and joy! see, Phœbus smile
More sooth through lucid clouds, the while
   Our woods and plains new lustres cheer,
   And double spring inspires the year.

O, happy land! his tenderest care
Thee, favour'd! the Creator yields,
And kindest smile: ne'er from thy fields
   Again may fate me fiercely tear!
   O, let my last sun light me there!

How sweet it is to hear the rain,
My love! so softly falling thus
On the low roof that shelters us!
   And the winds whistling o'er the plain
   And bellowings of the distant main.

Fill high my cup with golden wine;
Let cares and griefs be driven away;
That proved by thee, my thirst to stay,
   Will, my adored! more precious shine,
   So touch'd by those sweet lips of thine.

By thee on easy seat reclined,
My lyre how happy will I string; .
My love and country's praise to sing;
   My blissful lot, thy face and mind,
   And love ineffable and kind!

POESY, AN ODE.

Soul of the universe, bright Poesy!
Thy spirit vivifies, and, like the blast
   That's burning in the desert swiftly free,
In its course all inflames where it has past.
   Happy the man who feels within his breast
   The fire celestial purely is possess'd!
For that to worth, to virtue elevates,
   And to his view makes smile the shadowy forms
Confused of joys to come, and future fates:
   Of cruel fortune 'gainst the gathering storms
It shields him, causing him to dwell among
   The beings of his own creation bright:
It arms him daringly with wings of light,
   And to the world invisible along
Bears him, to wondering mortals to unseal
The mysteries which the horrid depths reveal.

   High inspiration! O, what hours of joy,
Deep and ineffable, without alloy,
Hast thou benign conceded to my breast!
On summer nights, with brilliant hues impress'd,

'T is sweet to break with sounding prow the wave
Of the dark surging sea, which shows behind
   A lengthen'd streak of light the current gave.
'T is sweet to bound where lofty mountains wind,
   Or on thy steed to scour along the plain;
But sweeter to my fiery soul 't is far
   To feel myself whirl'd forward in the train
Of thy wild torrent, and as with a star
   The brow deck'd proudly, hear thy oracles
Divine; and to repeat them, as of old
   Greece listen'd mute to those from Delphic cells
The favour'd priestess of Apollo told;
While she with sacred horror would unfold
The words prophetic, trembling to refer
To the consuming god that frenzied her.

There is of life a spirit that pervades
The universe divine: 't is he who shades
All Nature's loveliest scenes with majesty,
And glory greater: beauty's self 't is he,
Who robes with radiant mantle, and endows
Her eye with language eloquent, while flows
Soft music from her voice; 't is he who lends
   To her the magic irresistible,
And fatal, which her smile and look attends,
   Making men mad and drunk beneath her spell.

If on the marble's sleeping forms he breathe,
To life they start the chisel's touch beneath :
In Phædra, Tancred, Zorayde he wrings
The heart within us deep; or softly brings
Love-fraught delight, as do their strains inspire
Anacreon, or Tibullus, or the lyre
Of our Melendez, sweetest languishings.
Or wrapt in thunder snatches us away
With Pindar, or Herrera, or thy lay,
Illustrious Quintana ! to the heights,
Where virtue, and where glory too invites.
By him compels us Tasso to admire
Clorinda; Homer fierce Achilles' ire ;
And Milton, elevated all beyond,
His direful angel, arm'd of diamond.

O'er all, though invisible, this spirit dwells ;
But from ethereal mansions he descends
To show himself to men, and thus portends
 His steps the night rain, and the thunder tells.
There have I seen him : or perhaps serene
 In the sun's beam, he wanders to o'erflow
 Heaven, earth and sea, in waves of golden glow.
On music's accent trembles he unseen ;
 And solitude he loves, he lists attent
 The waters' rush in headlong fury sent :

The wandering Arabs o'er their sands he leads,
　And through their agitated breasts inspires
A feeling undefined, but great to deeds
　Of desperate and wild liberty that fires.
With joy he sits upon the mountain heights,
　Or thence descends, to mirror in the deep,
In crystal fixedness, or animates
　The tempest with his cries along to sweep :
Or if its clear and sparkling veil extend
　The night, upon the lofty poop reclined,
　With ecstasy delights to inspire his mind,
Who raptured views the skies with ocean blend.

　Noble and lovely is the ardour felt
For glory ! for its laurel pants my heart ;
And I would fain, this world when I depart,
　Of my steps leave deep traces where I dwelt.
　This of thy favour, spirit most divine !
I well may hope, for that eternal lives
Thy glowing flame, and life eternal gives.
　Mortals, whom fate gave genius forth to shine,
Haste anxious to the sacred fount, where flows
Thy fiery inspiration ; but bestows
　The world unworthy guerdon on their pains :
While them a mortal covering enshrouds,
Obscure they wander through the listless crowds ;

Contempt and indigence their lot remains,
    Perchance ev'n impious mockery all their gains:
At length they die, and their souls take the road
Of the great fount of light whence first they flow'd;
    And then, in spite of envy, o'er their tomb
A sterile laurel buds, ay, buds and grows,
    And thus protects the ashes in the gloom,
'Neath its immortal shade; but vainly shows
    To teach men justice. Ages onward fleet
    The lamentable drama to repeat,
Without regret or shame. Homer! thou divine,
Milton sublime, unhappy Tasso thine,
    The fate to tell it. Genius yet the while
Faces misfortune undismay'd; his ears
    Dwell only on the applauses to beguile,
His songs will happy gain in future years;
    His glory, his misfortunes will excite
    Sweet sympathy; posterity will requite
Justice against their sires, who thus condemn
Him now to grief and misery, shame on them!
From his tomb he will reign; his cherish'd name
Will beauty with respect and sighs proclaim.
    On her eye gleams the bright and precious tear
His burning pages then will draw from her,
    Kind-hearted loveliness! he sees it near;
His heart beats, he is moved; and strong to incur

The cruelty and injustice, is consoled;
And waiting thus his triumph to obtain,
   Enjoying it, though but in death to hold,
Flies his Creator's bosom to regain.

O, sweet illusion! who has had the power
To save himself from thee, who was not born
   Than the cold marble, or the rough trunk lower?
With ardour I embrace, and wait thee lorn.
   Yet of my Muse perchance some happier strains
Will me survive, and my sepulchral stone
Will not be left to tell of me alone!
   Perhaps my name, which rancour now detains
   Proscribed, will yet resound o'er Cuba's plains,
On the swift trumpet of enduring fame!
Correggio, when he saw his canvas flame
   With life, "a painter," it was his to cry,
   "I also am!"—A poet too am I.

ODE TO NIGHT.

   Night reigns; in silence deep around
Dreams whirl through empty space;
   Clothing with her pure light the ground,
The moon shows bright her face:

Soft hour of peace; without a trace
   Of Man, where rise these heights uphurl'd,
   I sit abandon'd of the world.

How Nature's quietude august
Delights the feeling mind,
   That heeds her voice, and learns to trust
Its joys with her to find!
Sweet silence! here I rest reclined,
   With but the river's murmurings heard,
   Or leaves by gentle breezes stirr'd.

Now its repose on languid wings,
Its freshness Night supplies;
   To shaded heaven which faithful clings,
And blaze of daylight flies:
Unseen by that, mysterious lies
   On mount and plain, to please though sad,
   Still beauteous ev'n in horrors clad.

How is the ecstatic soul impress'd
With melancholy thought!
   The lovely picture here possess'd
Sublime with sadness fraught!
How more its music to be sought,
   And peace, than all that may entrance
   The echoes of the noisy dance.

Around the proud saloon reflect
Each face the mirrors there;
   With diamonds, pearls, and gold bedeck'd,
Light dance the gentle fair;
And with their witching grace and air,
   O'er thousand lovers holding sway,
   Their vows and plaudits bear away.

   Lovely is that! I one day too,
When childhood scarce above,
   Through balls and banquets would pursue
The object of my love.
And from the young beloved I strove,
   As magic treasure, to obtain
   A passing look, or smile to gain.

   But now by cares subdued, and bound
By languor and disease,
   Than gilded halls, these plains around
Me more the night hours please:
To the gay dance preferring these,
   The calm asylum they supply,
   To meditate beneath this sky.

   O! ever shine on me the stars,
In a clear heaven as now!
   And as my Maker that avers,
There let me turn my brow.

O! God of heaven, to Thee I bow!
And raise by night my humble strain,
The voice of my consuming pain.

Thee, also, friendly Moon! I hail;
I always loved thee dear:
Thou, Queen of heaven! me ne'er didst fail,
In fortunes fair or drear,
To guide, to counsel, and to cheer:
Thou know'st how oft, to enjoy thy ray,
I chide the blaze and heat of day.

Oft seated on the wide sea-shore,
Whose waves reflected thee,
To muse alone, thou smiling o'er,
I pass'd the night hours free;
And 'midst my clouded hopes to see
Thy face serene, I found relief,
In sweet complaint to pour my grief.

For throbs, alas! my breast with pain,
Consumption's wounds to bear;
And pales my cheek, as thou must wane
Beneath the morning's glare.
When I shall sink, grant this my prayer,
That thy light ne'er to shine defer,
On thy friend's humble sepulchre.

But, hark! what dulcet notes arise
The neighbouring woods among?
 Causing these tender thoughts and sighs
My lonely breast to throng.
Sweet Nightingale, it is thy song!
 I always loved thy wood-notes wild,
 Like me from sorrow ne'er beguiled.

Perish whoe'er for thy soft note
Seeks thee to oppress or take.
 Why rather not like me remote,
Thee follow through the brake,
Where these thick woods our shelter make?
 Fly free and happy round thy nest;
 Enslaved I wish none, none oppress'd.

Night, ancient goddess! Chaos thee
Produced before the sun;
 And the last sun 't is thine to see
When the world's course is run;
And the Lord wills his work undone!
 Hear me, while this life's breath is raised,
 By me thou shalt be loved and praised.

Before time was, in Chaos vast
Thou laid perhaps mightst view
 Thy coming beauties, as forecast
Thy destined glories grew:

Looking thy veil of shadows through
  With face obscured, to meditate
  Calm on thy future power and state.

Thou camest, O Queen! from Ocean's bars
At the Creator's voice,
  With sceptre raised, and crown'd with stars,
And mantle glittering choice;
And bade the silent world rejoice,
  To see through space thy brow severe
  Shine with the kind moon's silvery sphere.

How many high truths have I learn'd
Beneath thy solemn shade!
  What inspirations in me burn'd
'Mid the wood's silence laid!
In thee I saw sublime display'd
  The Almighty's power, and seized my lyre,
  And fervid dared to Heaven aspire.

Great Goddess, hail! in thy calm breast
Let me soothe every care!
  Thy peaceful balm may give me rest
From ills my heart that tear.
Sweet pitying friend! to whom repair
  Poets and mourners for repose,
  O, Night! in soft peace end my woes.

XI.

JOSÈ DE ESPRONCEDA.

IN the introductory part of this work, while acknowledging the merits of the earlier poets of Spain, it may be remembered that a claim was made in favour of the still superior excellences of their successors in the present day. If the reader, who has followed us so far through these notices, has not already come to the same conclusion, his assent may be confidently expected to the assertion, in consideration of the surpassingly poetical genius of the two writers who have now to come under his review.

In considering the merits of their earlier poets, the best critics of Spain have not been so blinded by national partiality as to be led into awarding them unqualified commendations. In the very able prologue to the 'Moro Esposito' of the Duke de Rivas, said to have been written by the celebrated Alcalà Galiano, we find an estimation of them which we can adopt, as correct in judgement as it is unexceptionable for an authority. He says, "Though the tenderness of Garcilasso, the warmth of Herrera, the fancy, at once lively and thoughtful, of Rioja, and, above all, those strong feelings of devotion which give to Fray Luis de Leon a character so original, even when he is most an imitator, are sources of great perfections, and most glorious crowns of the Spanish Parnassus, yet we are obliged to confess, that in the Spanish poets, lyric and pastoral, we see too great a sameness, that their stock of ideas and images is limited and common to them all, and that if varied and choice in expression, they are uniform in their arguments and plans, founding their merit more in the gala and pomp of language, in the floridness and sonorousness of verse, and in the ingenious dexterity of making variations on one theme, than in the vigour and originality of their thoughts, or in the strength and profoundness of the emotions which they felt, or which their works excite in the minds of their readers."

Entirely coinciding in the opinions thus expressed, we feel, on the other hand, with regard to the modern Spanish poets, that while they have fully maintained the grace and beauty that distinguished their predecessors in former ages, their genius has expanded over far wider fields, and embraced subjects of as varied and powerful interest as the contemporary poetry of any other country can present to delight or captivate. As instances in support of this opinion, we have, in particular, to refer to the comparatively few but exceedingly brilliant compositions of Espronceda, whose early loss, at only thirty-two years of age, the whole literary world has to deplore.

We have great cause to be thankful to Ferrer del Rio that we have any account at all of this very eminent lyric poet, though the one he has given is far from being so full as the admirers of his genius might have desired. From that account, we learn that it was in the spring of 1810, during the most momentous period of the war of independence, a colonel of cavalry, after some long and harassing marches, was obliged to halt at the small town of Almendralejo, in the province of

Estremadura, in the face of the enemy, on account of his wife, who had followed him through the campaigns, having there had a son born, the subject of this narrative. We have no other particulars of his earlier years, than that on the conclusion of the war his parents settled at Madrid, where he was placed at an early age under the tuition of Lista, a writer who enjoyed considerable reputation at the time as a poet, but whose chief merit consisted in his critical and elementary works. Under such a preceptor, his natural genius found a congenial course of tuition, and verse-making seems to have been a part of his usual studies. It was remarked, that though he was by no means inclined to steady application, yet, that by the force of his quick comprehension, he shone as prominently as others of greater industry, and when a mere boy produced verses which gave tokens of future eminence.

When only fourteen years of age he joined a society of youths who called themselves Numantines, and was elected one of their tribunes. In their meetings, no doubt, there was much intended treason debated, for which, whether deservedly or not, the government of the day thought proper to proceed against them at law, and Espronceda, with others, was sentenced to three months' imprisonment in the convent of Guadalajera, in which town his father then resided. There, in the solitude of his imprisonment, his active mind found employment in poetry, and he was bold enough to begin an epic poem on the subject of the national hero, Pelayo. Of this poem there are fragments given among his works, from which we may judge favourably of what it might have proved when completed, containing as it does many striking passages. The representation of Hunger, and the Dream of the King, Don Roderic, are bold conceptions, and if they were not the additions of after-years, were truly remarkable as the productions of any one at so early an age.

On his release from the convent he returned to Madrid, but feeling himself under restraint as subject to the observation of the police, and desirous also of visiting other countries, he shortly afterwards went to Gibraltar and thence to Lisbon. There he seems to have been subjected to great privations, which, however, did not prevent his being involved in romantic adventures, characteristic of one of his temperament, such as he subsequently described with all the warmth of poetic feeling. But the ministers of the king, now restored to absolute power by French intervention, could not allow Spanish emigrants to be congregated so near to Spain, and at their instance Espronceda and others were obliged to go from Lisbon to London. How he maintained himself, during these wanderings, we are not informed, but his relatives probably had the means to afford him sufficient for his pressing necessities, and the love of adventure would lead him, oftentimes willingly, into situations from which most others would have recoiled.

In London, we are informed, that he enjoyed the happiest period of his life, though not abounding in resources; passing his time between his studies and gaieties, which resulted in confirmed dissipation. He learned to read Shakespeare and Milton, as well as Byron, and considering his inclinations, his habits and his writings, we need not be surprised to find him supposed to have taken the last for his model. There he began the series of compositions which place him in the first rank of lyric poets, though we have to lament that they are tinctured with a spirit of such evil character. His 'Elegy to Spain,' dated London, 1829, is in the original written with peculiar sweetness of expression, which Del Rio finds in the style of the Prophet of the Lamentations, and which, though not so well suited for translation as most of his other poems, has been chosen as the effusion of the patriotic muse of Spain, no less worthy of note than others of more general application.

From London he passed over to Paris, and happening to be there during the three memorable days of July 1830, he took part in the fearful scenes which then took place with all the ardour of his character as well as of youth. He joined afterwards the small band of emigrants who crossed the Pyrenees in the hopeless attempt of subverting the despotic sway that then prevailed, resulting in the death of Don Joaquin de Pablo, whom his friends regarded as falling heroically, and to whose memory Espronceda has left a poem of great beauty. Returning to Paris, he entered himself in the rank of the bold spirits who volunteered to lend their aid in the regeneration of Poland, from which, and other similar schemes, he was rescued by the promulgation of the first amnesty, of which he took advantage immediately to return to Spain.

On his arrival in Madrid, he entered himself in the Royal Guard, where he soon won the goodwill and affections of his officers and comrades, and might have risen to distinction, but for an unfortunate though characteristic occurrence. He had written some verses on passing events connected with the service, which were recited at a banquet, and having been much applauded and passed from hand to hand, came to the knowledge of the ministry, who thereupon, notwithstanding the efforts of his colonel to the contrary, dismissed Espronceda from the corps, and banished him to the town of Cuellar. There he composed a work, which he called a novel, under the title of the 'Sancho of Saldania,' but which, though containing some good sketches and descriptions, is only worthy of notice as having been one of his compositions.

"On the dawning of liberty in Spain with the promulgation of the Estatuto," by Martinez de la Rosa, he came forward as a journalist, connected with the paper published as 'The Age.' His proud spirit could not submit to the censorship previously existing, but even now he had to feel its influence. The fourteenth number of his paper, the most violent of the time, was found to contain some articles which were forbidden by the censor, and as the time pressed, the editors did not know how to supply the deficiency. The ready genius of Espronceda suggested a scheme, which, after a little hesitation, was adopted: this was to publish the sheet in blank, with merely the headings, which had not been struck out of the manuscript by the censor. Accordingly, the usual sheet appeared with the titles only of the subjects it had originally to bear, namely—"The Amnesty;" "Domestic Policy;" "Letter from Don Miguel and Don Manuel Bravedeed in defence of their honour and patriotism;" "On the Cortes;" "Song on the Death of Don Joaquin de Pablo." The effect was startling, and perhaps more powerful than the forbidden articles would have proved. The people supplied the deficiencies according to their individual feelings, and the ingenuity of the device had its fullest success. As the result, the publication of the paper was forbidden, and the managers had to hide themselves for a time to escape further prosecution.

In the years 1835 and 1836, there were several serious commotions in Madrid in which he joined, erecting barricades in the principal square, and making violent harangues to the people. On both occasions the disturbances were soon put down by the military, and he had to hide himself in the provinces, until, in the year 1840, Espartero having put himself at the head of the liberal party, the public principles prevailed for which Espronceda had so exerted himself. He then came forth again from his retirement, and made himself conspicuous by appearing as an advocate in a case in which a paper named the 'Hurricane' had been denounced at law for a seditious article it contained. Espronceda's speech in defence, from some passages of it given by Del Rio, appears to have been very energetic, and as inflammatory as the article accused, but he was successful, and the proprietor of the paper was acquitted.

In the same year, 1840, he published the volume of poems on which his fame rests, as perhaps the first lyric poet that Spain has produced. Most of the contents had been previously given in the periodical publications of Madrid, but it was a great service to literature to have them collected. They contained the fragment of the epic poem, 'Pelayo,' and a short dramatic piece, entitled, 'The Student of Salamanca,' in which his own character is supposed to have been depicted; as well as the lyric odes and other poems. They are comparatively few in number, not exceeding fifteen altogether, but of such rare excellence as to make us regret that so gifted a writer was to be so soon cut off, depriving the literary world of the hopes of still further excellence they gave reason to expect. In the following year, 1841, he published his poem, 'The Devil World, El Diablo Mundo,' in four cantos, to which three others were afterwards added, found among his papers after his death. His friends had long feared that he was not destined to attain a prolonged period of life, but their fears were unhappily realized much sooner than they had imagined.

In December 1841, Espronceda was sent to the Hague as Secretary of Legation, but the coldness of the climate affecting too severely his enfeebled constitution, he was obliged, almost immediately, to return to Spain. He had meanwhile been elected Deputy to the Cortes for Almeria, and he attempted to take accordingly his share of public duties. But his health and strength had been undermined by the life of hazard, of privations and excesses he had undergone, and the journey to the Hague in the depth of winter seemed to give the final shock to his frame, from which it could not recover. On the 23rd of May, 1842, his friends and admirers were thrown into unexpected grief by hearing that he had died that morning, after what was termed a four days' illness. The immediate cause was said to have been some disorder affecting the throat, and his sufferings have been described by an intimate friend and schoolfellow, who was with him at the time, as very painful. The loss to Spain and the whole literary world was as great as it was irreparable; and so the people seemed to feel it, by the general expression of regret over his fate, such as it seldom falls to the lot of any one to excite.

The moralist might dilate on the evil courses which probably hastened his death, and all must lament that a man of such extraordinary genius should have sunk under them; but before we judge any one severely, we should be certain of being able to form a right judgement. The utmost remark, therefore, we permit ourselves to make, may be to consider his history as a lesson to all under similar circumstances of life, that if they will not take heed to a moral in others, they may become a warning themselves. Every man's character may be taken as a whole, in which his good and evil qualities are often so blended together as to make them inseparable. The excesses of youth are often "the flash and outbreak of a fiery mind," which shows itself in its true characters in other respects, though often with the alloy of lower passions to lead them to a fatal end. Thus Byron and Espronceda, two kindred geniuses in our days, have sunk prematurely into the grave, most unhappily, when new fields of glory seemed to be opened before them to retrieve the past errors of life, and make it in future as honourable as they had already rendered it renowned.

The genius of Espronceda was kindred to Byron's, of whom he has been accused of having been an imitator. But this seems to me unquestionably a mistake. During his residence in England he had certainly acquired a good knowledge of the English language and literature, much to his advantage; but he could scarcely have acquired such a knowledge of either as to put him in the position of an imitator. The utmost that can be alleged of him in this respect is, that the style of Byron's writing was so congenial to his own taste and talent, as to make him imbibe it intuitively, and so obtain a more decided character for his own than perhaps it would have otherwise attained.

It is certain that Spanish poetry never before presented such depth of thought and feeling, and such fulness and vigour of expression, as he gave to it; and it is apparent, in every page of his works, that he had studied in a higher school and become imbued with a brighter inspiration than he could have done on the Continent. But what ordinary imitators would have considered the characteristics of Byron as models to follow, he had the good sense entirely to discard. He has none of the egotism and affectation which distinguish that school; and if he indulged in some of its propensities, it is clear that they were the natural results of the circumstances in which he was placed, and not the wilful perversions of misdirected abilities. His poem to Harifa is written with an earnestness of feeling that must be felt, even through the haze of translation, giving tokens of its origin too distinct to admit any supposition of its being a suggestion from any other source than his own experience of life. Neither in this poem nor in any other of his works is there any of those mysterious suggestions of dark histories, or of those morbid denunciations of imaginary wrongs which abound in the productions of the Byronian school. His complaints are the evident effusions of a mind maddened at finding itself in a state unworthy of its powers, and thus, instead of venting his rage on others, he turned it against his own misdeeds, in giving way to excesses that he scorned, and which he felt degraded him. But even in his aspirations for higher thoughts, he had the same leaven of earth to keep him from attaining them. He had not learned the lessons which Jovellanos inculcated in the Epistle to Bermudez, to seek wisdom where only it ought to be sought; as he might have done even from the heathen poet, that the hidden things of God could not be found out, though he were to traverse over all space in search of them.

> Ἀλλ' οὐ γὰρ ἂν τὰ θεῖα, κρύπτοντος Θεοῦ,
> Μάθεις ἂν, οὐδ' εἰ πάντ' ἐπεξέλθοις σκότων.

In somewhat of the same strain with these lines is the second canto of his poem, the 'Diablo Mundo,' addressed to Theresa, which, however, has no connexion with the rest of the poem to which it is attached. The verses 'To a Star,' contain also poetical thoughts no less exquisite, though perhaps not of so decided a character; and they are all valuable at least in this, that instead of gilding over vices and follies, they show the confession of one so highly gifted by nature, that the indulgences of sensual gratifications are in reality only sources of unhappiness.

Two other of his poems, 'The Mendicant' and 'The Executioner,' are no less distinguishable for the power of thought and expression they display; but they also unfortunately indicate such objectionable tendencies, as to make us regret that his extraordinary talents had not been directed to nobler subjects. Not so the two poems selected for translation,

'The Song of the Pirate,' and that of the 'Criminal Condemned to Die,' in addition to those previously mentioned. Of these, the latter is one of such peculiarly energetic character, as to need no comment. The other is one of the most favourite poems known in Spain, and having been set to music, is therefore heard repeated more frequently. It has been said to have been taken from the French, but I believe erroneously. It bears strongly the impress of Espronceda's genius; and if the poem intended be either of those by Floran or Victor Hugo, any one who will take the trouble of comparing them will observe that they are essentially different, as each also is from the song of Lord Byron's 'Corsair.'

At the first view of it, the 'Diablo Mundo' appears to be an imitation of 'Don Juan;' but it would be as unjust to declare it so, as to say the latter had been copied from the various Italian poems written in the same style. Espronceda might have had the idea suggested by reading Lord Byron's poem, or Goëthe's 'Faust,' or both, but he has carried it much higher, and given the outlines of a nobler conception than either. He begins by supposing that, absorbed in meditation, during the silence of the night, he hears an extraordinary noise, which calls back his feelings and arouses them. That confused noise, with sublime music and solemn sound, are all the passions of the world, all the interests found in life,—the affections and hatreds, love, glory, wealth, the vices and the virtues; they are, in fine, the complaint of the whole universe that comes like a revolving whirlwind, and displays before the fancy a thousand allegorical monsters, traced with inimitable facility and astonishing vigour.

The visions pass away, the noise goes gradually off, losing itself in the distance, until it ceases, where begins the introduction of the poem. The first canto is the exposition of the great drama proposed to be developed.

A man bowed down with age and embittered by sorrowful and useless experience, shuts in despair a book he was reading, and mournfully convinced of the barrenness of learning, falls asleep. Death then presents itself, and intones a hymn inviting him to the peace of the grave. With pleasure he feels his benumbed limbs growing stiff with cold, and is enjoying himself in the enervation of his spirit, when Immortality suddenly rises up before him and sings another hymn in opposition to that of Death, and like that also offering herself to the man about to die.

The election is immediate; he chooses Immortality, and is re-endowed with youth. The song of this deity, however, does not lead to the immortality of the spirit, but of the material part of man, and it is that he receives. The image of death is invested with melancholy beauty; it is soft and gentle; that which is desired when, free from prejudices, we feel the heart worn and the soul discontented. The immortality that rises over the pale front of death, effaces it with a magnificent lustre. "It is impossible," says Ros de Olano, who has written the prologue to this beautiful poem, "to approach, by any words of ours whatever, to the luxuriousness of thought, of expression, and of knowledge displayed in this sublime description, the most happy perhaps yet presented in the Spanish language." Grand, extended and immense is the field which the poet has displayed to trace out a course for his hero, and the variety of tones he employs are like the face of the world, over which he has to range. As the character is developed, the hero, with the body of a man and the soul of a child, is placed in situations equally original and interesting, and the whole scheme is one which gave full scope to the writer for an unlimited work, even if he had been permitted to live to the utmost period of human existence.

Del Rio states, that Espronceda was in his public discourses an ineffective speaker, and ascribes it to the physical weakness of his frame; he describes him as having been distinguished for sarcasms, and only at intervals powerful in declamation. "In conversation he made an affectation of laughing at the restraints and virtues which are necessary for the order of society, and yet in private life no one was more remarkable for kindness and generosity. When the cholera was raging in Madrid, he was one of the most active in disregarding its attacks, and in attending to the wants of those near him who were suffering from it." "All who knew him loved him, and even to his faults he knew how to give a certain impression of greatness." Del Rio proceeds to describe him as having been graceful in his bearing, endowed with manly beauty, and his countenance marked with a melancholy cast that rendered it more interesting. He concludes by observing, that notwithstanding the years that have passed since his friends had to lament his loss, a garland of everlastings never fails to be found renewed over his grave.

In 1848 Baudry published another edition of Espronceda's works, at Paris, but, with the exception of the fifth and sixth cantos of the 'Diablo Mundo,' there is no additional poem given, though Del Rio points out six other pieces published in different periodicals. This omission is much to be regretted, as undoubtedly every line that proceeded from his pen was worthy of being gathered together as a rare treasure. It is to be hoped that some admirer of his genius may soon collect those scattered relics, and give them in an edition worthy of their character in Spanish literature. Another Life of him also would be most desirable, as in the Paris edition there is only repeated the account given by Ferrer del Rio, which, though ably written as a sketch, is still on the same scale with a number of other writers in the same work of far inferior merits, and utterly unworthy of so great a genius as Espronceda. Spanish versification under his influence has become "revolutionized." He has extended the powers apparently even of the language itself, and by the force of his style as well as by the varied character of his poems, has certainly shown its capabilities more decidedly than any poet who preceded him.

JOSÈ DE ESPRONCEDA.

TO SPAIN, AN ELEGY.

LONDON, 1829.

How solitary is the nation now
    That peopled countries vast a former day!
That all beneath her sovereignty to bow,
    From East to West extended once her sway!

Tears now profuse to shed, unhappy one,
    Queen of the world! 'tis thine; and from thy face,
Enchanting yet in sorrow, there is none
    Its overwhelming traces to erase.

How fatally o'er thee has death pour'd forth
    Darkness and mourning, horrible and great!
And the stern despot in his madden'd wrath
    Exulted wildly o'er thy low estate.

Nothing or great or beautiful he spared,
    My country! the young warrior by him fell,
The veteran fell, and vile his war-axe glared,
    Pleased all its fury o'er thee to impel.

Ev'n the pure maiden fell beneath the rage
    Of the unpitying despot, as the rose
Condemn'd the summer's burning sun to engage
    Her bloom and beauty withering soon must close.

Come, O! ye inhabiters of the earth,
    And contemplate my misery! can there,
Tell me, be any found of mortal birth
    Bearing the sorrows I am doom'd to bear?

I wretched, banish'd from my native land,
    Behold, far from the country I adore,
Her former glories lost and high command,
    And only left her sufferings to deplore.

Her children have been fatally betray'd
    By treacherous brethren, and a tyrant's power;
And these her lovely fertile plains have made
    Fields o'er which lamentations only lower.

Her arms extended wide unhappy Spain,
    Her sons imploring in her deep distress:
Her sons they were, but her command was vain,
    Unheard the traitor madness to repress.

Whate'er could then avail thee, tower or wall,
    My country! still amid thy woes adored?
Where were the heroes that could once appal
    The fiercest foe? where thy unconquer'd sword?

Alas! now on thy children's humbled brow
    Deeply is shame engraved, and on their eyes,
Cast down and sorrowfully beating now,
    The tears alone of grief and mourning rise.

Once was a time for Spain, when she possess'd
    A hundred heroes in her hour of pride;
And trembling nations saw her manifest
    Her power and beauty, dazzling by their side.

As lofty shows itself in Lebanon
    The cedar, so her brow she raised on high;
And fell her voice the nations round upon,
    As terrifies a girl the thunders nigh.

But as a stone now in the desert's wild
    Thou liest abandon'd, and an unknown way
Through strangers' lands, uncertain where, exiled
    The patriot's doom'd unfortunate to stray.

Her ancient pomp and power are cover'd o'er
    With sand and weeds contemptuous; and the foe,
That trembled at her puissance before,
    Now mocks exulting and enjoys her woe.

Maidens! your flowing locks dishevell'd tear,
  To give them to the wandering winds; and bring
Your harps in mournful company to share
  With me the sorrowful laments I sing.

Thus banish'd from our homes afar away
  Still let us weep our miseries. O! Spain,
Who shall have power thy torments to allay?
  Who shall have power to dry thy tears again!

THE CONDEMNED TO DIE.

His form upon the ground reclined,
  With bitter anguish inward drawn,
Full of the coming day his mind,
  That soon will sadly dawn,
The culprit waits, in silence laid,
  The fatal moments hastening now,
In which his last sun's light display'd
  Will shine upon his brow.

O'er crucifix and altar there,
  The chapel cell in mourning hung,
From the dim candle's yellow glare
  A funeral light is flung;

And by the wretched culprit's side,
    His face with hood half cover'd o'er,
The friar, with trembling voice to guide,
    Is heard his prayers implore.

His brow then raises he again,
    And slowly lifts to heaven his eyes;
Perhaps a prayer for mercy fain
    May in his grief arise.
A tear flows: whence had that release?
    Was it from bitterness or fear?
Perhaps his sorrows to increase
    Some thought to memory dear?

So young! and life, that he had dream'd
    Was full of golden days to glide,
Is pass'd, when childhood's tears it seem'd
    As scarcely yet were dried.
Then on him of his childhood burst
    The thought, and of his mother's woe,
That he whom she so fondly nursed
    Was doom'd that death to know.

And while that hopelessly he sees
    His course already death arrest,
He feels his life's best energies
    Beat strongly in his breast;

And sees that friar, who calmly now
    Is laid, with sleep no more to strive,
With age so feebly doom'd to bow,
    Tomorrow will survive.

But hark! what noise the silence breaks
    This hour unseasonably by?
Some one a gay guitar awakes
    And mirthful songs reply;
And shouts are raised, and sounds are heard
    Of bottles rattling, and perchance
Others, remember'd well, concurr'd
    Of lovers in the dance.
And then he hears funereal roll,
    Between each pause in accents high,
"Your alms, for prayers to rest the soul
    Of him condemn'd to die."

And so combined the drunkard's shout,
    The toast, the strifes, and fancies wild
Of all that Bacchanalian rout,
    With wanton's songs defiled,
And bursts of idle laughter, reach
    Distinct into the gloomy cell,
And seem far off ejected each
    The very sounds of hell.

And then he hears, funereal roll
    Between each pause, those accents high,
"Your alms, for prayers to rest the soul
    Of him condemn'd to die."

He cursed them all, as one by one
    The impious echos each express'd;
He cursed the mother as a son
    Who nursed him at her breast:
The whole world round alike he cursed,
    His evil destiny forlorn,
And the dark day and hour when first
    That wretched he was born.

II.

The moon serene illumes the skies,
And earth in deepest stillness lies;
No sound is heard, the watchdog's mute,
And ev'n the lover's plaintive lute.

Madrid enveloped lies in sleep;
    Repose o'er all its shade has cast,
And men of him no memory keep
    Who soon will breathe his last.

Or if perchance one thinks to wake
    At early dawn, no thoughts whate'er
Rise for the wretched being's sake,
    Who death is waiting there.
Unmoved by pity's kind control,
    Men bear around the funeral cry,
" Your alms, for prayers to rest the soul
    Of him condemn'd to die."

Sleeps in his bed the judge in peace;
    And sleeps and dreams of how his store,
The executioner, to increase;
    And pleased he counts it o'er.
Only the city's silence breaks,
    And destined place of death portrays,
The harden'd workman who awakes
    The scaffolding to raise.

III.

Confused and mad his heated mind,
With raving feverish dreams combined,
The culprit's soul exhaustion press'd,
His head sunk heavy on his breast.

And in his dreams he life and death
    Confounds, remembers, and forgets;
And fearful struggling every breath,
    And sigh he gives besets.

And in a world of darkness seems
    As now to stray; feels fear and cold,
And in his horrid madness deems
    The cord his neck infold:
And so much more, in desperate fight,
    In anguish to escape his lot,
He strives, with so much more the might
    He binds the fatal knot:
And voices hears, confused the whole,
    Of people round, and then that cry,
"Your alms, for prayers to rest the soul
    Of him condemn'd to die!"

Or fancies now that he is free;
    And breathes the fresh pure air, and hears
Her sigh of love, the maid whom he
    Had loved in happier years:
Beauteous and kind as e'er of old,
    Sweet flower of spring-time's gay resort,
As could for love the meads behold,
    Or gallant April court.

And joyful he to see her flies,
    And seeks to reach her, but in vain;
For as with anxious hands he tries
    His hoped-for bliss to gain,
The illusion suddenly to break,
    He finds the dream deceitful fled!
A cold stiff corpse the shape to take,
    And scaffold in its stead.
And hears the mournful funeral knoll,
    And hollow voice resounding nigh,
"Your alms, for prayers to rest the soul
    Of him condemn'd to die!"

THE SONG OF THE PIRATE.

The breeze fair aft, all sails on high,
    Ten guns on each side mounted seen,
She does not cut the sea, but fly,
    A swiftly sailing brigantine;
A pirate bark, the 'Dreaded' named,
For her surpassing boldness famed,
On every sea well known and shore,
From side to side their boundaries o'er.

The moon in streaks the waves illumes;
　　Hoarse groans the wind the rigging through;
In gentle motion raised assumes
　　The sea a silvery shade with blue;
While singing gaily on the poop,
The pirate Captain, in a group,
Sees Europe here, there Asia lies,
And Stamboul in the front arise.

Sail on, my swift one! nothing fear;
　　Nor calm, nor storm, nor foeman's force
Shall make thee yield in thy career,
　　Or turn thee from thy course.
Despite the English cruisers fleet
　　We have full twenty prizes made;
And see their flags beneath my feet
　　A hundred nations laid.
My treasure is my gallant bark,
　　My only god is liberty;
My law is might, the wind my mark,
　　My country is the sea.

There blindly kings fierce wars maintain,
　　For palms of land, when here I hold
As mine, whose power no laws restrain,
　　Whate'er the seas infold.

Nor is there shore around whate'er,
    Or banner proud, but of my might
Is taught the valorous proofs to bear,
    And made to feel my right.
My treasure is my gallant bark,
    My only god is liberty;
My law is might, the wind my mark,
    My country is the sea.

Look when a ship our signals ring,
    Full sail to fly how quick she's veer'd!
For of the sea I am the king,
    My fury's to be fear'd;
But equally with all I share
    Whate'er the wealth we take supplies;
I only seek the matchless fair
    My portion of the prize.
My treasure is my gallant bark,
    My only god is liberty;
My law is might, the wind my mark,
    My country is the sea.

I am condemn'd to die! I laugh;
    For, if my fates are kindly sped,
My doomer from his own ship's staff
    Perhaps I'll hang instead.

And if I fall, why what is life?
   For lost I gave it then as due,
When from slavery's yoke in strife
   A rover I withdrew.
My treasure is my gallant bark,
   My only god is liberty;
My law is might, the wind my mark,
   My country is the sea.

My music is the north wind's roar,
   The noise when round the cable runs,
The bellowings of the Black Sea's shore,
   And rolling of my guns.
And as the thunders loudly sound,
   And furious as the tempests rave,
I calmly rest in sleep profound,
   So rock'd upon the wave.
My treasure is my gallant bark,
   My only god is liberty;
My law is might, the wind my mark,
   My country is the sea.

TO HARIFA, IN AN ORGY.

Thy hand, Harifa! bring it me;
  Come near, and place it on my brow;
As on some lava's boiling sea
  I feel my head is burning now.
Come, bring with mine thy lips to meet,
  Though they but madden me astray,
Where yet I find the kisses beat,
  There left thy loves of yesterday.

What is virtue, what is joy,
  Or love, or purity, or truth?
The false illusions of a boy,
  The cherish'd flatteries of my youth.
Then bring me wine; there let me try
  Remembrance drown'd to hold repress'd,
Without a pang from life to fly;
  In frenzy death may give me rest.

O'erspreads my face a burning flood,
  And red and glaring wildly start
My eyes forth out in heated blood,
  And forth leaps restlessly my heart.

Woman! I hate thee; fly thee—go:
   I feel thy hands my hands infold,
And feel them freezing, cold as snow,
   As snow thy kisses are as cold.

Ever the same, try, tempters weak!
   Other endearments to enthral;
Another world, new pleasures seek,
   For such your joys I curse them all.
Your kisses are a lie; a cheat
   Is all the tenderness you feign;
Your beauty ugly in deceit,
   The enjoyment suffering and pain.

I wish for love, ethereal, high,
   For some diviner joy my lot;
For such my heart will imaged sigh,
   For such as in the world is not.
And 't is that meteor light afar,
   The phantom that deceived my mind,
The treacherous guide, the vapour star,
   That leads me wandering and blind.

Why is my soul for pleasure dead,
   And yet alive to grief and care?
Why doom'd in listless stupor laid
   This arid loathing still to bear?

Why this consuming wild desire,
    This restless passion vague and strange?
That well I know I rave, 't is fire,
    Yet plunge in its deceitful range.

Why do I dream of love and joy,
    That I am sure a lie will prove?
Why where fantastic charms decoy,
    Will thus my heart delirious move,
If soon it finds for meads and flowers,
    But arid wastes and tangled thorns,
And soon a loathing rage o'erpowers
    The mad or mournful love it scorns?

Flung as a rapid comet wide,
    On ardent fancy's wings I flew,
Where'er my wayward mind espied
    Or joys or triumphs to pursue.
I launch'd myself, in daring flight,
    Beyond the world through heavenward space,
And found but doubt, and all so bright
    That seem'd, illusive proved the chase.

Then on the earth I anxious sought
    For virtue, glory, love sublime;
And my worn spirit found there nought
    But fetid dust and loathsome slime.

Mid clouds with heavenly hues o'ercast
    Women of virgin lustre shone;
I saw, I touch'd them, and they pass'd,
    And smoke and ashes left alone.

I found the illusion fled; but rife,
    Unquench'd desires their longings crave;
I felt the real, I hated life,
    And peace believed but in the grave.
And yet I seek, and anxious seek,
    For pleasures still I ask and sigh,
And hear dread accents answering speak,
    "Unhappy one! despair, and die.

"Die: Life is torment, joy a cheat,
    Hope not for good on earth for thee,
But fruitless struggles look to meet
    In thy vain longings endlessly!
For so God punishes the soul
    That in its madness dares espy
The unfathom'd secrets of the scroll
    Of truth, denied to mortal eye!"

O! cease: no more I ask to know,
    No more to see: my soul oppress'd
Is humbly bow'd, and prostrate low,
    Now only asks, and longs for rest.

In me let feeling then lie dead,
   Since died my hopes of happiness,
Nor joys nor griefs be o'er me spread
   My soul returning to depress.

Pass, as in magic optic glass,
   And other youthful hearts deceive,
Bright images of glory! pass,
   That crowns of gold and laurel weave.
Pass, ye voluptuous fair ones, on!
   With dance and mirthful songs attuned,
Like vaporous visions, pass, begone!
   No more my heart to move or wound.
And let the dance, and festal din,
   O'er my revolted fancy reign,
And fled the night, see morn begin,
   Surprised in senseless stupor's chain.

Harifa, come! Like me this woe
   Thou too hast borne! Thou ne'er dost weep!
But, ah! how wretched 't is to know
   Feelings so bitter and so deep!
The same our sufferings and care;
   In vain thou hold'st thy tears apart;
Like me thou also hast to bear
   A wounded and an aching heart!

XII.

JOSÈ ZORRILLA.

It has been said that "the life of a poet is ever a romance." Perhaps this observation may apply equally well to the history of every man of ardent genius who enters with characteristic enthusiasm into the affairs of life, so as to invest even ordinary circumstances with the glow and hue of his own excited imagination. But this is more especially the case with poets who make us participate in their feelings, their joys or their sorrows, so as to give a character of romance to incidents that with other persons would have passed away as unnoticed. In the course of the preceding narratives, no doubt, many instances may be remembered to verify this remark, and the life of the eminent and deservedly popular poet with which we have to close the series, even in his yet youthful career, may be found to afford a further exemplification of it.

On the 14th February, 1837, a funeral car, over which was placed a crown of laurel, had to traverse the streets of Madrid, bearing to their resting-place in the cemetery, the remains of the talented but wrong-minded Larra. The car was followed by an immense concourse of mourners, principally young men of the first classes of Madrid, who were so testifying their regret for the loss they had sustained. The whole scene presented a spectacle of homage paid to genius, such as had seldom been witnessed. It was such as power might have envied, and as worth scarcely ever attained. Melancholy as had been the end of the unhappy being they mourned, envy and hatred had become silenced, morality and charity joined in regret, and no one disputed the propriety of the funeral honours paid to the dead.

It was already late when the ceremonies were concluded, and the darkening shadows of the night, in such a place and on such an occasion, gave the countenances of all assembled an extraordinary character. The shock they had felt, to lose so suddenly from among them one so well-known to them all, in the fulness of youth and intellect, in the height of fame and popularity, without any apparent motive and enveloped in mystery, was of itself sufficient to penetrate their minds with sorrow. They felt that a bright light had been extinguished, and they feared there was no hope of another arising to shine in its place. A strange spell seemed to have come over the bystanders, and they lingered round the vault with an unaccountable disinclination to separate.

The eloquent Señor Roca de Togares, distinguished both as an orator and a poet, pronounced a discourse he had hastily prepared, in which he portrayed the general sensation of sorrow, as he eulogized the talents and the principal literary successes of the deceased. But his eloquence had only the effect of exciting still further the prevalent feeling, which was that of something still more appropriate being required to give expression to their grief, and they instinctively looked round for some one to give utterance to it in the language of mournful inspiration with which to take their final farewell.

At that moment, in the midst of, it may be supposed, almost painful silence, a young man, unknown to them, of a slight figure and boyish appearance, stood forward, and with a tremulous voice began reading some verses in unison with their feelings, which at the first accents seemed to seize irresistibly on the minds of the listeners. He was himself so much affected by the scene, and perhaps under the sense of his own temerity, that he could not finish his task, and Roca de Togares took the paper out of his hands and read the verses again audibly. Had they been possessed of only ordinary merit, they would no doubt, on such an occasion, have been favourably received; but expressed as they were in highly poetical language, with appropriate sentiments, the effect was to excite the utmost astonishment and admiration. The author's name, Josè Zorrilla, was eagerly called for and repeated on all sides with loud applauses, and they who had followed sorrowfully shortly before the remains of the man of genius they had lost, now returned to the city attending in triumph another poet they had found, with all the tokens of enthusiastic rejoicing. The young poet, on his part, had found an audience ready to welcome him, and he was at once launched forth into that "tide in the affairs of men which taken at the flood leads on to fortune."

The history of the new aspirant for fame was now an object of interest, and the public learned that he was the son of Don Josè Zorrilla, a person well known as an eminent lawyer who had held several judicial offices with credit in Spain. It was while holding one of those offices, in Valladolid, that his son, the subject of this narrative, was born there, the 21st of February, 1817. From Valladolid, the father having been promoted to other duties in Burgos, Seville, and finally at Madrid, the son followed him, and received his primary education in the various cities they inhabited, under circumstances which must have operated powerfully on his mind. On arriving at Madrid he was placed at the Seminary of Nobles, where he remained six years, thus giving that celebrated institution the just merit of claiming him, as well as so many others of the ablest writers and public men of Spain, among those they had educated. There he seems to have gone through his course of studies without apparently other distinction than an early inclination to write verses and attend the theatres, which predilection his tutors disapproved, but in consideration of his father's position passed over more leniently than they otherwise would have done. This indulgence, however, there is no doubt gave that decided turn to his mind which led to his subsequent career.

On leaving the Seminary, Zorrilla had to go to his father at his estate in the province of Castille, where he now lived in retirement, having lost the favour of the government. There soon a discordance rose between them as to his future course in life. The father wished him to graduate in the profession of the law, in which he had acquired wealth and fame, and sent him, notwithstanding his repugnance, to Toledo, to study in the university of that city. He passed accordingly a year there, but with only sufficient application to go through the ordinary routine respectably. Other studies, more congenial to his taste, engaged all his thoughts. Toledo is a city rich in historical and poetical remembrances and legends. Its monuments and ruins are among the most interesting that exist in Spain, and in the contemplation of these Zorrilla was constantly absorbed. To Toledo he owed his poetical education, as to it he has dedicated some of his sweetest poetry. He shunned the society of his fellow-students, and seemed to pass an eccentric and even mysterious life. Out no one knew where, at strange hours, disregarding the university rules and dress and etiquette, allowing his hair to grow long over his shoulders, and composing songs, not to the taste of his tutors, he was considered half-mad, and his father was informed of his strange conduct as not amenable to study and discipline. On going home for the vacation, his father therefore received him with coldness and displeasure, and made him read law with him, notwithstanding his continued disinclination to it, though in secret he made amends for the restraint by indulging in reading more agreeable to himself. It is recorded more especially that he then studied the Sacred Scriptures, in whose pages he found the truest inspiration of poetry, as he certainly seems in his writings generally to have imbibed the purest principles of morality and religion.

In the hope of his entering on a more diligent course of study at another place than Toledo, Zorrilla was then sent to Valladolid, as if by changing universities he could be expected to change the tendency of mind which urged him to his destiny. There he was watched on all sides by his father's directions, and it was reported to him that his son still continued his former course of conduct; that instead of passing his hours in study, he was ever out on lonely walks, lying under the shade of trees by the side of the river or the broken rock, absorbed in his own meditations. There is a hint also given, of even the discovery that he had found some dream of youthful love to indulge in, as if it were something extraordinary for one of his age and enthusiastic character. The father must have been one of the class that Chateaubriand suffered under, or Mirabeau; and happy it was for Zorrilla that he did not sink into the recklessness of the one or the inanities of the other, while he had also to submit to similar discouragements. As it was, the father came to the conclusion that no hope was to be entertained of his son's application to study, to take that position in the world which he had planned out for him, and in which were centred all his own ideas of honourable activity. He therefore resolved to take him from Valladolid, and sent a trusty messenger to bring him home.

On the way the messenger gave Zorrilla to understand that his father had resolved to employ him on his estate, to dress the vines and perform other labours of country occupation. It seems the father had even talked about fitting him out in a labourer's working garb, as not being calculated for nobler employment, while he himself was unconscious or careless of the wonderful power of mind which lay hid from his observation in the son's apparent inability to fulfil his expectations. On this intimation, however, Zorrilla at once formed his determination. Shortly before reaching home, he stayed at the house of a relative, where he collected together the few valuable things he could carry away, and appropriating to his necessity a horse belonging to his cousin, he hastened back to Valladolid. There he was fortunate enough to arrive and sell the horse before the messenger sent after him again could arrest him on his flight. He then transferred himself without loss of time to Madrid, where for a length of time he succeeded in escaping the vigilant search made for him by his friends, who not having seen him since he was a boy, were not able now to penetrate his disguise.

At Madrid under these circumstances, a fugitive from his father's house, he had now passed almost a year, when he came forth before the public, as we have narrated, on the occasion of Larra's funeral. How he had passed those months we are not informed further, than that he had to submit to every kind of annoyances and privations, which he surmounted by the firmness of his determination and the elevated character of his hopes. He had in the interval sent several pieces of poetry to the different periodicals, by which his name had already become sufficiently known to a number of those who hailed him on the 14th February as supplying the place of the popular writer they had lost.

On the following day, Zorrilla could say, like Lord Byron, that he awoke and found himself famous. The verses on Larra were in every one's mouth, and all others that could be obtained of his writing were eagerly collected. Editors and proprietors of periodicals were anxious to obtain his cooperation for their works, and his period of difficulties had passed away. Before the year closed, the first volume of his poems appeared with an introduction by Pastor Diaz, and that was so eagerly bought that he was induced to bring out others in succession, with a prolificness unknown almost even in Spain. Seven other closely printed volumes of his poems were published, including several plays, within about three years afterwards, and eight or nine other volumes have appeared since. His works have been reprinted in Paris and in various parts of Spanish America, and received everywhere with unbounded admiration, so as at once to prove him one of the most favourite poets that Spain has produced.

While he was thus rising to fame and competence, his father, on the other hand, had fallen into misfortune. A high prerogative lawyer, he had maintained the doctrines of absolutism, and at length openly espoused the cause of Don Carlos. On the failure of this prince's attempts to gain the throne, the elder Zorrilla, with other adherents, was proscribed and had his property confiscated. His son had not heard from him after this event for some years, when he received a letter from his father from Bayonne, stating that he was in difficulties, and requesting him to apply to a former friend, whom he named, for a loan for his assistance. Zorrilla wrote back to say that there was no occasion to incur an obligation from one not related to him, and that he himself was happy to have it in his power to send him the sum required, which he would repeat at stated intervals. This he accordingly did, until he received his father's directions to discontinue it, as not requiring it any more.

Another instance of Zorrilla's high-mindedness and true Castilian pride has been recorded. On his father's property having been sequestrated by the government, it was intimated to him that if he applied he might have the administration of it, which was tantamount to giving him possession of it. But he replied that he would neither apply for it nor accept it, for while his father lived, he could acknowledge no one else as entitled to it. His father having since died, Zorrilla has come by law into possession of his estates, and has thus had the rare fortune, for a poet, to be possessed of considerable wealth. He has had several offers of appointments from the government, but he has declined them, contented to live according to his own fancies and occupied with his own peculiar pursuits. His extraordinary facility for composing verses is such as scarcely to allow his compositions to be termed studies; but with them and his attendances at the theatre, and other recreations, or at literary reunions, he is said to pass away his hours in ease and contentment. The first volume of his poems, it has been already intimated, was published before he was twenty-one years of age. Within three years afterwards seven others were published; and in the eighth, to the poem of 'The Duke and the Sculptor,' was appended the following note to his wife:—"Dedicated to the Señora Matilda O'Reilly de Zorrilla. I began the publication of my poems with our acquaintance, and I conclude them with thy name. Madrid, 10 October, 1840."

What were the circumstances attending this acquaintance or union, we are not informed; but it is fortunate for the world that the intimation it might convey of its being the conclusion of his literary works has not been fulfilled. Since then he has published 'Songs of the Troubadour,' in three volumes, and other minor poems and plays separately. A larger work he meditated on the conquest of Granada, to be entitled 'The Cross and the Crescent,' has not been completed; and another he projected with the title 'Maria,' intending to celebrate the different characters under which the Holy Virgin is venerated in Roman Catholic countries, he has published, with the greater part supplied by a friend, all very inferior to what might have been expected from him.

It is much to be regretted that Zorrilla has in all his works allowed carelessnesses to prevail, which too often mar the effect of his verses, and still more that he has often inserted some that were of very inferior merit compared with the rest. It is not to be supposed that an author can be equally sustained in all his productions, but it is somewhat extraordinary in his volumes to find some poems of such transcendent merit, and others so inferior. These, however, are very few, and probably were hastily composed and hastily published, to supply the demand arising for the day. He is probably the only author in Spain who has profited by the sale of his writings to any extent, and to do this he must have been often under the necessity of tasking his mind severely, without regard to its spontaneous suggestions. Thus then, when he found his inspiration failing, he has often had recourse to memory, and repeated from himself, and even from others, verses previously published. It is to be hoped that he may be induced soon to give the world a revised edition of his works, in which the oversights may be corrected, and the poems unworthy of his fame may be omitted.

On reading over dispassionately the 'Lines to Larra,' by which he was first brought so prominently into notice, it may occasion some surprise to learn they had produced so remarkable an effect. If they had previously been read over alone to any one of the auditors, he probably might not have considered them so ideal, so beautiful, or so original as they seemed at the public recital. Some phrase might have appeared incomprehensible, some sentiment exaggerated or not true; some expression or line, hard or weak or forced. He might have observed a want of order or connection in the ideas, or the whole to be vague and leaving no fixed thought in the mind; or he might have pronounced them, as they have been since pronounced, an imitation of Victor Hugo or Lamartine. But to the auditors assembled, in the excited state of their feelings, there was no time for reflection or criticism. It was a composition of the hour for that particular scene,—for themselves, in language and feelings with which they could sympathize. Thus the verses seized on their minds and electrified them, so that they had no time to dwell on any discussion or dispute of their merits, but yielded at once to the fascination of the melodious verse they heard, and the appropriate application of the homage they testified.

In the first volume of poems that Zorrilla published, containing his earliest productions, are to be found all the selections made for translation in this work. They may not be so highly finished as some afterwards published, nor so marked by that distinctive character he has made his own; but they show the first promises of the fruit that was in store, to be afterwards brought to such maturity. As he had scarcely emerged from boyhood when he began to tread the path to fame, his first steps could scarcely fail to betray that sort of uncertainty which attends on all who are going on an unknown road. Thus then through the volume he appears to be seeking a ground whereon to fix his energies and build the temple for his future fame, without being able confidently to fix on any place in preference. His poetry from the first, always sonorous and easy, often evidently spontaneous and true to nature, at times is weak and deficient in the depth of thought that at other times distinguishes it, especially in the compositions of a philosophic cast, which require fuller age and reflection to give them with perfectness. Subject to these remarks, independently of the poems hereafter given in the translations, there are others, 'To Toledo,' 'The Statue of Cervantes,' 'The Winter Night,' more clearly portraying the peculiar character of his poetry as afterwards developed.

In the second volume published about six months afterwards, he seems already to have taken his ground and to proceed with a more decided step. The poem, 'The Day without Sun,' is full of poetic vigour and richness of description, and several tales of greater length and legendary character show the bent of his mind and the direction it was in future to take. In the third volume it was reserved for his genius to be fully developed. It opens with a magnificent composition, 'To Rome,' in which deep philosophy and reflection are combined with exquisite description, all so clear and distinct as fully to captivate the mind and leave an impression of complete satisfaction. But beyond this it contains the poem 'To the last Moorish King of Granada, Boabdil the Little,' which is generally considered his best. He was already recognized as an admirable descriptive poet, but he now proved his power of moving the inmost feelings to be as great as his power of imagination. It is undoubtedly a splendid composition and highly finished, so as to be well worthy of study for the Spanish reader, though too long for translation for this work. The same volume contains another poem, also worthy of mention, 'To a Skull,' as written with much force and effect, but in the style of the French imitators of Byron, whom Zorrilla has too much copied, though it must be stated without their affectation and exaggerations.

In the following volumes he continues the course now so markedly his own as a national poet. He avowedly chooses, as becoming him in that character, subjects taken from the traditions and legends current in Spain, and clothing them in glowing language reproduces them to his delighted readers as the dreams and remembrances of their youth. He is especially partial to the tales connected with the Moorish wars, and in so doing, with great poetic effect, always represents the Moors in the most favourable light. Thus he throughout makes them worthy rivals of the Christians, and thereby renders greater the merit of the conquerors. The richness of his diction is truly extraordinary, often so as to make us lose sight of the paucity of ideas contained in his poems, and that those again are too much the same repeated constantly over.

If it was a wonderful and admirable triumph for one so young to achieve by one bound the unqualified commendations of his countrymen, and to sustain the success then acquired by subsequent efforts, we have still to regret that there were evils attending that precocity to prevent his attaining apparently the highest excellence. Perhaps there is no one we can point out as so truly exemplifying the maxim " poeta nascitur." He was truly born a poet; and though he often writes showing that he had been reading Calderon or some other of the elder writers of Spain, or even some of the French poets, yet he always gives the colouring of his own mind to those imitations so as to make them his own. This often again leads him to a mannerism and repetition of himself; but notwithstanding these faults or occasional errors of carelessness, his compositions always remain uniformly and irresistibly captivating.

Besides his poems, Zorrilla has published upwards of twenty dramatic pieces, some of which have been repeatedly produced on the stage with the fullest success. They are all remarkable for the richness of versification and high tone of poetry which distinguish his lyrical compositions, and, like them, all tend to honour and promote the chivalrous spirit for which the Spanish nation has ever been renowned.

The modern poetry of Spain shows that her nationality is still as distinct, her genius as elevated, and her sense of honour as pure, as in any former period of her history. It shows itself in unison with the spirit that has always animated the people in their public conduct, in their loyalty and devotion, the same now as a thousand years since, making every hill a fortress and every plain a battle-field, to dispute the ground at every foot with the enemy till they were driven from their soil. The poets of Spain have still, as ever, the most stirring tasks before them, to commemorate the glories of their romantic country, and they are worthy of their task.

JOSÈ ZORRILLA.

THE CHRISTIAN LADY AND THE MOOR.

Hastening to Granada's gates,
    Came o'er the Vega's land,
Some forty Gomel horsemen,
    And the Captain of the band.

He, entering in the city,
    Check'd his white steed's career;
And to a lady on his arm,
    Borne weeping many a tear,

Said, "Cease your tears, fair Christian,
    That grief afflicting me,
I have a second Eden,
    Sultana, here for thee.

"A palace in Granada,
    With gardens and with flowers,
And a gilded fountain playing
    More than a hundred showers.

" And in the Henil's valley
  I have a fortress gray,
To be among a thousand queen
  Beneath thy beauty's sway.

" For over all yon winding shore
  Extends my wide domain,
Nor Cordova's, nor Seville's lands,
  A park like mine contain.

" There towers the lofty palm-tree,
  The pomegranate 's glowing there,
And the leafy fig-tree, spreading
  O'er hill and valley fair.

" There grows the hardy walnut,
  The yellow nopal tall,
And mulberry darkly shading
  Beneath the castle wall;

" And elms I have in my arcades
  That to the skies aspire,
And singing birds in cages
  Of silk, and silver wire.

" And thou shalt my Sultana be,
  My halls alone to cheer;
My harem without other fair,
  Without sweet songs my ear.

"And velvets I will give thee,
   And eastern rich perfumes,
From Greece I'll bring thee choicest veils,
   And shawls from Cashmere's looms:

"And I will give thee feathers white,
   To deck thy beauteous brow,
Whiter than ev'n the ocean foam
   Our eastern waters know.

"And pearls to twine amid thy hair,
   Cool baths when heat's above,
And gold and jewels for thy neck,
   And for thy lips be—love!"

"O! what avail those riches all,"
   Replied the Christian fair,
"If from my father and my friends,
   My ladies, me you tear?

"Restore me, O! restore me, Moor,
   To my father's land, my own;
To me more dear are Leon's towers
   Than thy Granada's throne."

Smoothing his beard, awhile the Moor
   In silence heard her speak;
Then said as one who deeply thinks,
   With a tear upon his cheek,

"If better seem thy castles there
   Than here our gardens shine,
And thy flowers are more beautiful,
   Because in Leon thine;

"And thou hast given thy youthful love
   One of thy warriors there,
Houri of Eden! weep no more,
   But to thy knights repair!"

Then giving her his chosen steed,
   And half his lordly train,
The Moorish chieftain turn'd him back
   In silence home again.

ROMANCE. THE WAKING.

No sound is in the midnight air,
   No colour in its shade,
The old are resting free from care,
   Duenna's voice is stay'd;
But when all else in slumber meet,
   We two are waking nigh,
She on the grated window's seat,
   And at its foot am I.

I cannot see her beaming eyes,
    Nor her clear brow above,
Nor her face with its rosy dyes,
    Nor yet her smile of love:
I cannot see the virgin flush
    That heightens her cheek's glow,
The enchantments of that maiden blush,
    She is but fifteen now.

Nor can my searching eyes behold
    Her form scarce wrapp'd about;
Nor from the flowing garment's fold
    Her white foot peeping out;
As on some gentle river's spring,
    To glide the foam between,
Spread forth her snowy floatsome wing,
    The stately swan is seen.

Nor can I see her white neck shine,
    Or shoulders as they part;
Nor from her face can I divine
    Her restlessness of heart;
While like a guard, too watchful o'er,
    The grated bars I find;
Audacious love is there before,
    Poor virtue is behind.

But in despite of that thick grate,
    And shades that round us twine,
I have, my dove, to compensate,
    My soul embathed in thine:
My lips of fire I hold impress'd
    On thine of roses free;
And well I feel there's in that breast
    A heart that beats for me.

But see along the East arise
    The unwelcome god of day,
Enveloped in the humid skies,
    The darkness drive away.
And when a maid has watch'd the night,
    With gallant by her side,
The bright red dawn has too much light
    Its coming to abide!

The smiling morn is shedding round
    Its harmony and hues,
And fragrant odours o'er the ground
    The breezes soft diffuse:
Robbing the rose, the lily fair,
    And cherish'd pinks they fly,
And leave upon the laurels there
    A murmur moaning by.

Murmurs the fountain's freshening spring,
    Beneath its crystal veil,
And the angelic turtles sing
    Their tender mournful tale;
The love-sick dove the morning light
    Drinks with enraptured throat,
Mixing the balmy air so bright
    With her unequal note.

Paces the while the noble youth
    The garden's paths along,
And lowly sings, his soul to soothe,
    His love-inspiring song;

"O! soundless midnight hour, again
    Come with thy kindly shade,
When rest thy old from cares, and when
    Duenna's voice is stay'd;
For then, while they in slumber meet,
    We two are waking nigh,
She on the grated window's seat,
    And at its foot am I."

ORIENTAL ROMANCE,—BOABDIL.

Lady of the dark head-dress,
   And monkish vest of purple hue,
Gladly would Boabdil give
   Granada for a kiss of you.

He would give the best adventure
   Of the bravest horseman tried,
And with all its verdant freshness
   A whole bank of Darro's tide.

He would give rich carpets, perfumes,
   Armours of rare price and force,
And so much he values you,
   A troop, ay, of his favourite horse.

" Because thine eyes are beautiful,
   Because the morning's blushing light
From them arises to the East,
   And gilds the whole world bright.

" From thy lips smiles are flowing,
   From thy tongue gentle peace,
Light and aërial as the course
   Of the purple morning's breeze.

"O! lovely Nazarene, how choice!
  For an Eastern harem's pride,
Those dark locks waving freely
  Thy crystal neck beside.

" Upon a couch of velvet,
  In a cloud of perfumed air,
Wrapp'd in the white and flowing veil
  Of Mahomet's daughters fair.

" O, Lady! come to Cordova,
  There Sultana thou shalt be,
And the Sultan there, Sultana,
  Shall be but a slave for thee.

" Such riches he will give thee,
  And such robes of Tunisine,
That thou wilt judge thy beauty,
  To repay him for them, mean."

———

O! Lady of the dark head-dress!
That him a kiss of thee might bless,
  Resign a realm Boabdil would! *
But I for that, fair Christian, fain
Would give of heavens, and think it gain,
  A thousand if I only could.

THE CAPTIVE.

I go, fair Nazarene, tomorrow
    To queenly Cordova again;
Then thou, my song of love and sorrow
    To hear, no longer mayst complain,
    Sung to the compass of my chain.

When home the Christians shall return,
    In triumph o'er the Moorish foe,
My cruel destiny wouldst thou learn?
    The history of my loves to know,
    The blood upon their hands shall show.

Better it were at once to close,
    In this dark tower a captive here,
The life I suffer now of woes,
    Than that today thou sett'st me clear;
    Alas! thou sell'st it very dear.

Adieu! tomorrow o'er, thy slave
    May never vex thy soul again,
But vain is all the hope it gave:
    Still must I bear the captive's chain,
    Thine eyes my prison still remain.

Fair Christian! baleful is my star;
    What values it this life to me,
If I must bear it from thee far?
    Nor in Granada's bowers may be,
    Nor, my fair Cordova, with thee?

Today's bright sun to me will seem
    A lamp unseasonably by:
Daughter of Spain, thy beauties gleam
    Alone my sun and moon on high,
    The dawn and brightness of my sky.

Since then I lose thy light today,
    Without that light I cannot live!
To Cordova I take my way;
    But in the doom my fortunes give,
    Alas! 't is death that I receive.

A paradise and houri fair
    Has Mahomet promised we shall prove:
Aye, thou wilt be an angel there,
    And in that blissful realm above
    We meet again, and there to love.

THE TOWER OF MUNION.

Dark-shadow'd giant! shame of proud Castille,
   Castle without bridge, battlements or towers,
In whose wide halls now loathsome reptiles steal,
   Where nobles once and warriors held their bowers!
Tell me, where are they? where thy tapestries gay,
   Thy hundred troubadours of lofty song?
Thy mouldering ruins in the vale decay,
   Thou humbled warrior! time has quell'd the strong:
Thy name and history to oblivion thrown,
The world forgets that there thou standst, Munion.

To me thou art a spectre, shade of grief!
   With black remembrances my soul's o'ercast;
To me thou art a palm with wither'd leaf,
   Burnt by the lightning, bow'd beneath the blast.
I, wandering bard, proscribed perchance my doom
   In the bier's dust nor name, nor glory know;
With useless toil my brow's consumed in gloom;
   Of her I loved, dark dwelling-place below,
Whom I was robb'd of, angel from above,
Cursed be thy name, thy soil, as was my love.

There rest, aye, in thy loftiness,
    To shame the plain around,
Warderless castle, matron lone,
    In whom no beauty's found.
At thee time laughs, thy towers o'erthrown,
    Scorn'd by thy vassals, by thy Lord
Deserted, rest, black skeleton!
    Stain of the vale's green sward.

Priestless hermitage of Castille,
    On thee no banners wave;
Unblazon'd gate, thy pointed vaults
    No more their weight can save:
Thou hast no soldier on thy heights,
    No echo in thy halls,
And rank weeds festering grow uncheck'd
    Beneath thy mouldering walls.

Chieftain dead in a foreign land,
    Forgotten of thy race,
While storm-torn fragments from thy brow
    Are scatter'd o'er thy place;
And men pass careless at thy feet,
    Nor seek thy tale to find;
Because thy history is not read,
    Thy name's not in their mind.

But thou hast one, who in a luckless hour
  Inscribed another's name on thy worn stone:
'T was I, and that my deep relentless shame
  Remains with thee alone.
When my lips named that name, they play'd me false;
  When my hands graved it, 't was a like deceit;
Now it exists not; in time's impious course
  'T was swept beneath his feet.

  And that celestial name,
    To time at length a prey,
  A woman for my sin,
    For a seraph snatch'd away;
  The hurricane of life
    Has left me, loved one, worse
  For my eternal grief,
    In pledge as of a curse,
Thy name ne'er from my thoughts to part,
Nor thy love ever from my heart.

THE WARNING.

Yesterday the morning's light
Shone on thy window crystal bright,
And lightsome breezes floating there
Gave richest perfumes to the air,
Which the gay flowers had lent to them,
All scatter'd from the unequal stem.

The nightingale had bathed his wing
Beneath the neighbouring murmuring spring;
And birds, and flowers, and streamlets gay,
Seem'd to salute the new-born day;
And in requital of the light,
Their grateful harmony unite.

The sun was bright, the sky serene,
The garden fresh and pleasant seen;
Life was delight, and thou, sweet maid,
No blush of shame thy charms betray'd;
For innocence ruled o'er thy breast,
Alike thy waking and thy rest.

Maiden, or angel upon earth,
Thy laugh, and song of gentle mirth,
In heaven were surely heard; thine eyes
Were stars, and like sweet melodies
Thy wandering tones; thy breath perfume,
And dawn-like thy complexion's bloom.

As phantoms then thou didst not find
The hours pass heavy on thy mind,
A poet, under Love's decree,
Sang melancholy songs to thee;
And of his griefs the voice they lend
Thou didst not, maiden, comprehend.

Poor maiden, now what change has come
O'er that glad brow and youthful bloom?
Forgotten flower, thy leaves are sere,
Thy fruitless blossoms dried appear;
Thy powerless stem all broken, low,
May to the sun no colours show.

O! dark-eyed maid of ill-starr'd birth,
Why camest thou on this evil earth?
Rose amid tangled briars born,
What waits thee from the world but scorn?
A blasting breath around thee, see,
Thy bloom is gone, who'll ask for thee?

Return, my angel, to thy sphere,
Before the world shall see thee here:
The joys of earth are cursed and brief,
Buy them not with eternal grief!
Heaven is alone, my soul, secure
The mansion for an angel pure.

MEDITATION.

Upon the obscure and lonely tomb,
Beneath the yellow evening's gloom,
To offer up to Heaven I come,
  For her I loved, my prayer!
Upon the marble bow'd my head,
Around my knees the moist herbs spread,
The wild flowers bend beneath my tread,
  That deck the thicket there.

Far from the world, and pleasures vain,
From earth my frenzied thoughts to gain,
And read in characters yet plain
  Names of the long since past;
There by the gilded lamp alone,
That waves above the altar stone,
As by the wandering breezes moan,
  A light's upon me cast.

Perchance some bird will pause its flight
Upon the funeral cypress height,
Warbling the absence of the light,
    As sorrowing for its loss;
Or takes leave of the day's bright power,
From the high window of the tower,
Or skims, where dark the cupolas lower,
    On the gigantic cross.

With eyes immersed in tears, around
I watch it silent from the ground,
Until it startled flies the sound
    The harsh bolts creaking gave;
A funeral smile salutes me dread,
The only dweller with the dead,
Lends me a hard and rough hand, led
    To ope another grave.

Pardon, O God! the worldly thought,
    Nor mark it midst my prayer;
Grant it to pass, with evil fraught,
As die the river's murmurings brought
    Upon the breezy air.

Why does a worldly image rise
    As if my prayer to stain?

Perchance in evil shadow's guise,
Which may when by the morrow flies
    Sign of a curse remain.

Why has my mind been doom'd to dream
    A phantom loveliness?
To see those charms transparent gleam,
That brow in tranquil light supreme,
    And neck's peculiar grace?

Not heighten'd its enchantments shine
    By pomp or worldly glow;
I only see that form recline
In tears, before some sacred shrine,
    Or castle walls below.

Like a forgotten offering lone,
    In ruin'd temple laid;
Upon the carved and time-worn stone,
Where fell it by the rough wind thrown,
    So bent beneath the shade.

With such a picture in my mind,
    Such name upon my ear,
Before my God the place to find,
Where the forgotten are consign'd,
    I come, and bow down here.

With eyes all vaguely motionless,
    Perhaps my wanderings view
The dead, with horror and distress,
As, roused up in their resting-place,
    They look their dark walls through.

'T was not to muse I hither came
    Of nothingness my part;
Nor of my God, but of a name,
That deep in characters of flame
    Is written on my heart.

Pardon, O God! the worldly thought,
    Nor mark it midst my prayer;
Grant it to pass, with evil fraught,
As die the river's murmurings brought
    Upon the breezy air.

NOTES.

1. Page 3. "Gaspar Melchor de Jovellanos."

This name (pronounced Hovellianos) was formerly written as two distinct names, Jove Llanos, as it is still by several members of the family, one, an Advocate, at present at Madrid, and another the Spanish Consul at Jamaica.

2. Page 3. "An able and distinguished writer," &c.

Antonio Alcalá Galiano, author also of the able article in the Foreign Quarterly Review on Jovellanos, afterwards mentioned. He was born at Cadiz, in 1789, the son of a distinguished officer in the Spanish navy, who was killed at Trafalgar. In his youth, Alcalá Galiano studied the English language so assiduously as to receive much benefit from his knowledge of it when he had to take refuge in London, on the various political changes that took place in Spain. He then wrote much for the Westminster and Foreign Quarterly Reviews, as well as other publications, and was subsequently named one of the Professors of Languages in the London University. Having returned to Spain, on the death of Ferdinand VII., he was appointed a Minister of State, with the Señor Isturitz, and has held, at various times, several high offices in the government. In the Cortes he was considered one of the most able orators of his time, having been put on a rivalry with Martinez de la Rosa and Argüelles. He has published a few poems, and contributed several valuable papers for the different learned societies of Madrid, besides having written much for the periodicals, according to the continental system for public men seeking to disseminate their opinions. His principal work as an author is a ' History of Spain.' Ferrer del Rio says of him, that " he writes Spanish with an English idiom, and though he puts his name to a history of Spain, it seems a translation from the language of Byron." Few foreigners have ever obtained so complete a knowledge of the English language ; in fact his writings in the several reviews might be pointed out as compositions which would do credit to our own best writers. As an instance of his knowledge of the state of literature in England, we may quote a few observations from an article bearing his name in the first number of the Madrid Review. He says, " The Bible and the Plays of Shakespeare, if they may be named together without profanation, are the two works which have most influence on the thoughts of the English ;" adding, that "classical literature is there better cultivated than in France, or at least cultivated with more profound knowledge," deducing the conclusion, "that the English drama is consequently radically different from the French."

3. Page 11. "Bermudez, his biographer."

This industrious writer was born at Gijon, in 1749, and died at Cadiz in 1829. He may be termed the Vasari of Spain, as the historian of the artists of his country. His two biographical works, the one on her painters, the other on her architects, are a rich mine of materials. The former was published in six volumes 8vo, in 1800: the latter, in four volumes 4to, was almost the last work on which he was engaged, and did not appear till 1829. Besides these, he was the author of various other publications on the principal edifices in Seville, and had completed a 'History of the Roman Antiquities in Spain ;' a 'General History of Painting;' a work on 'Architecture,' and other pieces, which yet remain unedited. As a fellow-townsman, as well as an artist of considerable genius, he was much assisted by Jovellanos, who, when Minister of State, gave him a valuable appointment at Madrid under the government. When that eminent individual fell, his friends had to suffer also, and Cean Bermudez, deprived of his appointment, had to return to Seville, where he instituted a school for drawing. It was no doubt under the feelings of regret, occasioned by the reflection of having his friends involved in his misfortunes, that Jovellanos wrote to him the Epistle selected for translation in this work.

4. Page 16. " Merit of first bringing into favour."

See Hermosilla, 'Juicio Critico de los principales Poetas Españoles de la ultima era,' vol. i. p. 11.

5. Page 18. "Epistle to Cean Bermudez."

From Works of Jovellanos, Mellado's edition, vol. iv. p. 226.

6. Page 30. "To Galatea's Bird."

From the same, p. 369.

7. Page 32. "To Enarda.—I."

From the same, p. 368. In submission to the recommendations of several friends to give the original of at least part or the whole of some one poem of each author, from whose works the translations have been made, selections of such as the English students of Spanish literature would probably most desire, are offered for their comparison.

> Riñen me bella Enarda
> Los mozos y los viejos,
> Por que tal vez jugando
> Te escribo dulces versos.
>   Debiera un magistrado
> (Susurran) mas severo,
> De las livianas Musas
> Huir el vil comercio.
>   Que mal el tiempo gastas!
> Predican otros,—pero
> Por mas que todos riñan
> Tengo de escribir versos.

> Quiero loar de Enarda
> El peregrino ingenio
> Al son de mi zampoña
> Y en bien medidos metros.
> Quiero de su hermosura
> Encaramar al cielo
> Las altas perfecciones;
> De su semblante quiero
> Cantar el dulce hechizo
> Y con pincel maestro
> Pintar su frente hermosa
> Sus traviesos ojuelos,
> El carmin de sus labios,
> La nieve de su cuello;
> Y vàyanse à la .... al rollo
> Los Catonianos ceños
> Las frentes arrugadas
> Y adustos sobrecejos,
> Que Enarda serà siempre
> Celebrada en mis versos

8. Page 33. "To Enarda.—II."

From Works of Jovellanos, vol. iv. p. 364.

9. Page 46. "Epistle to Domingo de Iriarte."

From Works of Tomas Iriarte, 1805, vol. ii. p. 56.

Domingo Iriarte was subsequently much engaged in the diplomatic service of Spain, and signed the treaty of peace with France of 1795, as Plenipotentiary, along with the celebrated M. Barthélemy.

10. Page 50. "But now the confines of," &c.

The following is the original of this passage:—

> Mas ya dexar te miro
> Los confines Germanos,
> Y el político giro
> Seguir hasta los ùltimos Britanos.
> Desde luego la corte populosa
> Cuyas murallas baña
> La corriente anchurosa
> Del Tàmesis, la imàgen te presenta

De una nacion en todo bien extraña:
Nacion en otros siglos no opulenta,
Hoi feliz por su industria, y siempre esenta:
Nacion tan liberal como ambiciosa;
Flemàtica y activa;
Ingenua, pero adusta;
Humana, pero altiva;
Y en la causa que abraza, iniqua ó justa
Violenta defensora,
Del riesgo y del temor despreciadora.
Alli serà preciso que te asombres
De ver (qual no habràs visto en parte alguna)
Obrar y hablar con libertad los hombres.
Admiraràs la rapida fortuna
Que alli logra el valor y la eloqüencia,
Sin que ni el oro, ni la ilustre cuna
Roben el premio al mèrito y la ciencia.
Adverteràs el numeroso enxambre
De diligentes y habiles Isleños
Que han procurado, del comercio Dueños
No conocer la ociosidad ni el hambre;
Ocupados en ùtiles inventos
En fàbricas, caminos, arsenales,
Escuelas, academias, hospitales,
Libros, experimentos,
Y estudios de las Artes liberales.
Alli sabràs, en fin, à quanto alcanza
La sabia educacion, y el acertado
Mètodo de patriòtica enseñanza,
La privada ambicion bien dirigida
Al pùblico provecho del Estado;
La justa recompensa y acogida
En que fundan las Letras su esperanza,
Y el desvelo de un pròvido Gobierno
Que al bien aspira, y à un renombre eterno.

This Epistle is addressed to his brother, as the reader may observe, in the second person singular, which, in Spanish, has a tone of more familiarity than in English, and understanding it so intended, I have altered it, in the translation, into our colloquial form of the second person plural.

The above extract is the same in his printed works of both editions; but I have in my possession a collection of his manuscripts, among which is a copy of this Epistle, with several variations, less flattering to England. Had he lived to superintend the second edition, these variations might probably have been adopted in it. They are not, however, of any material variance, but they seem to me to show that his eulogium had not been favourably received in some quarters, and that he had therefore thought it prudent to soften it in preparing for another edition. The publisher of the edition of 1805 does not seem to have been aware of these manuscripts, nor indeed to have taken the trouble of doing more for Iriarte's memory than merely to reprint the first edition, without even any biographical or critical notice of him or his writings, as he might well have done, Iriarte having been then deceased fourteen years.

For another eloquent and encomiastic description of English usages and institutions, the student of Spanish literature would do well to read a work, published in London in 1834, by the Marques de Miraflores, 'Apuntes historico-criticos para escribir la Historia de la Revolucion de España.' This distinguished nobleman was born the 23rd December, 1792, at Madrid, and succeeded to the honours and vast property of his ancient house in 1809, on the death of his elder brother, during the campaign of that year. He has been much engaged in public affairs, having held various offices in the state. He has been twice Ambassador to England; the last time, Ambassador Extraordinary on the coronation of Her Majesty Queen Victoriá. The Marques has written several works on political subjects, of which the one above-mentioned is particularly deserving of study.

11. Page 52. "Saying as Seneca has said of yore."

> Stet quicumque volet potens
> Aulæ culmine lubrico:
> Me dulcis saturet quies.
> Obscuro positus loco
> Leni perfruar otio.
> Nullis notus Quiritibus
> Ætas per tacitum fluat.

> Sic cum transierint mei
> Nullo cum strepitu dies,
> Plebeius moriar senex.
> Illi mors gravis incubat
> Qui notus nimis omnibus
> Ignotus moritur sibi.

Thyestes, Act II. The critical reader will observe, that the translation into English has been made from the Spanish rather than the Latin.

12. Page 53. "Fables."

The Fables translated are numbered respectively III., VIII., XI., LIII. and LIV., in the original collection. The two first, III. and VIII., having been given by Bouterwek as specimens of Iriarte's style, without any translation, I took them for my first essays, and had already versified them, before finding Roscoe had done the same also in his translation of Sismondi, and it was subsequently to that I became aware of other similar versions. Having, however, made those translations, I have, notwithstanding the others, allowed them to remain in this work. The fable of the Two Rabbits has been selected as particularly noticed by Martinez de la Rosa, and the others almost without cause of peculiar preference. The last one contains an old but good lesson, which cannot be too frequently and earnestly repeated:—

> Ego nec studium sine divite venâ
> Nec rude quid prosit video ingenium, alterius sic
> Altera poscit opem res et conjurat amicè.

13. Page 64. "Iglesias and Gonzalez."

Diego Gonzalez was born at Ciudad Rodrigo in 1733, and died at Madrid, 1794. Josè Iglesias de la Casa was born at Salamanca in 1753, and died there in 1791. His poems were first published seven years after his death, and have been several times reprinted. The best edition is that of Barcelona, 1820, from which the one of Paris, 1821, was taken. The poems of Gonzalez also were first published after his death, and have been several times reprinted.

Both wrote very pleasing verses, and are deservedly popular in Spain.

14. Page 69. "It was for his detractors," &c.

Hermosilla, author of a work, 'Juicio Critico de los principales Poetas Españoles de la ultima era,' published after his death, Paris 1840, gives in it, as Mr. Ticknor pithily observes, "a criticism of the poems of Melendez so severe that I find it difficult to explain its motive;" at the same time that he gives "an unreasonably laudatory criticism of L. Moratin's works." Hermosilla appears to have been a man of considerable learning, but little judgement. His criticisms are generally worthless, and the only excuse for him, with regard to his book, is, that he did not publish it. With regard to Melendez, taking every opportunity to depreciate his merits, he is constantly found constrained to acknowledge them, and sometimes even in contradiction to himself. Thus, having several times intimated, as at p. 31, that the erotic effusions of Melendez only were praiseworthy, he says, at p. 297, when speaking of his Epistles, that they are "his best compositions; thoughts, language, style, tone and versification, all in general are good." In another part he censures Melendez for his poems addressed to different ladies, especially some to 'Fanny,' who appears to have been an Englishwoman; and yet those epistles, addressed to her, on the death of her husband, are among the purest and most elegant specimens that can be pointed out of consolation to a mourner. It is but justice to his editor, Salva, to say, that he has expressed his dissent from these criticisms, though he thought proper to publish the work.

15. Page 73. "The Duke de Frias."

This estimable nobleman, who died in 1850, was descended from the Counts of Haro, one of the three great families of Spain. He was the munificent friend of literary men, and in the case of Melendez extended his protection to the dead, having taken much personal trouble to have his remains removed from the common burying-ground to a vault, where they might not afterwards be disturbed. He also wrote verses occasionally, of which have been preserved, by Del Rio, a 'Sonnet to the Duke of Wellington,' and by Ochoa, an 'Elegy on the Death of his Duchess,' whose virtues will be found hereafter commemorated by Martinez de la Rosa.

16. Page 76. "Best edition, that by Salvà."

In taking the edition of 1820 for the text, Salvà, in his edition, has exercised much judgement in giving some of the poems as they were originally published, rather than as Melendez afterwards had left them, weakened by over-correction.

Salvà was in early life distinguished for learning and study, having been, when only twenty years of age, named Professor of Greek in the University of Alcalà de Henares. On the French invasion he returned to his native city Valencia, and engaged in trade as a bookseller, in which occupation he continued in London, when obliged to emigrate hither in 1823, in consequence of his having joined in the political events of the times. He had been, during those events, Deputy from Valencia, and Secretary to the Cortes. In 1830 he transferred his house to Paris, where he continued his pursuits, publishing many valuable works of his own compilation, as a Grammar and Dictionary of the Spanish language, as well as editing and superintending the publication of many other standard works. He closed his useful life, in his native city, in 1850.

17. Page 77. "Juvenilities."

Works of Melendez, Salvà's Edition, vol. i. p. 39.

This piece was also taken for translation from Bouterwek, when first entering on a study of Spanish literature. From Bouterwek it was copied by Sismondi, when borrowing, as he did largely, from that compiler; but Mr. Roscoe has not given a translation of this, as he probably found it difficult to do so satisfactorily. It is in fact almost as difficult to translate Melendez as it is to translate Anacreon, their peculiar simplicity and grace being so nearly allied.

18. Page 79.   "The Timid Lover."

Works of Melendez, *ibid*, p. 263.

This poem having been particularly mentioned by Martinez de la Rosa as favourably characteristic of the style of the author, may be considered best to be selected as an exemplification of it. It is what is termed a Letrillia.

EL AMANTE TIMIDO.

En la pena aguda
Que me hace sufrir
El Amor tirano
Desde que te vi
  Mil veces su alivio
Te voy à pedir,
Y luego, aldeana,
Que llego ante ti,
   Si quiero atreverme
   No sè que decir.

Las voces me faltan
Y mi frenesí
Con miseros ayes
Las cuida suplir
  Pero el dios que aleve
Se burla de mi
Cuanto ansio mas tierno
Mis labios abrir
   Se quiero atreverme
   No sè que decir.

  Sus fuegos entonces
Empieza à sentir
Tan vivos el alma
Que pienso morir,
  Mis làgrimas corren,
Mi agudo gemir
Tu pecho sensible
Conmueve, y al fin
   Si quiero atreverme
   No sè que decir.

  No lo sè, temblando
Si por descubrir
Con loca esperanza

>   Mi amor infeliz,
>   Tu lado por siempre
>   Tendrè ya que buir:
>   Sellàndome el miedo
>   La boca: y asì
>   Si quiero atreverme
>   No sè que decir.
>
>   Ay! si tu, adorada,
>   Pudieras oir
>   Mis hondos suspiros
>   Yo fuera feliz.
>   Yo, Filis, lo fuera
>   Mas, triste de mi!
>   Que tìmido al verte
>   Burlarme y reir,
>   Si quiero atreverme
>   No sè que decir.

19. Page 81. "My Village Life."

This and the two following poems are taken from those at pages 94, 110 and 64 of the first volume of the Works of Melendez Valdes; the Disdainful Shepherdess from the one at p. 62 of vol. ii.

20. Page 95. "Merits of their national dramas."

For an excellent criticism on the Spanish drama, see the article in the twenty-fifth volume of the Quarterly Review.

21. Page 104. "There, says his biographer," &c.

In the sketch prefixed to the edition by Rivadeneyra, from which the two poems following are taken, at pages 581 and 582. The one to Jovellanos has been justly praised by Mr. Ticknor as one of his best, and from it we may in preference extract the commencement, as an exemplification of his style.

>   Si, la pura amistad, que en dulce nudo
>   Nuestras almas uniò, durable existe
>   Jovino ilustre, y ni la ausencia larga
>   Ni la distancia, ni interpuestos montes
>   Y proceloso mar que suena roco,
>   De mi memoria apartaràn tu idea.

Duro silencio à mi cariño impuso
El son de Marte, que suspende ahora
La paz, la dulce paz.   Sè que en obscura
Deliciosa quietud, contento vives,
Siempre animado de incansable celo
Por el pùblico bien; de las virtudes
Y del talento protector y amigo.
   Estos que formo de primor desnudos,
No castigados de tu docta lima,
Fàciles versos, la verdad te anuncien
De mi constante fe; y el cielo en tanto
Vuèlvame presto la ocasion de verte
Y renovar en familiar discurso
Cuanto à mi vista presentò del orbe
La varia escena.   De mi patria orilla
A las que el Sena turbulento bañia,
Teñido en sangre, del audaz Britano
Dueño del mar, al aterido Belga,
Del Rin profundo à las nevadas cumbres
Del Apenino, y la que en humo ardiente
Cubre y ceniza à Nàpoles canora,
Pueblos, naciones, visitè distintas
Util sciencia adquirì, que nunca enseña
Docta leccion en retirada estancia,
Que allì no ves la diferencia suma
Que el clima, el culto, la opinion, las artes,
Las leyes causan.   Hallaràsla solo
Si al hombre estudias en el hombre mismo.

22. Page 113.   "Juan Bautista de Arriaza."

This poet's name is pronounced Arriatha; the two poems selected for translation are taken, the first from p. 60 of Book III. of his works, edition of 1829. 'The Parting, or the Young Sailor's Farewell,' from *ibid.*, Book I. p. 77.

The eighth stanza; beginning in the translation, 'With venal aid of hate assists,' is in the original—

   Què de ministros vendes a su encono,
   Anglia infecunda! de las nieblas trono,
      Campos que el sol no mira,
   Que en sonrisa falsa, Flora reviste
   De esteril verde, en que la flor es triste,
      Y Amor sin gloria espira.

Which stanza is thus translated by Maury:—

> Combien te sied le mal, Angleterre inféconde,
> Amante de vapeurs, jetée où l'œil du monde
>   Te regarde si peu!
> Champs où la brume arrose une oiseuse verdure,
> Où Flore est sans gaieté, l'automne sans parure,
>   L'Amour sans traits de feu!

Of thirty-three stanzas in the original, Maury has only taken fifteen for his translation, and of 'The Parting' he has only taken eighteen out of twenty-five. The four concluding stanzas are in the original—

> Crisol de adversidad claro y seguro
> Vuestro valor probò sublime y puro,
>   O Marinos Hispanos!
> Broquel fue de la patria vuestra vida
> Que al fin vengada y siempre defendida
>   Serà per vuestras manos.
>
> Rinda al Leon y al Aguila Neptuno
> El brazo tutelar, con que importuno
>   Y esclavo al Anglia cierra:
> Y ella os verà desde las altas popas
> Lanzar torrentes de invencibles tropas
>   Sobre su infausta tierra.
>
> Bàsteos, en tanto, el lùgubre tributo
> De su muerte Adalid doblando el luto
>   Del Tàmesis umbrio,
> Que, si, llenos de honrosas cicatrices
> Se os ve, para ocasiones mas felices
>   Reservar vuestro brio.
>
> Sois cual leon, que en Libico desierto
> Con garra atroz, del cazador experto
>   Rompiò asechanza astuta;
> Que no inglorioso, aunque sangriento y laso
> Temido si, se vuelve paso à paso
>   A su arenosa gruta.

23. Page 145. "Described by Humboldt."

Political Essay on New Spain, Book II. chapter 5.

24. Page 145. "So popular a writer as Larra."

Mariano Josè de Larra was born at Madrid, 24th March, 1809. His father had joined the French army as a medical officer, and after the peace went to France, taking his son with him, where he forgot his native language, so that he had to learn it as a novice on his return to Spain. It is not improbable that his education in that country, where also he passed some time subsequently, gave Larra's mind that tendency for scepticism and perverted feeling which led to his miserable end. From his earliest years he showed great aptitude for learning, and had studied the Greek, English and Italian languages, before he went to Valladolid to prepare for the profession of the law. After a short residence there, he went to Valencia on some disappointment he suffered, which, to one of his temperament, seemed a greater misfortune than what perhaps any other person would have considered it. At Valencia he obtained employment in a public office, which, however, did not suit his taste, and having then married, he returned to Madrid and determined to write for the public. His first efforts were not successful, and have not been subsequently reprinted with his works, but after a short time he began writing a series of essays on passing events, under the signature of Figaro, which at once attained great popularity. He also wrote several plays and a few poems, which, as written by Figaro, were favourably received. But the essays, under that title, were the foundation of his popularity. They were in the style of our essayists of the reign of Queen Anne, containing criticisms, and sketches of manners and characters, written in a style of great ease and elegance, marked with much wit and humour, as well as vigour. These works have been very many times reprinted in Spain, and also in France and South America. The student who wishes to form a correct style in learning Spanish, cannot do better than take Larra for a model. By his writings he had attained a respectable place in literary society, and it was understood that his fortunes were thereby also in a state of competence. He was, however, possessed of an ill-regulated mind and headstrong passions, so that, as it seems intimated, baffled in some object of unlawful desire, he put an end to his existence by a pistol shot the 13th February, 1837.

In his review of Quintana's Life of Las Casas, he unreservedly subscribes to all the sentiments therein expressed.

25. Page 160. "From the proud castled poop," &c.

> Se alzò el Breton en el soberbio alcazar
> Que corona su indòmito navio;
> Y ufano con su gloria y poderio
> Alli estan, exclamò.

26. Page 161. "Conquerors of winds and waves."

> ...... sus nadantes proras
> Del viento y de las ondas vencedoras.

27. Page 163. "And Alcalà, Churruca, also ye!"

Of those who fell at Trafalgar, the names of Alcalà aud Churruca seem to be remembered with peculiar affection. The latter is referred to by Arriaza also, and seems to have been an officer of great skill and bravery in his profession, as well as of most amiable qualities in private life. Alcalà was an officer of very superior attainments. He was author of a learned Treatise on taking Observations of Longitude and Latitude at Sea, published at Madrid, 1796. With the copy of this work in my possession, there is bound up an unedited treatise of his original manuscript, 'On the Trigonometrical Calculation of the Height of Mountains.' He has already been referred to in Note 2.

• The Spanish navy is at the present day much distinguished for the superior attainments and character of the officers, as well as in former years. In addition to the poet Arriaza, they have to boast of the late learned Navarrete, one of the most eminent and industrious writers of our times, principally on scientific subjects connected with his profession, geography, hydrography, and voyages, though in various biographical works he has extended his labours to the memory of poets and others, as well as the naval heroes of his country: see his memoir in Ochoa, vol. ii. p. 586, copied from one by the Bishop of Astorga.

28. Page 164. "Yet fell ye not, ye generous squadrons."

> No empero sin venganza y sin estrago,
> Generoso escuadron allí caiste:
> Tambien brotando à rios
> La sangre Inglesa inunda sus navios.
> Tambien Albion pasmada
> Los montes de cadàveres contempla
> Horrendo peso à su soberbia armada.
> Tambien Nelson allí, Terrible sombra,
> No esperes, no, cuando mi voz te nombra
> Que vil insulte à tu postrer suspiro;
> Inglès te aborrecì, y hèroe te admiro.
> Oh, golpe! oh, suerte! El Tàmesis aguarda
> De las naves cautivas
> El confuso tropel, y ya en idea
> Goza el aplauso y los sonoros vivas
> Que al vencedor se dan. Oh suerte! El puerto
> Solo le verà entrar pàlido y yerto:
> Ejemplo grande à la arrogancia humana,
> Digno holocausto à la afliccion Hispana.

The two poems from Quintana are at pages 16 and 93 respectively of the fourth edition of his works, published in 1825.

29. Page 170. "The Conde de Toreno."

This able and enlightened statesman was born at Oviedo in 1786, and died at Paris in 1845. His work, on the 'Rising, War, and Revolution of Spain,' is one well deserving of the fame it has attained, having been translated into all the principal languages of Europe.

30. Page 170. "The celebrated Pacheco."

Born at Ecija, near Seville, in 1808, he came to Madrid in 1833, and was admitted an Advocate in the courts of law, but has been since engaged actively in conducting various publications, principally of a political character. He has been several times chosen member of the legislature, and had to undertake his share of public duties, but he has declined office, and in his whole public life shown a freedom from ambition, remarkable, as Del Rio intimates, from the contrast it presents with the conduct of other men of far inferior abilities. He has announced 'A History of the Regency of Queen Christina,' of which he has published a preliminary volume, comprising a detail of antecedent events. He has also written various plays and poems, but not of such a character as to be worthy of his fame as a public speaker and journalist. His life of Martinez de la Rosa, given in a publication entitled 'Galeria de Españoles celebres contemporaneos, 1842,' (which work has now extended to many volumes, including persons of distinction in all ranks of life,) is very pleasingly written, and has been taken as the principal authority in this compilation.

31. Page 176. "Rights of the Basque people."

For a just statement of these rights, see the late Earl of Carnarvon's 'Portugal and Galicia,' vol. ii.

32. Page 180. "Observation may apply to English verse."

Our best poets, and Milton especially, afford many exemplifications of this practice.

> O'er many a frozen, many a fiery alp,
> Rocks, caves, lakes, fens, bogs, dens and shades of death
> * * * * * * *
> Perverse, all monstrous, all prodigious things
> Abominable, inutterable and worse.

Many of our syllables also are in effect double syllables, as in the words *brave, grave, clave,* &c., as singers often have to regret, causing them, on that account, to slur over them. But these rules are only a continuation of Quinctilian's maxim, "Optime de illa judicant aures. Quædam arte tradi non possunt."

33. Page 181. "The Roman friend," &c.

See note 23 to the Fourth Canto of Childe Harold.

34. Page 183.   "I saw upon the shady Thames."

Vi en el Tàmesis umbrio
Cien y cien naves cargadas
    De riqueza;
Vi su inmenso poderio
Sus artes tan celebradas
    Su grandeza.

Mas el ànima afligida
Mil suspiros exhalaba
    Y ayes mil;
Y ver la orilla florida
Del manso Dauro anhelaba
    Y del Genil.

Vi de la soberbia corte
Las damas engalanadas
    Muy vistosas;
Vi las bellezas del norte
De blanca nieve formadas
    Y de rosas.

Sus ojos de azul del cielo,
De oro puro parecia
    Su cabello;
Bajo transparente velo
Turgente el seno se via
    Blanco y bello.

Mas que valen los brocados
Las sedas y pedreria
    De la ciudad?
Que los rostros sonrosados
La blancura y gallardia
    Ni la beldad?

Con mostrarse mi zagala,
De blanco lino vestida,
    Fresca y pura,
Condena la inutil gala
Y se esconde confundida
    La hermosura.

Dò hallar en climas helados
Sus negros ojos graciosos,
   Que son fuego?
Ora me miren airados
Ora roben cariñosos
   Mi sosiego.

Dò la negra caballera
Que al èbano se aventaja?
   Y el pie leve
Que al triscar por la pradera
Ni las tiernas flores aja,
   Ni aun las mueve?

Doncellas las del Genil
Vuestra tez escurecida
   No trocara
Por los rostros de marfil
Que Albion envanecida
   Me mostrara.

Padre Dauro! manso rio,
De las arenas doradas,
   Dignate oir
Los votos del pecho mio,
Y en tus màrgenes sagradas
   Logre morir!

Works of Martinez de la Rosa, edition of Barcelona, 1838, vol. iv. p. 1. The other translations are taken from the same, pages 113, 104, 48 and 34 respectively.

In the prologue, he enters on the discussion, so common a few years since, as to the relative merits of what were called the Classical and Romantic schools of poetry, which discussion, it is to be hoped, may now be considered at an end. The pretensions of different writers, who affected to range themselves under one or other of these denominations, were in fact generally only the devices of mediocrity to shelter their deficiencies. Those who write spontaneously from the true inspiration of genius, will never submit to the shackles of any system, and for all writers the wisest aim is to seek the clearest style of expressing those thoughts which they have to convey. As Martinez de la Rosa has well observed in this prologue, "I do not remember any one sublime passage, in whatever language it may be, that is not expressed with the utmost simplicity; and without this most essential quality, they cannot excite in the mind that lively and instantaneous impression which distinguishes them."

35. Page 184. "The light foot that never stirs," &c.

An Andalusian poet may be excused entering into hyperbolical praise of his countrywomen, but we find an English traveller almost as hyperbolical in praise of them also. "It is beyond the power of language to describe those slow and surpassingly graceful movements which accompany every step of the Andalusa; her every attitude is so flowing, at the same time so unforced, that she seems upborne by some invisible power that renders her independent of the classically moulded foot she presses so lightly on the ground."—*Murray's Cities and Wilds of Andalusia.*

36. Page 216. "His biographer, Pastor Diaz," &c.

In the work already mentioned, 'Galeria de Españoles contemporaneos,' under his own superintendence, and from which the notices in this compilation are principally taken. Pastor Diaz was born at Vivero in Galicia, in the year 1811, and was educated at Alcalà de Henares. Having been admitted an Advocate in the courts of law, he engaged, in 1833, in the public service, and has held various offices under the government in the provinces. In 1847 he published a volume of poems, of which two,—one, 'The Black Butterfly,' and the other, an 'Ode to the Moon,'—Ochoa declares, in his opinion, "two of the most beautiful pieces that have been written for many years in Spain." Disagreeing very much with this opinion, it is only quoted in token of the estimation in which Pastor Diaz is held among his countrymen. (Ochoa, vol. ii. p. 628.)

37. Page 216. "The advantages he enjoyed there."

In his poem of the 'Moro Esposito,' the Duke has inserted an interesting episode referring to his residence in Malta, "whose good and honest inhabitants he found under the dominion of the most wealthy, free, enlightened, noble and powerful nation that the sun admires from the zodiac." (Book VI.) In the notes he details the particulars under which he arrived there, acknowledging gratefully the hospitality he had received.

38. Page 222. "Pedro, surnamed the Cruel."

This name is pronounced Ped-ro. The true character of the monarch is yet a disputed question, and has only within the last year been offered as a subject for inquiry by the Spanish Academy. The learned Llorente, in his 'Historical Notices,' vol. v., has, I think, clearly shown that Pedro was no more deserving of the epithet peculiarly than others of his age, including his half-brother and successor, by whose hand he fell, in retributive justice for the death of their other brother Fadrique. The legend of this prince's death has been variously given, and thus Salvador Bermudez de Castro, who has also a poem on the subject, takes some different details to those repeated by the Duke de Rivas. The traditions of the people have handed down Don Pedro's memory more favourably, and, perhaps, more justly, than the historians of the time, whose accounts no doubt were tinctured as darkly as they could be, partly to please the reigning monarch, and partly because Don Pedro had not been so submissive to priestly rule as they had desired.

39. Page 227. "'Yet, ah! those lovely bowers along," &c.

> Mas, ay! aquellos pensiles
> No he pisado un solo dia
> Sin ver (sueños de mi mente!)
> La sombra de la Padilla,
>   Lanzando un hondo gemido
> Cruzar leve ante mi vista,

> Como un vapor, como un humo
> Que entre los àrboles gira :
>   Ni entrè en aquellos salones
> Sin figuràrseme erguida
> Del fundador la fantasma
> En belada sangre tinta ;
>   Ni en vestibulo oscuro
> El que tiene en la cornisa
> De los reyes los retratos,
> El que en colunas estriba,
>   Al que adornan azulejos
> Abajo, y esmalte arriba
> El que muestra en cada muro
> Un rico balcon, y encima
>   El bondo arteson dorado
> Que lo corona y atrista,
> Sin ver en tierra un cadaver.
> Aun en las losas se mira
> Una tenaz mancha oscura
> Ni las edades limpian !
> Sangre ! sangre ! oh, cielos, cuantos
> Sin saber que lo es, la pisan !

This romance was originally printed with the 'Moro Esposito,' Paris 1834, vol. ii. p. 451. It was subsequently included among the 'Romances Historicos,' Madrid 1841, p. 19. The Alcazar of Seville has been described by so many travellers that it is unnecessary to add to their accounts of it, or to the graphic details of the romance. The stain on the floor may remind the reader of the legends of Holyrood and the Alhambra, as well as of other places.

40. Page 233. "Darting round fierce looks," &c.

This description of anger, as again at p. 241, seems a favourite one with the Duke, as well as other poets; thus Virgil—

> Totoque ardentis ab ore
> Scintillæ absistunt, oculis micat acribus ignis.

41. Page 234. "The crackling of his arms and knees."

From the peculiarity of this formation, the king was recognized by an old woman who had witnessed his killing a man he had met in a night rencontre in the street opposite her house, and she having given evidence to that effect, he ordered his statue to be beheaded, and so placed in the street in memorial of the sentence against himself.

42. Page 236.

> "And more than Tello madly hates,
> And more than Henry too."

The two brothers of Fadrique, of whom Henry was his successor on the throne, after he had killed Don Pedro in fight by his own hand. In another romance, the Duke de Rivas describes this "fratricide," and represents that Don Pedro had the advantage at first, but that the page of the other came to his master's assistance, and attacking Don Pedro from behind, diverted his attention so as to enable him to give the King the death-wound. From the accounts handed down to us, it is clear that Don Pedro had sufficient grounds for suspecting treason from the brothers, which occasioned his animosity against them and their adherents, for which they afterwards blackened his memory.

43. Page 259.   "Meagre soup bouillie."

In the original, Gazpacho, "the name of a dish universal in and peculiar to Spain. It is a sort of cold soup, made of bread, pot-herbs, oil and water. Its materials are easily come by, and its concoction requires no skill." Mr. W. G. Clark has taken this name for the title of his lively 'Sketches of Spain,' London 1850.

44. Page 260.   "Whene'er Don Juan," &c.

> Siempre que tiene una broma
>   El señor don Juan me olvida
> Como si estuviera en Roma;
>   Y à un entierro me convida
> Para matarme de pena!
>   Sea enhorabuena.

Despues de melindres mil
  Canta Celestina el duo
Que le han puesto en atril,
  Y aunque canta como un buho
Todos la llaman Sirena.
      Sea enhorabuena.

Cien abejas sin reposo
  Labrando à porfia estàn
El dulce panal sabroso.
  Ay! que un zàngano holgazàn
Se ha de tragar la colmena!
      Sea enhorabuena.

El hombre à su semejante
  Mueve guerra furibundo,
Cual si no fuera bastante
  Para despoblar el mundo
El escuadron de Avicena.
      Sea enhorabuena.

Hay en España usureros
  Hay esbirros à montones,
Y chalanes y venteros,
  Y dicen que los ladrones
Estan en Sierra Morena!
      Sea enhorabuena.

En vano à tu puerta, Conde,
  Llegan los pobres desnudos,
Que el perro solo responde,
  Y gastas dos mil escudos
En un baile y una cena!
      Sea enhorabuena.

Basta por hoy de sermon.
  Aqui mi pluma suspendo
Hasta mejor ocasion.
  Si el vicio en vano reprendo
Y escribo sobre la arena,
      Sea enhorabuena.

The selections from Breton de los Herreros are taken from the edition of 1831, at pages 61, 63 and 71 respectively.

45. Page 269. "The celebrated Lista."

This celebrated writer was born at Seville in 1775, and in early life adopted the ecclesiastical profession, having therein principally dedicated himself to the education of youth, in which he has been eminently successful. He has written a continuation of Mariana's 'History of Spain,' and translated from the French Segur's 'Universal History,' besides several mathematical and other elementary works. In 1822 he published a volume of poems, of which a second edition has been since published, highly praised by the different writers who have treated of modern Spanish literature. They are however avowedly of the classical school, and their greatest merit must be supposed to consist in their elegance of expression. His critical writings are numerous and valuable.

46. Page 271. "Twelve out of the nineteen stanzas."

The stanzas 6, 9, 10, 11, 16 and 17 seem to be of his addition, and it must be acknowledged that they are in no respect inferior to the others. One stanza in Pindemonte he has not taken into his version.

47. Page 272. "Part of his first volume is taken up with imitations."

Before observing that this part had been so expressed at the beginning, I made a translation of one small piece, which may give an idea of the others.

En el Album de una Senorita.

Cual suele en màrmol sepulcral escrito
Un nombre detener al pasagero,
Pueda en aquesta pàgina mi nombre
Fijar tus ojos, ay! por los que muero.
   Miralo, cuando ya de ti apartado,
No te pide mi amor mas recompensa;
De mi te acuerda como muerte y piensa
Que aqui mi corazon queda enterrado.

In a Lady's Album.

As on sepulchral marble writ
    A name to stay the passer-by,
So let my name on this page meet
    Thine eyes, for which, alas! I die.
Look on it when I am far from thee;
    My love asks no return more dear;
As of one dead remember me,
    And think my heart is buried here.

It was only on translating the last line that I recognized them as Lord Byron's.

Written in an Album.

As o'er the cold sepulchral stone
    Some name arrests the passer-by,
Thus when thou view'st this page alone
    May mine attract thy pensive eye.
And when by thee that name is read
    Perchance in some succeeding year,
Reflect on me as on the dead,
    And think my heart is buried here.

48. Page 275. "Sonnet, Dedication," &c.

A mi Esposa.

    Cuando en mis venas fèrvidas ardia
La fiera juventud, en mis canciones
El tormentoso afan de mis pasiones
    Con dolorosas làgrimas vertia.
    Hoy à ti las dedico, Esposa mia,
Cuando el amor mas libre de ilusiones
Inflama nuestros puros corazones,
    Y sereno y de paz me luce el dia.
    Asi perdido en turbulentos mares
Mìsero navegante al cielo implora,
Cuando le aqueja la tormenta grave;
    Y del naufragio libre, en los altares
Consagra fiel à la Deidad que adora
Las hùmedas reliquias de su nave.

This sonnet, and the two following translations, are taken respectively from pages 8, 18 and 46 of the first volume of the

Toluca edition. The imitation of Lord Byron is at page 83 of the same. The Odes to 'Poesy' and to 'Night' are at pages 13 and 72 of the second volume.

49. Page 282. "Milton elevated all beyond."

    Y Milton mas que todos elevado
    A su angel fiero de diamante armado.

50. Page 305. "Josè de Espronceda."

This name is to be pronounced Esprontheda. The translations, taken from the original poems, may be found in the Paris edition of 1848, at pages 49, 58, 73 and 79 respectively. The one translated, 'The Condemned to Die,' El Reo de Muerte, literally, 'The Guilty of Death,' has the signification given to this phrase by our translators of the New Testament, and it may be necessary to explain that the refrain "Your alms for prayers," &c., is in the original merely "To do good for the soul of him who is about to be executed."

    Para hacer bien al alma
    Del que van à ajusticiar!

In Spain, when a criminal is about to be executed, it is the custom for the Brothers of the religious order De la Humanidad, to go about the public ways, in their peculiar garb, with salvers for receiving alms for masses to be said for him, repeating words to the effect above given.

51. Page 315. "Sail on, my swift one, never fear."

    Navega, velero mio,
        Sin temor,
    Que ni enemigo navio,
    Ni tormenta, ni bonanza,
    Tu rumbo à torcer alcanza
    Ni à sujetar tu valor.
        Veinte presos
        Hemos hecho
        A despecho
        Del Ingles,

>   Y han rendido
>   Sus pendones
>   Cien naciones
>   A mis piès.
> Que es mi barco mi tesoro,
> Que es mi Dios la libertad,
> Mi ley la fuerza y el viento,
> Mi ùnica patria la mar.
>
> Allà muevan feroz guerra
>   Ciegos reyes
> Por un palmo mas de tierra;
> Que yo tengo aqui por mio
> Cuanto abarca el mar bravio
> A quien nadie impuso leyes.
>   Y no hay playa
>   Sea cual quiera
>   Ni bandera
>   De esplendor
>   Que no sienta
>   Mi derecho
>   Y dè pecho
>   A mi valor.
> Que es mi barco mi tesoro ....
>
> A la voz de 'barco viene!'
>   Es de ver
> Como vira, y se previene
> A todo trapo à escapar;
> Que yo soy el rey del mar
> Y mi furia es de temer.
>   En las presas
>   Yo divido
>   Lo cogido
>   Por igual:
>   Solo quiero
>   Por riqueza
>   La belleza
>   Sin rival
> Que es mi barco mi tesoro ....
>
> Sentenciado estoy à muerte!
>   Yo me rio;
> No me abandone la suerte,
> Y al mismo que me condena

  Colgarè de alguna entena
  Quizà en su proprio navio.
   Y si caigo
   Que es la vida?
   Por perdida
   Ya la di,
   Cuando el yugo
   Del esclavo
   Como un bravo
   Sacudì.
  Que es mi barco mi tesoro . . . .

  Son mi música mejor
   Aquilones;
  El estrépito y temblor
  De los cables sacudidos,
  Del negro mar los bramidos,
  Y el rugir de mis cañones;
   Y del trueno
   Al son violento,
   Y del viento
   Al rebramàr,
   Yo me duermo
   Sosegado,
   Arrullado
   Por el mar.
  Que es mi barco mi tesoro,
  Que es mi Dios la libertad,
  Mi ley la fuerza y el viento,
  Mi ùnica patria la mar.

52. Page 323. "Josè Zorrilla."

The name of this eminently great poet is to be pronounced as Thorrillia; the translations made from his works are of the poems at pages 62, 99, 34, 97, 102, 28 and 65, respectively, of the first volume, as stated in the memoir, published at Madrid in 1837. The headings, for the sake of distinction, have been given somewhat differently from the originals, where they are generally only entitled 'Oriental,' or 'A Romance;' and the piece named 'The Warning' is but part of a longer poem, the conclusion of which is not in the same good taste as the beginning. All the other selections translated in this work, of the different authors, have been given fully.

53. Page 347. "The Tower of Munion."

This tower is a shapeless ruin, the remains of an ancient castle in the plain of Arlanza near Burgos. The history of the castle is unknown, further than that Don Fernan Gonzalez assembled there, on one occasion, the Grandees of Castille, during his wars with the Moors.

54. Page 352. "Meditation."

La Meditacion.

Sobre ignorada tumba solitaria,
A la luz amarilla de la tarde,
Vengo à ofrecer al cielo mi plegaria
    Por la muger que amè.
Apoyada en el màrmol mi cabeza,
Sobre la hùmeda yerba la rodilla,
La parda flor que esmalta la maleza
    Humillo con mi piè.

Aquì, lejos del mundo y sus placeres,
Levanto mis delirios de la tierra,
Y leo en agrupados caractères
    Nombres que ya no son;
Y la dorada làmpara que brilla
Y al soplo oscila de la brisa errante,
Colgada ante el altar en la capilla
    Alumbra mi oracion.

Acaso un ave su volar detiene
Del fùnebre ciprès entre las ramas
Que a lamentar con sus gorjeos viene
    La ausencia de la luz:
Y se despide del albor del dia
Desde una alta ventana de la torre
O trepa de la cùpula sombria
    A la gigante cruz.

Anegados en làgrimas los ojos
Yo la contemplo inmòvil desde el suelo
Hasta que el rechinar de los cerrojos
    La bace aturdida huir.
La funeral sonrisa me saluda
Del solo ser que con los muertos vive,
Y me presta su mano àspera y ruda
    Que un fèretro va à abrir.

Perdon! no escuches Dios mio
    Mi terrenal pensamiento!
Deja que se pierda impio
Como el murmullo de un rio
    Entre los pliegues del viento.

Por que una imàgen mundana
    Viene à manchar mi oracion?
Es una sombra profana
Que tal vez serà mañana
    Signo de mi maldicion.

Por que ha soñada mi mente
    Ese fantasma tan bello?
Con esa tez transparente
Sobre la tranquila frente
    Y sobre el desnudo cuello.

Que en vez de aumentar su encanto
    Con pompa y mundano brillo,
Se muestra anegada en llanto
Al piè de altar sacrosanto
    O al piè de pardo castillo.

Como una ofrenda olvidada
    En templo que se arruinò
Y en la piedra cincelada
    Que en su caida encontrò
La mece el viento colgada.

Con su retrato en la mente,
    Con su nombre en el oido,
Vengo à prosternar mi frente
Ante el Dios omnipotente
    En la mansion del olvido.

Mi crimen acaso ven
    Con turbios ojos inciertos,
Y me abominan los muertos,
Alzando la hedionda sien
    De los sepulcros abiertos.

Cuando estas tumbas visito,
    No es la nada en que naci,
No es un Dios lo que medito,
Es un nombre que está escrito
    Con fuego dentro de mi.

Perdon! no escuches Dios mio
    Mi terrenal pensamiento!
Deja que se pierda impio
Como el murmullo de un rio,
    Entre los pliegues del viento.

THE END.

PRINTED BY RICHARD TAYLOR,
RED LION COURT, FLEET STREET.

www.ingramcontent.com/pod-product-compliance
Lightning Source LLC
Chambersburg PA
CBHW020543300426
44111CB00008B/772